D0435460

2006 Edition

THE
TAO
OF
WAR

Other Books by Ralph D. Sawyer

Author

Tao of Deception:
A History of Unorthodox Warfare in China

Fire and Water:
The Art of Incendiary and Aquatic Warfare in China

The Tao of Spycraft:
Intelligence Theory and Practice in Traditional China

Translator

One Hundred Unorthodox Strategies:
Battle and Tactics of Chinese Warfare

The Seven Military Classics of Ancient China

The Art of War (by Sun-tzu)

Military Methods (by Sun Pin)

THE
TAO
OF
WAR

TRANSLATED BY RALPH D. SAWYER
WITH MEE-CHÜN LEE SAWYER

BARNES
& NOBLE

NEW YORK

Originally published as The Tao of Peace

© 1999 by Ralph D. Sawyer

This 2006 edition published by Barnes & Noble, Inc.,
by arrangement with Perseus Books, Inc.

ISBN-13: 978-0-7607-9095-3
ISBN-10: 0-7607-9095-7

Printed and bound in the United States of America

1   3   5   7   9   10   8   6   4   2

To Nathan Sivin
    with profound appreciation for enlightenment
    and friendship over many decades

Contents

Preface   *XI*
Introduction   1

Wang Chen and His Time   1
Assumptions and Contradictions   7
The Tao of Government   13
Problems   18
    The Root Cause of Disorder   18
    The Baleful Nature of Weapons and Warfare   27
    The Actuality of Warfare   31
Solutions   36
    Virtue and Knowledge   38
    The Army's Employment   41
    Martial Noncontention   46
    Pliancy in Conquest   51
    The Role of the Sage   54
    Positive Measures   61

TAO CHING

1 The Tao That Can Be Spoken of   70
2 All Under Heaven Know   73
3 Do Not Esteem Worthies   78
4 The Tao Is Vacuous   81
5 Heaven and Earth Are Not Benevolent   83
6 The Valley Spirit Does Not Die   85

7   Heaven Persists; Earth Endures   87

8   The Highest Good Is Like Water   89

9   Holding and Filling   93

10   Regulating the Earthly Soul to Embrace Unity   96

11   Thirty Spokes Collectively Form a Hub   98

12   The Five Colors Compel Humans   101

13   Be Startled at Favor and Disgrace   103

14   Looked at but Unseen   105

15   Those in Antiquity Who Excelled as Officers   108

16   Realizing the Pinnacle of Vacuity   110

17   Those Beneath the Ultimate Know   113

18   The Great Tao Abandoned   115

19   Eliminate Sagacity, Abandon Wisdom   118

20   Eliminate Learning and There Will Be No Worry   120

21   Vast Encompassing Virtue   122

22   The Curved Will Be Preserved   124

23   Sparse Words Are Natural   127

24   Those on Tiptoe Do Not Stand   129

25   There Is Something Turbidly Complete   130

26   Weightiness Is the Root of Lightness   132

27   Those Who Excel in Moving Have No Tracks   133

28   Know the Masculine   136

29   About to Seize All Under Heaven   138

30   Assisting the Ruler with the Tao   140

31   Superlative Weapons   144

32   Tao Eternal, Unnamed   147

33   Knowing Men Is Wisdom   149

34   The Great Tao Overflows   152

35   Grasp the Great Emblem   154

36   Wanting to Reduce Something   156

37   Tao Eternally Actionless   158

TE CHING

38	Superior Virtue Is Not Virtuous	164
39	Those in Antiquity Who Realized the One	167
40	Reversal Is the Movement of the Tao	169
41	When Superior Officers Hear About the Tao	172
42	Tao Gave Birth to the One	175
43	The Most Pliant Under Heaven	178
44	Fame or the Body, Which Is More Intimate?	180
45	Great Achievement Seems Deficient	182
46	When the Tao Prevails Throughout the Realm	184
47	Without Going Out the Door, Know All Under Heaven	186
48	Those Who Study Daily Increase	188
49	The Sage Has No Preset Mind	190
50	Going Forth Into Life, Entering Death	192
51	Tao Gave Them Birth	195
52	All Under Heaven Had a Beginning	197
53	If I Minutely	199
54	Those Who Excel at Establishing Are Not Pulled Out	201
55	Abundantly Embodying Virtue	203
56	The Knowledgeable Do Not Speak	207
57	With Government, Order the State	209
58	The Government Is Morosely Quiet	213
59	Governing the People and Serving Heaven	215
60	Governing a Great State	218
61	Great States Defer to the Flow	220
62	Tao of the Myriad Things	222
63	Act Actionlessly	224
64	The Tranquil Is Easily Grasped	227
65	In Antiquity, Those Who Excelled in the Tao	231

66 How Rivers and Seas Can Be
   Kings of the Hundred Valley Streams   234
67 All Under Heaven Term Me Vast   236
68 Those Who Excel as Warriors Are Not Martial 241
69 Those Who Employ the Military Have a Saying 244
70 My Words Are Very Easy to Comprehend   248
71 Knowing, Not Knowing   250
72 People Do Not Dread Awesomeness   251
73 One Courageous in Daring Slays   253
74 The People Do Not Dread Death   256
75 The People's Hunger   258
76 Life of the People   260
77 The Tao of Heaven   263
78 The Pliant and Weak Under Heaven   265
79 Harmonizing Great Rancor   267
80 A Small State with Few People   269
81 Credible Words Are Not Beautiful   272

Index   275
Suggested Further Reading   287

Preface

Since the *Tao of War* takes Wang Chen's commentary as its focus and many readers are already familiar with one of the readily available *Tao Te Ching* translations, we did not intend to append our own version of this famous classic. However, studying Wang's thoughts in detail convinced us that his understanding of the *Tao Te Ching* necessitates a contextually modified translation to prevent considerable puzzlement about his exact meaning. We therefore decided to commence each chapter with the relevant verses rendered in accord with his vision and orientation, as well as his particularized pronouncements.

In many instances the resulting translation differs somewhat from our basic inclinations. (Being a laconic and often enigmatic text, unless compelled to struggle with variant textual understandings and even mutually exclusive possibilities, one tends to read nebulously and unconsciously, somehow simultaneously absorbing the many implied and alternative meanings. However, definitive choices must be made in order to render problematic passages into English, thereby accounting for the significant variations in wording and style seen among contemporary versions.) Not only does Wang Chen sometimes choose unusual textual variants, but he occasionally diverges dramatically from one or another "accepted" understanding. At times his choices seem consciously intended to conform, if not contort, the text to his purposes and vision, but in fact many of them enjoy support from one or another antique commentary, as well as certain tomb text rearrangements. On reflection we found no instances in which his perspectives and interpretations were precluded.

Translations of the *Tao Te Ching* abound which might be consulted in conjunction with *The Tao of War*. The classic versions (with their accompanying introductions) by Arthur Waley (*The Way And Its Power*) and Wing-tsit Chan (*The Way of Lao-tzu*) still hold great appeal. Wing-tsit Chan also includes incisive textual notes and some brief commentaries, all of which were expanded upon in Ellen M. Chen's focused version, *The Tao Te Ching: A New Translation with Commentary*. John Wu's *Tao Te Ching* is marked by a more political tone, one much closer to Wang Chen's understanding. However, several relatively recent renditions also merit pondering, including D.C. Lau's hybrid *Tao Te Ching*, Robert G. Henrick's *Lao-tzu Te-Tao Ching*, Victor Mair's *Tao Te Ching*, and Stephen Mitchell's *Tao Te Ching*. Comprehensive studies continue to appear, such as Michael LaFargue, *The Tao of the Tao Te Ching*, and Livia Kohn and Michael LaFargue, *Lao-tzu and the Tao-te-ching*; the discovery of Han dynasty tomb texts has stimulated numerous conferences and a much revised view of the text's historical evolution; and the pioneering work of Bruce and Taeko Brooks compels radical reinterpretation.

Wang Chen's text may be found in the great compilation of Taoist writings known as the *Tao Tsang*, the major collected editions, and even the recently published *Chung-kuo Ping-shu Chi-ch'eng*. Textual variations among the accessible editions are surprisingly few, easily emended wherever obviously corrupt or erroneous. (Although we have assiduously researched the text and pondered the translation and commentaries for some two years, the final work, being intended for readers with diverse interests and orientations rather than solely sinologists, has been spared the usual philological footnotes.) While it is uncertain which *Tao Te Ching* edition Wang Chen primarily employed — he clearly chose among variants in a number of cases — his comments suggest he was aware of Wang Pi's version but normally gave preference to Ho-shang Kung's. From his line by line notes, chapter arrangement, and chapter titles, he doubtlessly collated his comments to an eighty-one chapter version similar to the many presently available.

Thanks are due to Lee T'ing-rong for honoring the work with his calligraphy; to Max Gartenberg for his wise counsel over the years; and to our Saint Bernard, Zeno, for illuminating certain aspects of the *Tao Te Ching*.

Ralph D. Sawyer

Introduction

WANG CHEN AND HIS TIME

Stirred by the many sorrows warfare had inflicted upon China over the preceding two thousand years, the T'ang dynasty border commander Wang Chen pensively observed:

> The armies of the Three Kings all acted in accord with the requirements of the moment. When their efforts were complete, they desisted. After standing down, their armies were not again employed. Yet some of their later descendants were arrogant, uncouth, brutal, dissolute, angry, greedy, boastful, or evil, so they created personal armies, regiments, states, and families. When they acted, it was to seize the strong; when they employed their armies, they sought victory. Even though their troops became weary and their provisions were exhausted, they still advanced and fought. Some did not desist and were engulfed; some were never satisfied and brought extermination upon themselves, exposing the people's livers and brains on the road. Because of a single man's anger or desire, all within the seas were poisoned and in pain, and disaster was rife throughout the land.

His words, universal in their depiction, could well have been written in any postwar period, in any age or country, East or West, including this very day.

Perturbed by the carnage that had again plagued even the glorious T'ang dynasty in the preceding eighth century, Wang Chen sought a solution that would end warfare and eliminate the horrendous destruction it wrought. Although ostensibly a Confucian, he found the means to rectify humanity's self-destructive tendencies in the doctrines of the *Tao Te Ching*, a brief, already ancient philosophical work that had, at least in part, provided the initial intellectual inspiration for what evolved into the various forms of Taoism over the centuries from the late Warring States period (403–221 BCE) onward. The choice must be considered astonishing, not only because there were well-established, alternative possibilities—Confucianism and Buddhism—with strongly grounded theories of human nature and conflict, but also because prevailing interpretations of the *Tao Te Ching* had come to emphasize its mystical and even nihilistic aspects. However, the text must have appealed to Wang Chen because it provided a cosmological anchor for the patterns of human society and a transcendent explanation for the psychodynamics of conflict and contention, whose eradication had to be thorough to prove successful.

In the quest for a method to end warfare and coerce peace amid a world of selfish interests and conflicting desires, Wang Chen's treatise constitutes a striking, worldly meditation upon the patterns and principles of the *Tao Te Ching*. It therefore also offers a highly nontraditional interpretation of the text itself (although growing evidence shows that at least some schools of thought understood the *Tao Te Ching* as a political, rather than purely individualist, writing). Wang clearly inclined to true pacifism but found its solution of deference and humility, of simply refusing to engage in combat and warfare, inadequate when confronted by great evil, by the extinction of one's family and the extermination of the state. He read the *Tao Te Ching* closely for solutions and thoroughly embraced its concepts and ideas, but not without probing them within the context of a bureaucratized world of competing views and incessant bickering. Obviously struggling with the contradictions found within life and the *Tao Te Ching* itself, his commentaries sometimes vacillate between pure noncontention and a modified position of deference through power, as well as undertaking inactivity or actionless measures that participate in cosmic patterns and therefore entail no repercussions.

Little being known about the author of the extensive *Tao Te Ching* commentaries that comprise *Essential Explanations of the* Tao Te Ching's *Martial Discussions,* herein titled the *Tao of War,* context must be sought in the wider history of the T'ang dynasty. From the date of 809 CE appended to his overview, it can be concluded that Wang Chen lived in the second half of the T'ang dynasty, an era when its initial glory had already declined under weak emperors who often immersed themselves in Taoist studies rather than exercise control of the government. Moreover, the empire had sustained an enormous blow from An Lu-shan's violent rebellion, which had virtually torn the state asunder and caused the death of millions over nearly a decade, commencing in 755 CE. Although central government control had been restored by the time of Wang's writing a half century later, unrest still continued even then: in more remote areas, recalcitrant military leaders retained substantially independent power, and in the border region, various steppe peoples, termed "barbarians" by the imperial government (in comparison with China's vaunted civilization and culture), constantly posed threats and mounted incursions. Wang Chen's own words show he personally witnessed the turmoil and travail in these remote areas, having been posted there in a subordinate military capacity during his career as a central government bureaucrat.

By the T'ang dynasty, whose founders have traditionally been viewed as semibarbarians themselves, essentially Confucian views had come to characterize state orthodoxy. Actual administrative practice, however, was a complex matter: imperial attitudes and policies fluctuated between activist intervention marked by caustic "realist" or "Legalist" practices and deliberate Taoist quietism, whose inactivity verged on a power vacuum. Although other avenues were available, Wang Chen would presumably have pursued his career as a bureaucrat by passing at least one or two government examinations and gradually being advanced through a series of general posts, coming at some point to be appointed an imperial censor (or inspector) charged with scrutinizing behavior in a designated provincial area. In this capacity, he was eventually assigned command responsibilities, suggesting he either had some background in military studies or subsequently came to know the military writings in the course of his duties. However, since his commentaries rarely quote the military classics but do cite passages from the Confucian canon, he may well have been entrusted with command without any martial expertise. This could account for his lack of interest in the *Tao Te Ching*'s intriguing tactical concepts and unorthodox military principles.

His years of service on the border just when the central government was once again building strong armies and wresting back full control of the peripheral regions apparently impressed Wang Chen with the horrors of warfare firsthand. Certainly this experience was far more intense than any he was likely to have experienced in his childhood years, when he may have encountered remnants of the general suffering resulting from An Lu-shan's rebellion. Apparently these sorrows prompted him to envision a realistic program for reducing conflict and ending warfare in the *Tao Te Ching*, whose text was much favored by the avowedly Taoist T'ang dynasty. This provided Wang with a ready, acceptable justification for his ideas, as did the fact that the T'ang dynasty had also established China's first semilegendary strategist, the T'ai Kung of early Chou fame, as its revered, state-sanctioned martial patron, in conjunction with Confucius as its cultural patron. His afterword, here somewhat abridged by deleting much honorific language of little interest, briefly discusses his motives and rationale:

> I have heard that in antiquity, after Pao Hsi had completed Heaven and Earth and created patterns for the myriad things, he still felt that the August Tao was insufficient. Accordingly, he silently pondered the transformations, his vital essence moved to penetration and, without having spoken, Heaven began giving birth, without having spoken, Earth began nurturing. Therefore the Ho River gave forth the Dragon Diagram and the Luo River spewed forth the Turtle Books in order to display their writings. From these they were able to draw the hexagrams and images [of the *I Ching*], and govern written characters.

When the sprouts of wisdom and intelligence emerged, true simplicity submersively diminished, so the principles of these writings again became insufficient. Therefore was born our Emperor of the Dank Mysterious Origination, Lao-tzu, to speak for Heaven and Earth and excel in rescuing the distressed. For this reason, the sections comprised by his five thousand characters again and again express his earnestness and sincerity. They can be said to open the root and source of *Tao* and *Te* [Virtue], and reject the leaves and branches of language. Compared to essays, they are like the sun, moon, and stars shining in their revolutions in the Heavens; compared with the animals and plants, they are like the myriad things that fill up the Earth. If we speak about their instructions and admonitions, all behavior is completely prepared for men.

Now the civil rules the martial, while the martial prepares for the civil. These two handles must be implemented together. They come out together and always occupy the left and right [sides in court], so who can abandon them? Thus [in the *Ssu-ma Fa*] it is said, "One who forgets warfare will be endangered, one who is enthralled with warfare will perish." From this one knows that armies can be employed, but cannot be loved. They can engage in combat, but cannot be forgotten. From the time the Yellow Emperor repressed the chaos brought about by Shao Hao, no age has lacked them. When the Three Kings flourished, even though they all possessed Sagacious Virtue, they still settled the realm with weapons. However, the armies of the Three Kings all acted in accord with the requirements of the moment. When their efforts were complete, they desisted. After standing down, their armies were not again employed. Yet, some of their later descendants were arrogant, uncouth, brutal, dissolute, angry, greedy, boastful, or evil, so they created personal armies, regiments, states, and families. When they acted it was to seize the strong; when they employed their armies, they sought victory. Even though their troops became weary and their provisions were exhausted, they still advanced and fought. Some did not desist and were engulfed, some were never satisfied and brought extermination upon themselves, exposing the people's livers and brains on the road. Because of a single man's anger or desire, all within the seas were poisoned and in pain and disaster was rife throughout the land. Lao-tzu felt grief over the situation, but rulers still could not abandon military forces, having no alternative but to employ them.

Now Sages do not employ the military out of indignation or anger, to fight to seize terrain, from greed or love, or to avenge enmity. They order and discipline their troops, nurture and store them, in order to be prepared against evil and overawe the unwise. They do not employ them in battlefield deployments, nor use them in aggressive attacks, nor for hunting in the wilds, nor for great strength. This is the profound principle of the Sage's employment of the military.

Furthermore, anger is a contrary Virtue, weapons are baleful implements, and combat is strongly abhorred by all men. How can it be easy to employ baleful implements through contrary Virtue and thereby undertake what people strongly abhor? Thus, it is said, "All under Heaven will give their allegiance to one of superior Virtue; all within the four seas will give their allegiance to one of superior benevolence; an entire state will give their allegiance to one of superior righteousness; and a village will give their allegiance to one who esteems the rites. No man will give his allegiance to one who lacks these four virtues." When men do not give their allegiance, rulers then employ the military. Employing the army being the way to endangerment, it is therefore said to be "a baleful implement." Moreover, battlegrounds are termed "fatal terrain" ["ground of death"]. Therefore, kings must first concentrate upon *Tao* and *Te* [Virtue] and take the employment of the military very seriously.

I have also heard it said that rulers who establish dynasties are fervent in completing their achievements, whereas those who succeed them merely preserve them, holding on to their positions. Therefore, when the Sage takes what is necessary to be unnecessary, his armies and weapons can be disbanded. However, when ordinary men take the unnecessary to be necessary, combat and aggression will increasingly flourish. Thus, Lao-tzu was not simply satirizing the dukes and kings of his age but probably also cautioning rulers of later ages against lightly employing their armies. For this reason, he specially established these five thousand characters and first raised the essentials of Great Tao, Highest Te, self-cultivation, patterning the state, actionless affairs, and unspoken teachings, only after several tens of chapters beginning to truly speak about the military's origins. Amid his deep sincerity and subtle instructions, there isn't a chapter that does not entail some concept of the military. How is this? Probably because when rulers marked by the Tao came down to the end of the Shang dynasty, campaigns of aggression came to be mounted by the feudal lords. By Lao-tzu's time, kings had long lost the masses and correct Tao. However, he could not directly upbraid them, so he fervently discussed the Tao of soaring vacuity and noncontention and the Virtue of pliancy and weakness, of being humble, in order to admonish them.

Now contention is the source of military combat, the foundation of disaster and chaos. The Sage wants to restrain it at its source and sever its foundation; therefore, throughout the *Tao Te Ching,* from beginning to end, Lao-tzu repeatedly takes noncontention as the essence. When no one contends, how will weapons and armor arise? For what purpose will forces be deployed for combat? Therefore, Lao-tzu repeated this over and over. How sincere his instructions, how sincere his instructions!

ASSUMPTIONS AND CONTRADICTIONS

In the traditional form already defined by the T'ang dynasty, the *Tao Te Ching* consisted of two parts, whose very titles reflect their thematic focus; the thirty-seven chapters of the *Tao Ching,* or *Classic of the Tao,* and the remaining forty-four of the *Te Ching,* or *Classic of Te.* The *Tao Ching* tends to ponder issues from a cosmological and metaphysical perspective, anchoring its observations and implications for humanity in the Tao's ineffable pervasiveness throughout the phenomenal universe. The *Te Ching,* in contrast, is more oriented to questions and practices of government, emphasizing modes of action within the mundane realm, resolving the problems besetting society. The recent discovery of tomb texts with the traditional order reversed and minor variations in the wording and arrangement of some verses, as well as variant editions compiled by different commentators that have come down through the years, provides evidence that the *Tao Te Ching*'s basic format and contents were finalized by the Han dynasty. The tomb texts are inherently interesting and apparently suggest that the *Tao Te Ching* was originally conceived, at least by some interpretive schools, as a political text rather than the Taoist voyage of self-cultivation and metaphysical discovery it has long been considered. For our purposes, however, the book's interpretation is defined by Wang Chen's version, structured and informed solely by his understanding.

Scholarly opinion on the nature of the *Tao Te Ching*, its compilation process, and its probable composition date—presumably the fourth to third centuries BCE, during the Warring States period—differs significantly and vociferously. Despite its traditional attribution to the legendary Lao-tzu, who at best may have provided inspiration and some core material, it does not seem to stem from a single mind. Instead, it appears to be a much reworked and synthesized contemplation of various threads and contributions from several authors that achieves a defined but not entirely homogeneous perspective. Although several distinct voices are melded and incorporated into the *Tao Te Ching*, those voices are not totally integrated, with some remaining dramatically contradictory. Whether the resulting conceptual conflicts can be resolved by some greater vision or subsumed in some surpassing transpersonal power, concept, or entity that perhaps pervades the universe depends upon one's assumptions and perspective. Even Wang Chen, who undertakes a consistent, envisioned reading of the text, at times seems to simply ignore or obscure difficulties. In most cases, though, his enthusiasm allows a cogent interpretation advocating the actionless course of virtue that leads to his ultimate objective of eliminating conflict. In addition, many difficulties easily dissolve in a maze of "chain arguments" whereby the reader is enticed through a sequence of conditions, each of which is presented as a highly plausible, if not necessary, consequence of the preceding situation. Since movement from premise to apparent conclusion is normally bereft of delimiting conditions and constraints, in an extreme case black can even be convincingly transformed into white. Moreover, the *Tao Te Ching*'s particularistic nature tends to elicit focused comments defined solely by each chapter's unique concerns, with little or no reference to the greater text. Discrete but divergent views may therefore be enthusiastically espoused by the *Tao Te Ching* and promoted by Wang Chen without ever being perceived or pondered as contradictory.

Even though he often comments upon fundamentally metaphysical issues, for Wang Chen the *Tao Te Ching* is not an ethereal, nihilistic, contemplative work. Rather, it is an exposition of the Tao's universal forces that provides a guide to resolving the horrendous problems plaguing humanity: greed, desire, militarism, and especially warfare. Moreover, he does not view it as a work intended for the weak and powerless or for recluses fearful of sullying themselves with the world's affairs. He clearly regards it as being for rulers (honored with the rubric of "Sages") acting from a position of power whose fundamental concerns include the people's welfare and loss of their own positions. (As will be seen, humility and pliancy prove ideal redresses for power but simply doom the inherently weak to extinction.) For example, key verses of the chapter entitled "Know the Masculine" obviously speak to individuals in positions of ultimate temporal power:

> *Know the masculine, cleave to the feminine,*
> *Be a watery ravine to All under Heaven.*
> *By acting as a watery ravine to All under Heaven,*
> *Eternal Virtue will never be estranged,*
> *And you will revert back to being a child.*
> *Know the white, cleave to the black,*
> *Be a model for All under Heaven.*

By acting as a model for All under Heaven,
Eternal Virtue will never err,
And you will revert back to the unbounded.
Know glory, cleave to disgrace,
Be a valley to All under Heaven.

Since rulers are invariably tempted to lives of false glory and opulence through abusing their powers, actions that easily rebound and sow the seeds of calamity, Wang Chen's commentary to this chapter stresses the importance of cleaving to the dark, silent, and lowly as a necessary corrective:

> Now anyone ruling men already has heroic talent, strategic ability, robust demeanor, and fierce spirit [*ch'i*]. Moreover, since they dwell in the realm's most honored position at the pinnacle of millions, are protected by six armies, and attended by the hundred officials, even without being evil they will be severe, even without getting angry will be awesome. Thus, Lao-tzu wants them to constantly cleave to feminine tranquillity, being just like a watery ravine to All under Heaven, because watery ravines are void, empty, and receptive, terrain that stores illness and accepts contamination. In this way, their Virtue will never depart from their bodies.

Similarly, in commenting upon "Holding and Filling," Wang observes:

> Human nature relies upon weapons. Thus, when an ordinary fellow carries a sharp three-foot sword or brandishes a dagger several inches long, he may even succeed in insulting the Son of Heaven or coercing the feudal lords into sanctioning visible alliances and accepting clandestine orders. How much more so anyone who occupies the ultimate position of imperial power and possesses a million-man army?

Surprisingly, in "There Is Something Turbidly Complete," the *Tao Te Ching* cosmologically and metaphysically anchors the ruler in the Tao, Heaven, and Earth:

There is something turbidly complete,
Spawned before Heaven and Earth.
Silent and still,
Solitary and unchanging,
Everywhere active, unimperiled.
It can act as the mother of All under Heaven.
I do not know its name but designate it as Tao.
If I am forced to characterize it,
It is called great.
Being great, it goes beyond;
Going beyond, it is distant;
Being distant, it then reverts.
Thus, the Tao is great;
Heaven is great;
Earth is great;
The king is also great.
In the cosmos, these are the four greats;
The king dwells among them.
Man models on Earth;
Earth models on Heaven;
Heaven models on Tao;
Tao models on the natural.

Wang Chen then proceeds to validate the king as an active participant in the universe's unfolding and therefore the progenitor of political programs that will benefit the people:

Now "great" refers to being inexhaustible, unbounded. Moreover, among the multitudinous directions, there isn't anywhere that the expansive, great Tao does not go. This "going" is like dispersing [going beyond]. Endlessly dispersing, it must go far. When it goes far and reaches the pinnacle, it invariably returns, so this is termed "reversion." This states that the Tao is active and present everywhere and thus acts as the mother of All under Heaven. The mother is the ancestor of the Tao, while the ancestor is the One. Thus, [in "Those in Antiquity Who Realized the One,"] the *Tao Te Ching* states, "Kings and lords realized the One and thereby exemplified truth for All under Heaven." This is what is meant by saying that one who can rectify the masses can be king. For this reason, the three realms of Heaven, Earth, and Man model on each other in order to attain the Tao. The Tao models on naturalness, so if the king models on naturalness, he will be able to complete his affairs.

Wang Chen's interpretive method is thus based on a focused understanding of the text as describing political measures derived from the metaphysical patterns of the very cosmos itself that can resolve the apparently insurmountable problems of warfare and stop its endless carnage. His comments therefore comprise an envisioned reading structured in terms of certain parameters. More than a simple amalgamation of derivable principles and bureaucratic practices, it is a synthesis that turns out to be grounded upon essentially Confucian assumptions of the efficacy of true Virtue rather than the debased form witnessed in contemporary practice. (This view of virtue reflects the *Tao Te Ching*'s repeated condemnation of pedantic, hypocritical virtue in contrast to real, original Virtue.) In formulating comments that advance this overall vision, Wang Chen tends to gloss over—or simply not be troubled by—contradictions within the *Tao Te Ching* itself. He also ignores serious clashes between some of its bold statements and Confucian premises and remains largely oblivious to the text's implications for personal survival and the quest for transcendence in a troubled age. Moreover, even though Wang clearly attained a penetrating grasp of the abstruse observations and metaphysics of the *Tao Te Ching*—the focus of Wang Pi's and other traditional commentaries—his notes deemphasize them. Except when deliberately appealing to what might be termed "Taoist protoscience" to justify explanations, he concentrates instead upon more mundane issues of diminishing government and ending conflict.

Although Wang Chen titles his work *Essential Explanations of the* Tao Te Ching's *Martial Discussions,* his treatise—for that is what his extensive commentaries really compose, a dispersed but distinct volume keyed to the *Tao Te Ching*'s chapters—is driven by his major concern for ending warfare, humanity's great scourge. In consequence, he never discusses the tactical and strategic principles found in the *Tao Te Ching* that are mirrored in the two late Warring States military classics known as the *Six Secret Teachings* and *Three Strategies*. Moreover, he assumes, if subconsciously, that human nature is essentially consistent, free of significant anomalies; therefore, when the government implements appropriate measures and ensures that certain values and practices are embraced, they will be universally accepted and applauded. Thus, in concord with Mencius, he believes that because the appeal of true righteousness is universally strong and undeniable, the Virtuous ruler can successfully counter violent incursions merely through his great righteousness, which will shame the enemy into withdrawing. Such belief obviously reflects radical faith rather than simple naïveté, for Wang was certainly aware of innumerable historical villains and incorrigibles yet apparently continued to assume that everyone shared a common humanity, that no one would fall outside the domain of the affectable and affected. Such faith could only derive from the Tao's pervasiveness, for if the Tao, although ineffable and transcendent, provides the patterns for the universe and its workings, it is inescapably applicable to all human beings. No real theory of human nature would be required, even though there were many such theories by Wang Chen's time, ranging from viewing man as inherently evil to inherently good, with variations on admixtures and indeterminacy. An assumption similar to Confucius's famous statement that "by nature, men are alike; in practice, they differ" would suffice.

THE TAO OF GOVERNMENT

Contrary to nihilist and anarchist readings of the *Tao Te Ching* bent on discerning some sort of idealized, free-form social existence uncontaminated by any government, the book's authors assume the presence of a ruler exercising administrative control over a functioning bureaucracy. "With Government, Order the State" clearly annunciates this principle:

With government, order the state;
With the unorthodox, employ the military;
Without mounting affairs, seize All under Heaven.

Wang Chen's comments simply reiterate the lines, emphasizing the *active* Confucian virtue of uprightness: "States are ordered through government. Here 'government' means uprightness. When the ruler leads with uprightness, who will dare not be upright?"

The *Tao Te Ching* and Wang Chen's commentaries portray the ideal government and its impact upon the people in a coherent, if not always consistent, manner. At its core lies an image of government existent but virtually imperceptible, effective but amorphous, only sensed, never really perceived. The defining vision in "Those beneath the Ultimate Know" expresses this image:

Those beneath the ultimate know it exists;
The penultimate attracts them and their praise.
The next they fear,
While the lowest they detest.

· · ·

Achievements successful and affairs complete,
The hundred surnames all view it as naturally stemming
* from their efforts.*

Wang Chen's exegesis draws upon the *Tao Te Ching*'s highly visible theory of historical devolution, discussed below, to explicate the concise meaning of the verses:

When the Great Tao was implemented in remote antiquity, the highest Virtue was not regarded as Virtue. Therefore, the people below knew only that there was a ruler above them, nothing more. They were employed every day but simply didn't know it.

By middle antiquity, benevolence and virtue were simultaneously bespread. Benefits and beneficence reached them daily, so the people loved the ruler and gave him their allegiance.

Since they praised his attractiveness, his activities gradually became apparent.

Kings subsequently governed with righteousness, inflicting punishments and imposing fines for minor offenses, wielding shields and armor for major ones, so the people feared them. Next in order came those who governed with the *li* [rites, rituals, and forms of socialized behavior], but the li grew vexatious and brought confusion to sincerity. Death cheated life, so the people reviled the ruler. Moreover, people do not trust sincerity that does not proceed from the inner heart. Language was embellished in the quest for mutual deception, and some people valued words alone. How tragic!

For this reason, the king ought to complete tasks he does not dwell in, cleave to undefeatable affairs, and cause the people to be ignorant of his imperial power. This would then be viewed by everyone as "naturally stemming from their efforts." Excellent.

A slightly earlier chapter entitled "Those in Antiquity Who Excelled as Officers" describes the nebulous appearance of ancient rulers who realized the highest forms of government:

> *Those in antiquity who excelled as officers*
> *Were subtle, ethereal, dankly mysterious, and penetrating,*
> *Profound beyond recognition.*

Wang immediately links them to the ethereal Tao: "'Those in antiquity who excelled as officers' refers to those superior officers known as Sages and Worthies who occupied royal positions. 'Subtle, ethereal, dankly mysterious, and penetrating' all being aspects of the Tao's employment, they cannot really be grasped."

In this simple hierarchy of governments, the worst is detested because it causes rancor and annoyance, pain and suffering, and generally violates the Tao, conceived as oriented toward benefiting rather than harming. Although unmentioned in the *Tao Te Ching*, people oppressed and on the verge of extinction will react by fomenting revolution and overthrowing the ruler, resulting in great turmoil and suffering for all living creatures. However, somewhat short of this dire extreme looms caustic government, counseled against in "People Do Not Dread Awesomeness":

> *Do not vex them in their dwellings;*
> *Do not repress their means to life.*
> *Only when there is no repression*
> *Will they be unoppressed.*

Furthermore, according to "The Government Is Morosely Quiet," a direct relationship apparently exists between harsh governments—with their intrusive laws and measures, onerous ordinances, and required observances—and the nature of the people:

> *When the government is morosely quiet,*
> *The people will be heartily substantial.*
> *When the government is caustically intrusive,*
> *The people will be morally deficient.*

Wang's commentary then seizes upon the fundamental *Tao Te Ching* theme of keeping the people simple by abandoning wisdom:

> Those who would practice the Tao of rulership must conceal their wisdom and intelligence, be liberal in their instructions and commands, and constantly be morose, for then the people will naturally be simple and unadorned. When superiors have caustic, pedantic minds, the people below will invariably be deceptive and contrary, sneaky and irresponsible, neither sincere nor trustworthy.

The most detestable government veers far beyond merely onerous and annoying measures by callously exploiting its citizens solely to profit the ruling class, thereby destroying the people as well as compelling them to commit criminal acts to survive:

The people are famished because their superiors consume
excessive taxes,
Making them hungry.
The people are difficult to administer because their supe-
riors are active,
Making them difficult to govern.
The people are untroubled by death because their superiors
seek life's abundance,
Making them oblivious to death.

Wang Chen aptly concludes his notes to "The People's Hunger" by stating, "This chapter asserts that misery and famine stem from the ruler's establishing numerous labor services, heavy military impositions, and onerous taxes, thus taking in a great deal. This certainly is true!"

In "If I Minutely," a similar portrait is preserved—one that no doubt reflects conditions in the Warring States period, when many rulers mercilessly exploited the common people while themselves pursuing pleasure and practicing debauchery:

The court is thoroughly scoured,
The fields extremely weedy,
The granaries very empty.
They wear colorful, embroidered clothes,
Bear sharp weapons,
Surfeit themselves with drink and food,
And have wealth and goods in surplus.
This is termed the boasting of robbers;
It is not the Tao!

Wang Chen sympathetically observes:

Although the court and offices have been swept clean and scoured, the fields are heavily overgrown, the storehouses and granaries exceedingly empty, but militant ministers and martial generals are unlimited. Whether merited or not, they all wear fine silks and bear weapons such as daggers and swords. Sated with drink and food, they store away the goods and bribes that they rapaciously seize. The people, despite their own insufficiency, still have to support the houses of those who enjoy excess. This truly may be described as the "boasting of robbers and brigands." How could it ever be termed the Great Tao? Thus, Lao-tzu sighed deeply over the distress besetting his degenerative era and created this chapter to caution and upbraid the world about excess.

PROBLEMS

The Root Cause of Disorder

The *Tao Te Ching*'s authors discerned two causes for human suffering: man's tendency to conceptualize and thereby impute values, and the existence of desire. The former unfolds in "All under Heaven Know," a chapter whose initial verses became so famous as to enter the language as a common saying:

> *All under Heaven know the beautiful as beauty, so there is ugliness;*
> *All under Heaven know goodness as the good, so there is the not good.*
> *Therefore, being and nonbeing mutually produce each other;*
> *Difficult and easy complete each other;*
> *Long and short shape each other;*
> *High and low contrast each other;*
> *Notes and echoes harmonize with each other;*
> *Front and rear follow each other.*

In unveiling the relative, mutually defining nature of all concepts, its first verse furnishes Wang Chen with a well-founded, viable explanation for the origin and development of human conflict itself:

> The *Tao Te Ching* speaks of beauty in contrast to ugliness. When all the people under Heaven "know the beautiful as beauty," they will have long recognized ugliness. When all the people under Heaven "know goodness as the good," they will

have long known the ungood. . . . As soon as things have names and people have emotions, right and wrong, other and self already exist in their midst. When right and wrong, other and self exist in their midst, love and hate will arise and attack each other. When love and hate arise and attack each other, warfare will flourish. However, combatants do not invariably employ shields and halberds, hatchets and axes. Ordinary men confront each other with their hands and feet, insects and animals with their claws and teeth, and birds with their beaks and talons. All of them are disciples of combat. But when it comes to kings and nobles' taking action, there isn't one who doesn't employ metal [weapons] and leather [armor]. No calamity exceeds this!

The desires, being an inherent part of human nature, were viewed by Wang Chen and some of the later Taoists as ineradicable and problematic. (In his comments to "Eliminate Sagacity, Abandon Wisdom," Wang Chen observes, "Moreover, the great outlines of human nature are preserved in thought and desire, so they can be constrained but cannot be eliminated. Thus, Lao-tzu encourages kings and feudal lords to minimize them.") According to the *Tao Te Ching*, difficulty arises because the desires easily come to obsess people and compel immediate action to satisfy them, irrespective of the imminent consequences. Thus, "The Five Colors Compel Humans," another extremely well known chapter, fulminates succinctly:

The five colors cause human eyes to go blind;
The five notes cause human ears to go deaf;
The five flavors cause human mouths to err;
Racing horses and hunting cause human minds to go mad.
Products difficult to obtain cause human activities to be
  hindered.
For this reason, the Sage acts for the belly and not the eyes,
So he rejects that and takes this.

A part of Wang's commentary emphasizes the key concept of "products difficult to obtain"—objects that come to be desired because people value them due to the process of conceptualization—in stimulating antisocial actions: "When rulers value 'products difficult to obtain,' thieves and brigands will be spawned. When thieves and brigands appear, armies will arise. There is no greater harm than armies being mobilized. This will 'cause human activities to be hindered.' Certainly this is true." Thus, the desires not only debilitate the body and perturb the mind but also create the impetus for theft and violence, for men's seizing and forcefully pursuing what they believe essential to their happiness.

Apart from any innate tendency to drift away from the natural harmony and tranquillity of a life lived in accord with the Tao, the abrasive government actions reviewed above constitute the second cause of disorder. Active, caustic administrations not only stimulate disquiet but impel the people to anger and misery. However, "creating values" and "esteeming wisdom" impinge even more pervasively, if indirectly, upon the people. An explanation provided by "In Antiquity, Those Who Excelled in the Tao" includes an ideal solution:

> *In antiquity, those who excelled in the Tao*
> *Did not intend to enlighten the people but to stupefy them.*
> *People are hard to govern when their wisdom is manifold.*
> *Thus, one who governs a state with wisdom is the state's*
> *   brigand;*
> *One who does not govern with wisdom is the state's*
> *   benefactor.*

Wang's commentary concisely unfolds the psychodynamics and implications:

> By nature, the common masses are shallow and debased. Before wisdom and thought emerged, sly deceptions were first practiced. Did the resulting rancor and murmuring discriminate between right and wrong, contrary and according? The common people preferred to know who soothed, who brutalized. Some of them gathered like ants to form parties in the provinces; others arose like hornets amid the rivers and mountains. Ten thousand men responded to every evil leader

who laid plots. Campaigns of rectification were constantly mobilized against them, so isn't this indeed what is meant by "one who governs a state with wisdom is the state's brigand"? This says that if you increase the knowledge of the common masses, they will all become thieves capable of harming the state. Therefore, anyone who ensures the people preserve their stupidity, directness, simplicity, and purity can achieve good fortune and blessings for the state.

Since wisdom facilitates the appearance of evil and disorder, minimizing and rejecting it provide an obvious solution, just as advocated in "Eliminate Sagacity, Abandon Wisdom" (although both *sagacity* and *wisdom* should probably be understood in mundane terms, as skillful techniques and the ordinary knowledge of Confucian bureaucrats, rather than as penetrating understanding of the Tao):

> *Eliminate sagacity, abandon wisdom,*
> *The people will benefit a hundredfold.*
> *Eliminate benevolence, abandon righteousness,*
> *The people will revert to filiality and parental love.*
> *Eliminate skill, abandon profit,*
> *Robbers and brigands will be no more.*
> *As civilizing influences, these three being inadequate,*
> *Cause the people to have something to which they adhere.*
> *Display simplicity;*
> *Embrace the unadorned.*
> *Diminish yourself;*
> *Minimize your desires.*

In envisioning such highly visible Confucian virtues as righteousness and benevolence, combined with the effects of wisdom, contributing to the problem, these verses strongly reflect the devolution-from-virtue sentiment prominent throughout the *Tao Te Ching*. In his exegesis, Wang Chen therefore immediately perceives that an end to violence and harmful acts could be achieved by rejecting righteousness and benevolence in their debased forms:

This chapter advocates eliminating visible sagacity and abandoning boastful, deceptive wisdom, for then the people will receive great benefits said by the chapter to be "a hundredfold." Moreover, benevolence stems from inhumanity, righteousness from unrighteousness. If you eliminate wanton benevolence and cunning righteousness and ensure [that] relatives naturally unite in harmony, filiality and parental love will be restored. Furthermore, if you eliminate licentious artifice and abandon selfish profit, weapons and armor will not be flourished. When weapons and armor are not flourished, robbers and brigands will not arise.

While emphasizing the concept of simplifying the people's desires and knowledge, the third chapter, "Do Not Esteem Worthies," expands the specific measures any government should undertake:

Do not esteem Worthies
To keep the people from being contentious.
Do not value products difficult to obtain
To keep the people from committing robbery.
Do not display what is desirable
To keep the people's minds from being perturbed.
For these reasons, the Sage's administration
Makes their minds vacuous but satiates their bellies,
Weakens their intentions but strengthens their bones.
He constantly causes the people to have neither knowledge
    nor desire,
Ensures the wise dare not act.
Acting through actionlessness,
Nothing will be unordered.

Wang's extreme explanation, which follows, clearly reflects his belief that the *Tao Te Ching* presumes not only the imposition of government but also significant activity, often in very Confucian terms. (That activity, however, continues to be termed inactive or actionless, as will be further discussed.)

Clearly this does not mean that rulers avoid employing the Worthy and capable to keep the people from becoming contentious. Moreover, the legendary Sage Rulers, Five Emperors, early kings, and hegemons without exception all esteemed the three affairs [of serving Heaven and Earth and governing men] above and respected the hundred officials below, regarding the harmonious assistance of their court ministers, chancellors, and inner palace women as valued resources. Does this suggest they didn't esteem the worthy? Certainly not!

Moreover, "products difficult to obtain" are always unusual items from distant regions. If the ruler unrestrainedly esteems them, the people will supply and transport them endlessly. When they then start to seek them out and seize them from each other, if this isn't robbery, what is? When robbers and brigands begin to flourish, weapons and armor will appear.

Furthermore, everyone wants precious items and beautiful women, but the Sage, penetrating to the principles of things, doesn't allow them to perturb his inner self, to throw his mind into chaos. Accordingly, the Sage "makes their minds vacuous," eliminating the dross and stopping conception. He "satiates their bellies" so that they cherish loyalty and embrace sincerity. He "weakens their intentions" so that they are humbly compliant and externally inoffensive. He "strengthens their bones" so that they are solid and secure and internally prepared. "He constantly causes the people to have neither knowledge nor desire," leading by example in order to rectify them. He "ensures the wise dare not act." Accordingly, the *Tao Te Ching* subsequently speaks about being inactive to directly warn rulers not to undertake military affairs and warfare. As the *Analects* states, "What did Emperor Shun do? Making himself reverent, he correctly faced south, that's all." If every ruler could attain Shun's Virtue, how would All under Heaven not be ordered? Thus, the chapter concludes, "acting through actionlessness, nothing will be unordered."

In the Warring States period, civilization suddenly burgeoned with new ideas, technical skills, materials, and even population, while the people were simultaneously being decimated and the terrain laid waste. Yet it might be remarked that outside the few growing cities, the landscape was populated with small villages and towns, much as described in "A Small State with Few People." For the vast majority of people, life would have been extremely simple; therefore, further simplifying it would require little effort and few "sacrifices." However, by Wang Chen's time, two centuries of high T'ang culture had seen extensive developments in many aspects of civilization, both material and cultural (including the early stages of printing), that had created a dramatically more varied style of life and an opulent culture filled with music, literature, and foreign curios. Returning to simplicity would therefore have required vast changes, considerably transforming urban life and even village practices, where timeless ways still fundamentally prevailed. Wealthy families, powerful temples, and a growing bureaucracy all enjoyed an unshakable presence by the time of Wang's writing in the early ninth century CE, creating a complex world with a markedly advanced infrastructure that affected every aspect of the people's lives. In this context, his continued advocacy of the *Tao Te Ching*'s core vision of simplicity becomes a drastic measure, one unlikely to have received any real support even if it provided a solution to the factionalizing forces confronting and debilitating the T'ang.

One other chapter, "With Government, Order the State," provides further insights into the psychodynamics of disorder, concluding with four lines that formulate the essence of Sagely policy:

As the realm's prohibitions and interdictions
  are multiplied,
The people grow increasingly impoverished.
As the people's sharp implements multiply,
The state becomes increasingly muddled.
As human skill and artifice multiply,
Rarities are increasingly brought forth.
As laws and edicts are further publicized,
Robbers and brigands are increasingly numerous.

Somewhat abridged, Wang's commentary surprisingly ventures into fundamental economic issues, decrying the pernicious results of government impositions and excesses in causing unrest:

> Lao-tzu speaks about the realm's prohibitions and interdictions' being multiplied because whenever [the ruler's] fishing and hunting exhaust the marshes and numerous prohibitions are imposed on other sources, the people's material resources will be insufficient and profits will not circulate below. Since the people become increasingly impoverished, isn't Lao-tzu's lament appropriate! Moreover, if forcing All under Heaven to display tactical plans and take up sharp implements isn't muddled, what is? "Muddled" is like chaotic.
>
> "As human skill and artifice multiply, rarities are increasingly brought forth" that will inevitably perturb the minds of superiors. "As laws and edicts are further publicized, robbers and brigands become increasingly numerous," meaning that the people do not fear death.

Wang Chen often attributed the causes of strife and conflict to extensive breakdowns in the social values and fundamental courtesies defined by the conventions of his time, on the assumption that the original core of Confucian virtues, such as righteousness and benevolence, should prevail. (He little valued the debased, merely conscious or hypocritical, forms of virtue, as his commentary to several of the devolution chapters reveals.) In a remarkable meditation prompted by a chapter that merely mentions noncontention, "The Highest Good Is Like Water," he postulates strife as innate and goes on to reprise the causes of conflict:

> *In dwelling, focus on terrain;*
> *In mind, focus on profundity;*
> *In associates, focus on benevolence;*
> *In speech, focus on sincerity;*
> *In administration, focus on governing;*
> *In affairs, focus on capability;*

In movement, focus on timeliness.
Only by not contending
Will there be no rancor.

Now human nature cannot avoid strife; only Sages can be free from conflict. Furthermore, the disciples of combat are legion. Whenever I examine the causes of strife, I find that they all originate in being thoughtless, neglecting the *li* and the laws, not being fearful, and not exercising forbearance. Therefore, the chaotic and contrary invariably fight, the resolute and strong invariably fight, the brutal and overbearing invariably fight, the enraged invariably fight, the extravagant and profligate invariably fight, the braggarts and boastful invariably fight, those who would conqueror invariably fight, the contrary and perverse invariably fight, the ambitious invariably fight, the courageous and fierce invariably fight, love and hate invariably fight, the purely licentious invariably fight, and the favored and favorites invariably fight. If a king is marked by any one of these, armies will be raised within the four seas; if a feudal lord is marked by any one of these, armies will certainly clash within his state; if a high official is marked by any of one of these, brigands will bring chaos and defeat to his family; if a common man is marked by any one of these, harm will befall him personally. For this reason, any king who knows the Tao for appointing officials and bringing security to the people must first eliminate these diseases. If he brings it about that there is no contention, warfare can be extinguished. When warfare can be extinguished, weapons will naturally be put away. Therefore, the crux lies in not being contentious.

Although a number of works composed in the Warring States period conclude that warfare is innate to man and society, no such view characterizes the *Tao Te Ching*, despite its acknowledgment that strife and conflict inimically pervade human society. However, Wang Chen perceives conflict as inherent to human nature: it inevitably erupts whenever the forms governing the social and political realms—in particular, the laws and the li—are neglected, allowing minor selfish acts to irritate others and major offenses to result in combat. Since his analysis of strife prompts him to advocate the simple social constraints mentioned in the chapter as correctives for contentiousness, the only problem becomes how to implement them.

The Baleful Nature of Weapons and Warfare

The history of China being essentially one of warfare, and the *Tao Te Ching* having been composed during the aptly named Warring States period, the famous opening verse of "Superlative Weapons" not surprisingly condemns weapons:

> *Superlative weapons being inauspicious implements,*
> *There are things that detest them.*
> *Thus, those who attain the Tao do not dwell among them.*

Unfortunately, China's tenuous geopolitical history bears stark witness to the *Tao Te Ching*'s perspicacity because millions perished in repeated dynastic upheavals, millenarian revolts, and foreign invasions. Soldiers were slain and ordinary people died, both directly and indirectly, as famine followed destruction and pestilence ravaged the countryside.

"Assisting the Ruler with the Tao," one of the *Tao Te Ching*'s crucial antiwar chapters, extends warfare's condemnation to the army itself, decrying the calamities associated with its presence and passage:

> *One who assists the ruler with the Tao*
> *Does not coerce the realm with weapons.*
> *Such affairs easily rebound.*
> *Wherever the army has encamped,*
> *Thorny brambles will grow.*
> *After large armies have flourished,*
> *There will certainly be baleful years.*

Wang Chen's commentary, here somewhat abridged, cites several historical giants who eventually perished through relying upon force:

This whole chapter specifically admonishes generals, chancellors, and ministers who would assist their rulers by saying, "One who assists the ruler with the Tao does not coerce the realm with weapons, [for] such affairs easily rebound." In explication, I would like to raise a few examples—men such as Li Ssu, Chao Kao, Pai Ch'i, and Meng T'ien. None of them assisted their rulers in accord with the Tao but directly, through martial strength, were brutal and strong. They bit off and swallowed up territory, seized and struck, burned the *Book of Odes* and *Book of Documents,* buried Confucian scholars, and slaughtered more than four hundred thousand troops from Chao. Wherever they encamped, they ravaged and massacred, causing nothing to be left behind. The first Ch'in emperor, although alone in imperial power, looked down upon the realm like a great bird of prey but still wasn't satisfied in his heart. Even when Heaven's emolument was exhausted [and his dynasty collapsed], the poisonous remnants still resulted in mutual destruction and harm. In no time at all, the earth itself was cracked and rotting. . . .

Furthermore, "Wherever the army has encamped, thorny brambles will grow. After large armies have flourished, there will certainly be baleful years." In addition, the daily expenses for mobilizing an army of one hundred thousand will be a thousand catties of gold. When an army of a hundred thousand is in the field, a million men will wander the roads. Add to this the murderous spirit, impulse to harm, and drought and pestilence that follow, no disaster exceeds this.

In view of warfare's baleful effects, "About to Seize All under Heaven" warns against seizing the empire by force, contrary to efforts visible throughout the Warring States period:

> *Those about to seize All under Heaven and act upon it*
> *I perceive will not succeed.*
> *All under Heaven is a Spiritual vessel;*
> *It cannot be acted upon,*
> *It cannot be held.*
> *Those who would act on it, defeat it;*
> *Who would hold it, lose it.*

"To act on it" refers to mobilizing the army and flourishing weapons. Thus, Lao-tzu says that "All under Heaven is a Spiritual vessel; it cannot be acted upon." "Cannot be acted upon" means that shields and halberds cannot be employed to capture it; anyone who proceeds in this fashion will certainly be defeated. Even someone who temporarily gains hold of it will still quickly turn about and lose it.

A later chapter, "Those Who Study Daily Increase," directly restates these consequences in terms of pursuing actionlessness:

> *Those who would seize All under Heaven*
> *Always do so with the absence of affairs,*
> *For the presence of affairs*
> *Makes it impossible to seize All under Heaven.*

Wang Chen then analyzes the core teaching in terms of how war efforts affect the people:

> When a ruler mounts affairs, he confiscates the people's wealth through military and civil taxes; when he acts, he harms the people's basic nature and their very lives with shields and halberds. Under such conditions, his relatives will be estranged and his troops rebellious, the state extinguished and the people endangered, so how will he be able to seize the minds of All under Heaven? Thus, the *Tao Te Ching* states he will be "incapable of seizing All under Heaven."

As he observes in his commentary to "The Highest Good Is Like Water," "when armies fight for a city, the slain will fill the city; when they struggle for territory, the dead will fill the fields." Furthermore, his notes to "Realizing the Pinnacle of Vacuity" conclude: "A monarch incapable of knowing the truly constant Tao—who indulges his tastes and desires, wantonly initiates inauspicious activities, mobilizes the shields and halberds, and circulates his poisonous venoms—will certainly be repaid with calamity and disaster."

Based upon "Tao Gave Birth to the One," Wang sees the army's employment as invariably self-defeating because strong armies, as will be seen below, entail their own destruction:

> *Thus, some things, being diminished, are augmented;*
> *Some, being augmented, are diminished.*
> *What people teach I also teach:*
> *"The strong and powerful do not attain a natural death."*
> *I take this as my chief instruction.*

When Lao-tzu says that he must use the admonitory teachings of others to instruct men, he means that people who don't understand the Tao of augmenting and diminishing simply rely upon troops and love weapons. The brutally strong who slight their enemies will inevitably suffer the humiliation and destruction of defeat, will overturn their armies and bring about the slaughter of their cities. Since it is obvious that they will prematurely lose their lives, he comments, "the strong and powerful do not attain a natural death." Since no calamity greater than this can befall state rulers, Lao-tzu concludes, "I take this as my chief instruction," thereby asserting that no admonition is more important than this.

Apart from the immediate consequences, the existence and employment of weapons have a ripple effect that engulfs even ordinary men, according to Wang's expansion on "The People's Hunger":

Now when one family has weapons, it affects their village. When a village has weapons, it affects their state. When a state has weapons, it affects All under Heaven. When All under Heaven have weapons, chaos is preordained. Farmers then abandon their hoes to take up staffs and halberds, and women abandon their weaving work. Among the common people and registered households, more than half thus engage in military activities. Fathers and sons, elder and younger brothers, neighbors and clans, villages and cliques all become armed knights and perpetrate villainy. Even among those tempted to goodness, who speaks about Confucius and the *I Ching*? Therefore, they are said to be "difficult to govern."

The Actuality of Warfare

The *Tao Te Ching* condemns weapons and warfare and paints an idealized picture of handling invaders. (See "Those Who Employ the Military Have a Saying.") Yet at the same time, in Wang Chen's view, it regards the army as indispensable, both as a deterrent and because fighting may sometimes be the only alternative. As noted earlier, in his afterword, he remarks, "Sages do not employ the military out of indignation or anger, to fight to seize terrain, from greed or love, or to avenge enmity. They order and discipline their troops, nurture and store them, in order to be prepared against evil and overawe the unwise. They do not employ them in battlefield deployments, nor use them in aggressive attacks, nor for hunting in the wilds, nor for great strength."

The penultimate chapter, "A Small State with Few People," unfolds an idyllic vision of natural, strife-free harmony. Yet key lines clearly note the presence of military weapons and organizations, evidence that even in this romanticized tranquillity, the *Tao Te Ching* authors envisioned the need for a deterrent force in order to be truly untroubled, to preclude warfare's rearing its ugly head:

> *Given a small state with few people—*
> *Cause them to have military organizations of ten and a*
> * hundred*
> *But not employ them,*

Even though they have armor and weapons, they will then have no place to deploy them.

While acknowledging that the military should only be employed when circumstances truly require, Wang's expansion also recognizes a need to maintain it whenever a ruler cleaves to the Tao of humility. Thus, he implies that deference and yielding, otherwise seen as the key to actionless conquest, may also tempt enemy invasions:

> This chapter speaks about the Tao of rulership. Even with the strength of a large state, it is necessary to always make oneself humbly insignificant. Even with the strength of innumerable commoners, it is similarly necessary to always display solitary weakness.
>
> Now one who makes himself humbly insignificant and avoids the error of boasting about his greatness will never neglect the Tao of humility and pliancy. One who manifests solitariness and weakness and lacks the worry of relying upon others will not neglect defensive preparations. Even if the state has leaders for every ten men, or captains for a hundred, they will similarly not be employed except when given birth by necessity. This being the case, every man will embrace and cherish his life, respect and value his death. When they are already settled amid their village lands, why would they want to travel or move far off? Moreover, when it's unnecessary to transport military rations, boats and wagons will be useless. When warfare has ceased, armor and weapons will not be deployed. People will then naturally attain great tranquillity.

Thus, in pondering the well-known meditation upon the functionality of emptiness, "Thirty Spokes Collectively Form a Hub," Wang Chen explicitly raises the concept of deterrence despite the absence of any military themes:

> *Thirty spokes collectively form a hub,*
> *But through nonbeing, the chariot can be employed.*
> *Clay is thrown to make a vessel,*
> *But through nonbeing, the vessel is useful.*
> *Doors and windows are chiseled for a room,*
> *But though nonbeing, the room has use.*
> *Thus, through being, there is benefit;*
> *Through nonbeing, use.*

These three—chariots, vessels, and rooms—all become useful through nonbeing. They rely on being but employ nonbeing, so Lao-tzu adduces them as evidence. What about this? Through nonbeing, the five weapons similarly have their martial employment. Moreover, bows and arrows need not harm anyone before being advantageously employed to overawe All under Heaven. Thus, those who understand the army regard preparation as being, cessation as nonbeing, and thus exploit the army's nonemployment. "Through nonbeing, [there is] use" is thus clear!

Clearly Wang did not believe in abandoning the army to naively rely upon an enemy's goodwill but instead assumed that proper preparation (coupled with Sagely rule) would ensure the state's survival and deter warfare. Accordingly, "The state's sharp implements cannot be displayed to the people," found in "Wanting to Reduce Something," prompts a further assertion:

When the Former Kings manifested their scintillating Virtue, they never inspected the army because the army is the state's sharp implement and must not be displayed to the people. However, the army is also something that, although not employed in warfare, should be preserved, never abandoned. Still, it must only be prepared and maintained within, not exhaustively exposed outside, because when externally displayed to the people, the shame of defeat will inevitably follow. Shouldn't one be careful?

Moreover, although the *Tao Te Ching* never attributes any beneficial aspects to the army, Wang Chen finds occasion for evoking its merits in "The Highest Good Is Like Water," whose initial verse states, "The highest good is like water. Water excels in benefiting the myriad things without contending with them."

This chapter, which particularly discusses the essentials of directing the army, is most profound. Now the truly excellent army may be compared with water. Overflowing water produces the disaster of inundation and erosion, disordered armies the calamity of distress. When controlled, water irrigates and nurtures the myriad things while allowing passage for boats with oars. When well disciplined, the army settles the common people and protects the state. A disciplined army that can imitate the noncontentiousness of water and also occupy detested terrain without encroaching upon enemy territory or causing harm will approach the Tao.

Key verses in "Superlative Weapons" prescribe the attitude of sorrow that should be maintained whenever the army must be employed, thereby (in harmony with the Tao) de-emphasizing martial activities and quashing the common tendency to glorify them so as to preserve the fruits of victory:

> *Weapons are inauspicious implements,*
> *Not the instruments of the perfected man.*
> *But when he has no alternative but to employ them,*
> *He esteems calmness and equanimity.*
> *Victories achieved are not glorified,*
> *For glorifying them is to take pleasure in killing men.*
> *One who takes pleasure in killing men*
> *Cannot achieve his ambitions under Heaven.*
> *Auspicious affairs esteem the left;*
> *Inauspicious affairs esteem the right.*
> *Subordinate generals occupy the left;*
> *Commanding generals the right.*
> *This states that one treats military affairs as rites of*
> *   mourning.*
> *After killing masses of the enemy's men,*
> *Weep for them with grief and sorrow.*
> *After being victorious in battle,*
> *Implement the rites of mourning.*

Wang Chen unpacks the implications, pointing out that even the enemy's soldiers should be considered one's own within the context of the Tao:

"Weapons" include such things as swords, halberds, and spears. "Superlative" means excellent. In speaking of implements, Lao-tzu means these weapons. The chapter thus says that these polished and decorated hides, these marvelous, sharp weapons, are actually not good implements. Moreover, left and *yang* are auspicious, right and *yin* baleful. When the perfected man absolutely cannot avoid employing them, he should "esteem calmness and equanimity." "Calmness" means being settled and tranquil; "equanimity" means acting without relish. This says that even when deployed forces score a victory, the commander should remain placid and not relish it, "not glorify it." One who glorifies victory delights in killing men. Moreover, all those killed are actually one's own men. How can anyone take pleasure in killing his own men? Even when warfare is necessary, how can any king who takes pleasure in killing "achieve his ambitions under Heaven"?

Moreover, in antiquity, "After killing great masses of the enemy's men, [they wept] for them with grief and sorrow. After being victorious in battle, [they] implemented the rites of mourning." Since those killed were all their own men, how could they not hold the rites of mourning for them?

Wang basically adheres to the theory that Virtue will attract and subdue all enemies (as discussed in the chapter commentaries). Interestingly, in his remarks on "Those Who Employ the Military Have a Saying," he nonetheless notes dejectedly that most rulers, being far more ordinary, require strong military forces to survive:

> Although Sage rulers truly have no enemies under Heaven, if one speaks about ordinary rulers, about their order and disorder, their enemies are numerous. As the *Book of Documents* states, "Those who soothe us we regard as our ruler; those who oppress us we regard as our enemy." If this is so, then All under Heaven may be one's enemy. A single state may be the enemy, a village the enemy, a family the enemy, a person the enemy.

This passage reverts attention to the dilemma of managing evil and protecting the people with less than ideal government leadership.

SOLUTIONS

Apart from simply parading an idealized vision of government, whether ancient or contemporary, the various chapters of the *Tao Te Ching* counsel two basic solutions to the problem of strife and disorder. The first is active government measures (conceived as nonactivity) to reverse the pernicious effects of sensory stimuli and social competition; the second, imparting the doctrine of sufficiency, causing people to satisfy themselves with minimal material achievement. The former emphasizes non-competition, although in Wang Chen's more energetic conception, it embraces the original Confucian virtues, whereas the latter requires and is oriented toward individual awakening.

Realizing the stupidity of mindlessly pursuing desirable objects and interminably seeking the sensual pleasures (as described in the "The Five Colors Compel Humans") stems from understanding that the body is not immortal and unbreakable but instead easily subject to misery and pain. As "Be Startled at Favor and Disgrace" points out, "The reason we have great misery is that we have bodies. If we did not have bodies, what misery would we have?" Accordingly, "Fame or the Body, Which Is More Intimate?" suggestively ponders the implications:

> *Fame or the body, which is more intimate?*
> *The body or goods, which more numerous?*
> *Gain or loss, which more debilitating?*
> *For this reason, extreme love will certainly incur great*
> *   expense,*
> *Abundant storing certainly entail severe loss.*
> *To know sufficiency is to avoid disgrace;*
> *To know stopping is to be unimperiled*
> *And thus able to long endure.*

The liberating realization of knowing sufficiency, also expressed in the common Chinese saying that "those who know the point of sufficiency will have everlasting contentment," allows Wang Chen to envision it as one key to warfare's cessation as well as an end to personal misery and anxiety. Unfortunately, this lesson apparently remains incomprehensible to the average man:

> "Fame" entails salary and position, so those who contend for them forget their bodies. "Goods" refer to material wealth and treasures, so those who covet them slight their own deaths. Even the stupidest person understands that fame is something apart from his body, and his body much greater than mere goods, but in the incipient moment between gain and loss, at the edge of giving and taking, even the reasonably wise are not always able to avoid confusion. Only the Sage is capable of knowing that war can be halted and therefore does not fight for fame; that wealth and material goods can be sufficient and therefore does not harm his body to obtain them; and that by not abundantly storing things away, he will not suffer severe loss. Thus, to the very end of his life, harm, disgrace, and danger cannot touch him personally. Therefore, he can long endure.

According to "When the Tao Prevails throughout the Realm," when the ruler himself knows sufficiency instead of attempting to fulfill all his desires, tranquillity will become pervasive:

> *When the Tao prevails throughout the realm,*
> *Swift steeds are released to fertilize the fields.*
> *When the Tao does not prevail throughout the realm,*
> *War horses multiply amid the suburbs.*
> *No misfortune is greater than not knowing sufficiency,*
> *No calamity greater than being covetous.*
> *Therefore, the contentment of knowing sufficiency*
> *Is everlasting contentment.*

When swift steeds are released to fertilize fields of thorny brambles, isn't the Tao attained? When war horses multiply amid the many fortresses in the four outer districts, isn't the Tao absent?

When the ruler of men indulges his heart of desire, All under Heaven suffer punishment. When his tastes and desires are awakened but he does not know the boundary of stopping and sufficiency, then All under Heaven suffer misfortune. Moreover, when the ruler of men obtains all that he desires, All under Heaven will inevitably be ensnared in disaster and calamity. When the ruler knows the contentment of being sufficient, who among the people under Heaven will not always be content?

Virtue and Knowledge

Vastly simplified, the *Tao Te Ching* itself envisions Virtue (*Te*)—variously defined and characterized, but basically the power derived from embodying the Tao—as essential to all creatures and the realm of man. For Confucians, Te is primarily moral, although when sufficiently cultivated, it can become a surpassing and nearly transcendent power that radiates and overwhelms. Taoist Virtue is similar in many respects to the radical, pristine virtues of Confucius's original conception. In interpreting the text, Wang Chen discerns a cosmological explanation and justification for true Confucian virtues such as benevolence. In its natural form, before consciousness intervened, benevolence was integral to man and society even according to the *Tao Te Ching;* thus, Wang posits a functional role for virtue in general. Despite limitations, Wang considers the fundamental virtues all-encompassing and forceful rather than impotent and worthlessly confined to naive "do-gooders." This is in sharp contrast to modern attitudes, which find that virtue is irrelevant or simply results in societies that are sterile, constrained, and uninteresting, albeit safe. In his conception, Virtue thus constitutes a vital force for forming and reforming, requiring only a deep commitment to its implementation. For example, the chapter entitled "Governing the People and Serving Heaven," which tangentially introduces the concept of

Virtue, still prompts an essay emphasizing the effective power of benevolence and righteousness in converting and subduing the people:

For governing the people and serving Heaven, there is
nothing like frugality.
Now only through frugality will they early submit.
Early submission is termed doubly accumulated Virtue.
For one of doubly accumulated Virtue, there are none
unconquered.
Since there are none unconquered, no one knows their
pinnacle.
Since no one knows their pinnacle,
They can possess the state.
Those who possess the mother of the state
Can long endure.
This is referred to as deepening the roots and solidifying
the base,
The Tao to longevity and enduring vision.

To be frugal is like loving. This says that in governing the people and serving Heaven, the king must take benevolence and righteousness as his progenitor. Thus, the *Tao Te Ching* advises, "Nothing is like frugality." When the Tao of benevolence and righteousness is implemented, All under Heaven will early submit. Since All under Heaven early submit, it is referred to as "doubly accumulated Virtue." One marked by "doubly accumulated Virtue" will be victorious in warfare and solid in defense. Thus, the *Tao Te Ching* states, "there are none unconquered. Since there are none unconquered, no one knows their pinnacle. Since no one knows their pinnacle, they can possess the state. Those who possess the mother of the state can long endure." "Mother" here refers to the Tao. This means that if the king realizes the Tao in preserving the state, his roots and foundation will naturally be deep and solid, and he will enjoy the blessings of longevity and enduring vision.

Moreover, in the last part of his commentary to "Heaven Persists; Earth Endures," Wang praises the real effects of embracing and implementing benevolence, long the focal Confucian virtue:

> Now if the ruler conquers himself, adheres to the li, and compels All under Heaven to embrace benevolence, he will gain the willing allegiance of millions, barbarians will bow in submission, and shields and halberds will naturally be put aside. His ancestral temple will be secure and tranquil. Thus, the chapter concludes, "Isn't this being without selfishness? Therefore, he is able to complete his personal aims."

Coupled with the implementation of virtue is the attainment of knowledge. Despite despising and frequently condemning it, the *Tao Te Ching* is clearly premised upon acquiring surpassing knowledge of the transcendent, ineffable Tao and thereby becoming a Sage, a player in the realm of universality. Even commentators who stress the book's lessons for individual self-cultivation feel compelled to see the possibility and process of awakening as being dependent upon a profound understanding of the Tao, of the patterns and principles of activity, so that one can become attuned and in harmony. The Tao itself may be beyond words, ineffable and amorphous, but it can still be studied, still penetrated—and necessarily so if rulers and Sages are to be effective agents for good rather than instruments of disorder and chaos. Wang Chen premises his approach upon the Tao's knowability and a sustained effort toward attaining knowledge of it, coupled with an assumption of power that makes its actualization possible. However, apart from the overall presupposition and emphasis upon gaining awareness of the Tao's principles, a few *Tao Te Ching* verses also imply and even acknowledge the necessity for achieving it. This, of course, constitutes the defeatable paradox plaguing all enlightenment-dependent approaches to spiritual freedom. A late chapter, "Knowing, Not Knowing," typifies the need for knowledge:

Knowing, while acting as if one doesn't know, is superior;
Not knowing, while acting as if one knows, is an illness.

Despite the thrust of the *Tao Te Ching's* initial chapter, in "My Words Are Very Easy to Comprehend," Lao-tzu suggests that his teachings are readily understood and effected:

My words are very easy to comprehend,
Exceedingly easy to implement.
None under Heaven are able to comprehend them,
None capable of implementing them.
My words have a progenitor;
My actions have a master.
Only because they lack knowledge
Do others not know me.
Those who know me are rare,
Who model on me are honored.

Knowledge is thus possible and moreover requisite for acting in an appropriate manner in an otherwise difficult and perverse world.

The Army's Employment

Among the few *Tao Te Ching* chapters that acknowledge a need to employ the army in dire circumstances, a couple discuss the appropriate attitude and measures so that the commander may preclude Heaven's retribution for harming living beings as well as escape the reversal that invariably accompanies extremes. Wang Chen's commentaries further define advantageous courses of action, while several chapters unfold the methodology of the Sage's paradoxically inactive course. Naturally all these are fraught with contradictory aspects, which will be briefly raised below. However, attention should first be turned to "Assisting the Ruler with the Tao," a chapter that in implicitly recognizing the army's use, proclaims the inherently self-defeating nature of strength:

One who excels rests in the results, that's all,
Not daring to exploit his strength.
He attains without bragging;
He attains without boasting;
He attains without becoming arrogant.
He attains because he has no alternative;
He attains but does not manifest his might.
When things are strong, they grow old.
This is termed contrary to Tao.
What is contrary to Tao early perishes.

Wang Chen interprets the verses as referring to military commanders who, having excelled in the field, should desist and never dare to exploit their strength:

"He attains without bragging; he attains without becoming arrogant. He attains because he has no alternative." This is what is meant by achieving one's objective but not exploiting strength. "Having no alternative" is the essential Tao of the Sage's employment of the military. Thus, it is appropriate that he should be decisive and implement the Tao of not exploiting his power, not boast about his achievements, and not take pleasure in killing men. Placidity is uppermost; even victory is not glorified. This is the meaning of achieving results and not exploiting strength.

"When things are strong, they grow old." This refers to the army's becoming curved [fatigued]. What is termed "early perishing" speaks about armies that lack the Tao. They should be halted early on and never again advanced for employment. If Li Ssu and Pai Ch'i had been compelled early on to plan their withdrawal and standing down, how would they ever have suffered the calamity of incinerating themselves?

The image of a pliant and flexible infant lies behind the two chapters just quoted because old age and death are considered synonymous with stiffness and rigidity, with being easily broken. Armies long exposed to the hardships of campaign, even if victorious, would often suffer from broken spirits and exhaustion, the exhilaration of inflicting defeat insufficiently lasting. "Abundantly Embodying Virtue" provides the paradigm expression, one that Wang envisions as the basis for actual survival as well as cause not to employ the army a second time:

> One who abundantly embodies Virtue
> Is comparable to an infant.
> . . .
> Augmenting life is called auspicious;
> Mind manipulating ch'i is called strong.
> When things are strong, they grow old;
> This is termed contrary to Tao.
> What is contrary to Tao early perishes.

This chapter states that rulers marked by abundant Virtue invariably preserve their essence and harmonize their ch'i, just as an infant does. Free from impulses and contemplation, in themselves they are sincere and enlightened. Accordingly, nothing can harm them. . . . Furthermore, sustaining and augmenting life is termed "auspicious." This means that the ruler should constantly diminish his body and constrain his mind, making them pliant and weak, loving and compassionate, rather than manipulating his ch'i or relying upon power for strength. The *Tso Chuan* states, "A single drumming arouses the ch'i; a second time and it declines; a third and it is exhausted." This makes it clear that those who employ their ch'i cannot long endure. In addition, while the strong are sturdy, the sturdy become old. The meaning of the phrase "old armies are crooked" similarly lies in this. Thus, the *Tao Te Ching* advises desisting early and refraining from employing the army a second time.

A late *Tao Te Ching* chapter, "Life of the People," similarly concludes that strong armies cannot endure because they contravene the Tao of pliancy:

> Human life is pliancy and weakness;
> Death is stiffness and strength.

Alive, the myriad things, grasses, and trees are pliable
  and fragile;
Dead, they are dry and withered.
Thus, the firm and strong are disciples of death;
The pliant and weak are disciples of life.
For this reason, strong armies will not be victorious;
Strong trees will break.
The strong and great dwell below;
The pliant and weak dwell above.

Wang Chen's commentary not only reiterates these
principles but translates them into the concrete reality of human tendencies and historical examples:

This chapter once again speaks about employing pliancy and
weakness and elucidates the partisans of life and death. In my
ignorance, I think its profound essence lies in the idea that
strong armies will not be victorious. Moreover, the chapter
subsequently states, "Strong trees will break. The strong and
great dwell below; the pliant and weak dwell above." This is
another severe warning against misfortune arising from
armies' being too strong. Why? Armies are termed baleful,
dangerous implements, tools for fighting and conflict, the
scope of their impact being the enemy opposite. Accordingly,
when their armies are strong, rulers are unworried. When
rulers are unworried, their generals are arrogant. When generals are arrogant, their troops are brutal. When a complacent
ruler controls arrogant generals who in turn command brutal
troops, before long they will be defeated and overturned, so
how will they conquer the enemy?

The decline of the Hsia and Shang resulted from raising
massive armies and overturning all within the four seas. In the
end, Ch'in Shih-huang unified the realm but lost the Nine
Regions. Hsiang Yü suddenly became hegemon and then
raced toward extinction. Wang Mang of the Hsin usurped imperial power and was obliterated. Fu Chien was indecisive at
Huai-shang [and was destroyed], while Sui Yang-ti was torn
asunder in Ch'u Palace. The largest of their forces surpassed a

million; the least attained it. Since every single one of them seized defeat through relying on achievements, they furnish explicit evidence of the strong's not being victorious. Moreover, wresting military victory is not hard, but preserving it is!

Only a ruler who has realized the Tao can hold on to victory. These rulers were all defeated because they failed to hold on to victory. Isn't this truly the case!

In contrast, Wang Chen sees the core verses of "Those Who Excel in Moving Have No Tracks" as referring to the superior army, one that is both formless and successful:

Those who excel in moving have neither tracks nor traces;
Those who excel in speaking, no blemishes or defects.
Those who excel at calculating use no tallies or counters.
Those who excel at closing have no locks yet cannot be
opened;
Those who excel at knots use no ropes yet cannot be untied.

One who has "neither tracks nor traces" moves without movement. "No blemishes or defects" signifies cleaving to the middle. "Uses no tallies or counters" means that he will invariably be victorious in battle. "Cannot be opened" means his defenses must be solid. "Cannot be untied" means there are no beginnings or ends. Excelling in these five, the Sage secretly plans and clandestinely acts. He doesn't expose his ability, exhibit himself, manifest his traces, or reveal his shape. He always wants to effect the army's demobilization before the moment of action, end warfare before conflict begins.

Wang's final line conveys the essence of Taoist military strategy—avoiding actual conflict and achieving victory before deployment is even required. Accordingly, in "Knowing Men Is Wisdom," he concludes that attaining the strength level essential to victory would actually obviate any need for conflict because it requires gaining the willing allegiance of the people (a somewhat surprising contention in the face of numerous examples from the Warring States period):

It is said [that] "one who would achieve hegemony or kingship must be victorious." To be victorious, one must be strong. To be strong, one must be able to employ the strength of men. To employ the strength of men, one must gain their hearts. To be able to gain their hearts, one must realize himself. One who is able to realize himself will certainly be pliant and weak. Thus, when the strong and great realize the Tao, they conquer without warfare; when the small and weak attain the Tao, they are successful without combat.

Moreover, contrary to the fatal tendencies to arrogance seen in rulers with strong armies, the corrective of according with the Tao, being humble and apprehensive over insufficiency, surprisingly results in self-preservation, according to "Those in Antiquity Who Realized the One":

Now anyone who does not take himself to be strong and great will not be contentious. When rulers are not contentious, armies and warfare will cease by themselves. When armies cease by themselves, rulers will long preserve their Heavenly emoluments.

Martial Noncontention

Although Wang Chen does not expand the *Tao Te Ching*'s tactical and strategic military implications, he does comment on several verses that depict the army's utilization. Gathered together, they furnish coherent principles and best practices generally premised on avoiding strength's becoming excessive and the specter of warfare's leading only to carnage and suffering. (Although he bemoans the latter, as also noted in his afterword, the presence of true evil seems to be just cause for action within the constraints of the Tao's unfolding. States and rulers need not simply submit to evil tyrants and perverse forces, while deference generally proves viable only from a significant power base, not from weakness or fear.) However, as Wang Chen notes in "All under Heaven Had a Beginning," "When, in governing the state and controlling the army, things are not harmed, what misfortune will there be?"

In consonance with the idea that the Tao is amorphous and the best governments nearly imperceptible, Wang Chen understands "Grasp the Great Emblem" as outlining the fundamental technique for employing the army so that it may unexpectedly vanquish the enemy, much as advocated in the Chinese military classics:

> *Words spoken about the Tao*
> *Are placid and flavorless.*
> *Looked at, it is insufficient to be seen;*
> *Listened to, it is insufficient to be heard;*
> *But employed, is insufficient to ever exhaust!*

> If the ruler controls and maneuvers the army in accord with the subtle, ethereal Tao—stressing placidity, equanimity, and nonzealousness—he will naturally lack shape and traces, thus causing onlookers and listeners to be unable to hear or see it. Furthermore, the more the Great Tao is practiced, the more inexhaustible and unimpoverished it becomes. Thus, the *Tao Te Ching* says, "employed, is insufficient to ever exhaust." "Exhaust" here means to use up, to be finished.

The main question, however, is reconciling the *Tao Te Ching*'s strong advocacy of noncontention, of not competing, with the acknowledged need to employ the military. Several chapters espouse the idea that the strong can conquer through deference and yielding—apparently psychologically winning against outmatched enemies through the unexpected maneuver of deference—and that when properly prepared and commanded, the army need not even be deployed, much less engage in combat. For example, "Those Who Employ the Military Have a Saying" not only expresses this idea but also provides Wang Chen with an opportunity to effusively discuss the power of Virtue and righteousness as well as what might be termed Taoist operational principles for warfare—being defensive and reactive rather than aggressive and proactive:

Those who employ the military have a saying;
"I dare not act as the host but act as the guest;
I dare not advance an inch but withdraw a foot."
This is termed deploying without lines,
Displaying one's arms without laying them bare,
Being extant without enemies,
Grasping without weapons.
No disaster is greater than slighting the enemy,
For slighting the enemy borders on the loss of one's
*   treasures.*
Thus, when mutually opposing armies attack each other,
Those who feel grief will be victorious.

Lao-tzu, being humbly deferential, could not directly express himself, so he borrowed the phrase "Those who employ the military have a saying." Now armies invariably regard those who mobilize first as the "host," those who respond thereafter as the "guest." Moreover, Sages employ their armies only when there is no alternative, so they mobilize only in response to an enemy. Since they arise only in response to enemy forces, they always act as guests. Advancing little but withdrawing much is the concealed crux and mysterious employment of the military, evidence of its serious treatment of the enemy.

Thus, when an enemy draws up, even though the Sage excels in military affairs, he does not deploy. Since he excels in military affairs but does not deploy, he does not mount aggressive attacks. Thus, the *Tao Te Ching* states that he "deploys without lines." Since he does not employ aggressive formations while his infantry forces embrace righteousness and maintain a defensive posture, what "baring of arms" is there?

Now rulers who embody the Tao initially allow perverse, brutal invaders to wantonly advance, after which the army formally charges them with their offenses and performs martial dances with shields and arrows. The enemy will certainly respect such righteousness and withdraw, so naturally sagacious rulers will not have any enemies. Thus, the *Tao Te Ching* says, "extant without enemies." When the enemy has withdrawn, shields and halberds are put aside. Thus, it states, "grasping without weapons." Once weapons are stored away, Lao-tzu fears people will forget warfare, so he again admonishes, "No disaster is greater than slighting the enemy, for slighting the enemy borders on the loss of one's treasures." "Slighting the enemy" refers to being enthralled with conducting warfare outside the state while lacking preparations within it. However, rather than lacking preparations within the state, it is better to be enthralled with conducting warfare outside it because engaging in external battles will just result in victory or defeat, but lacking preparations within inevitably results in loss and extinction. . . .

"When mutually opposing armies attack each other, those who feel grief will be victorious." Whenever Lao-tzu speaks of grief, he means the solicitude and love that are sincerely manifest from within. If the ruler preserves a compassionate, loving mind and does not neglect the rites in employing his subordinates, they will exert themselves in the measures of loyalty and courage and fully realize the meaning of serving their ruler. Then, in what direction will the ruler not be victorious? Thus, the chapter concludes, "those who feel grief will be victorious."

Moreover, noncontention is modeled upon Heaven, which (because of its unopposable power) thereby excels at conquering, as the critical chapter "One Who Is Courageous in Daring Slays" reveals:

> *One courageous in daring slays;*
> *One courageous in not daring gives life.*
> *Among these two,*
> *One is beneficial, one harmful.*
> *For what Heaven abhors,*
> *Who knows the reason?*
> *For this reason, the Sage still regards it as difficult.*
> *The Tao of Heaven is to not contend, yet excel at*
>   *conquering;*
> *Not to speak, yet excel at being responsive;*
> *Not to summon, but come by itself;*

To be lax, yet excel at strategy.
Heaven's net is spaciously wide,
Expansive without any losses.

This chapter asserts that decisively daring and courageously fierce rulers are always enthralled with forging the strongest armies possible under Heaven and killing men. However, if they were instead decisively daring without being courageously fierce, they would invariably concentrate upon implementing the Tao throughout their region and preserving the people's lives. Thus, the chapter states that in knowing these two, there is benefit and harm.

"What Heaven abhors" are those who love to slay men. Since the Sage has long known this, to intensify his admonition, Lao-tzu reiterates that "he still regards it as difficult." Modeling on Heaven and implementing the Tao, the Sage undertakes actionless affairs and establishes unspoken instructions. How could there be any contention anywhere in the realm? Since there isn't any contention, how could there be anyone he wouldn't conquer? Thus, the chapter states, "Without contending, he excels at conquering."

Wang Chen's commentary then skillfully transforms Heaven's ability to conquer into an assertion of actionless noncontention. Accordingly, in meditating upon core verses in "The Curved Will Be Preserved," he concludes:

> Only by embracing the curved, the Tao of completion, can the Sage be a model for All under Heaven. Moreover, the four lines starting with "he doesn't manifest himself" all elucidate the Tao of not competing. Thus, the chapter states, "Only because he does not compete, no one under Heaven can contend with him." Since no one under Heaven can contend with him, combat between armies will naturally cease. Thus, Lao-tzu asks, "was the ancient saying 'the curved will be preserved' empty words?" Truly, he took the curved to be the Tao for preservation, abiding in it to be rooted in true tran-

quillity. Making this foremost in the Tao for controlling the army and governing the state is acting ethereally!

However, as we observe in the chapter notes, Wang Chen frequently asserts that when someone refuses to compete, no one can compete with him. Although his view undeniably evinces a certain intuitive cogency and inherent veracity, for ordinary people trapped in a mundane reality, such merely semantic victories might only entail death. The views expressed here by Wang Chen and the *Tao Te Ching* fundamentally presuppose the existence and indirect exercise of vast, surpassing power on the part of the Sage ruler. Not surprisingly, this is possible because he participates—both metaphysically and actually, through temporal power—in the activity of the universe: he structures its flow while ever maintaining an unobtrusive profile to avoid stirring rancor and annoyance, the latter a refrain found in several chapters. His stance, behavior, and course therefore differ dramatically from the options available to ordinary men, who lack transcendent attainments or awesome position and are therefore compelled to remain humble out of powerlessness.

Pliancy in Conquest

One strain of thought within the *Tao Te Ching* portrays the most skillful warriors, the most talented commanders, as dramatically violating normal expectation. For example, "Those Who Excel as Warriors Are Not Martial" envisions the ideal mode of conquest as unsullied by combat and violence:

> *Those who excel as warriors are not martial.*
> *Those who excel in combat do not get angry.*
> *Those who excel in conquering the enemy do not do battle.*
> *Those who excel in employing men act deferentially to them.*
> *This is what is termed the Virtue of nonconflict.*
> *This is what is termed employing the strength of men.*
> *This is what is termed matching Heaven,*
> *The pinnacle of antiquity.*

In addition to the idea of noncontention's irresistibly over-whelming others, several chapters of the *Tao Te Ching* and Wang Chen's commentaries as well strongly advocate employing visible deference to gain an enemy's willing submission rather than subjugating the enemy with force. Verses in "Great States Defer to the Flow" furnish the most straightforward formulation:

> *Great states should defer to the flow*
> *Where All under Heaven intersect,*
> *The realm's feminine.*
> *Through tranquillity, the feminine constantly overcomes*
>   *the masculine,*
> *Employing tranquilly to be deferential.*
> *Thus, when great states act deferentially to small states,*
> *They seize the small state.*
> *When small states defer to great states,*
> *They seize the great state.*
> *Thus, one seizes by being deferential;*
> *One seizes through its subordination.*
> *Great states want no more than to unify and nurture*
>   *people;*
> *Small states want only to enter the service of others.*
> *Since they both gain what they desire,*
> *The great should act deferentially.*

The path of deference presumes a massive degree of power—the verses specifically speak about "great states"—so that humility and yielding do not prove counterproductive or become construed as a virtual invitation to attack. Many commentators, however, have extrapolated yielding into an absolute principle, holding that the deferential will ever emerge victorious rather than plunge further into danger. Their views are premised upon weakness and pliancy's invariably conquering the hard and stiff, certainly a principle that the *Tao Te Ching* clearly asserts in "The Most Pliant under Heaven" by stating, "The most pliant under Heaven gallop over the firmest under Heaven." However, Wang Chen provides a more "realistic" or power-oriented interpretation in his comments to "Wanting to Reduce Something":

> *If you want to reduce something, you must certainly stretch it.*
> *If you want to weaken something, you must certainly strengthen it.*
> *If you want to abolish something, you must certainly make it flourish.*
> *If you want to grasp something, you must certainly give it away.*
> *This is referred to as subtle enlightenment.*
> *The pliant and weak will conquer the hard and strong.*
> *Fish cannot abandon the depths;*
> *The state's sharp implements cannot be displayed to the people.*

Although the chapter would seem to exploit the well-known pattern of "reversal being the movement of the Tao," after emphasizing the importance of apprehensiveness and attentiveness, Wang clearly interprets the verses as applying to the powerful, not the weak:

> This entire chapter explicates the meaning of Heaven and Earth, ghosts and spirits, harm and fullness, blessings and humility. It states that anyone who would govern the state and control the army must certainly contemplate the Tao of Heaven above and investigate human affairs below. . . . Those kings and lords who manage to be wary and cautious from beginning to end in this way may be said to understand the subtle and know the illustrious. Thus, the chapter subsequently states, "The pliant and weak will conquer the hard and strong." This really does not refer to the practitioners of the flexible and soft invariably being able to control and conquer hard and strong enemies but directly points out that kings and lords who already dwell in the hard and firm ought to preserve the intention to conquer through pliancy. For this reason, the humble and lowly, the parsimonious and constrained, will long

enjoy their years, while the arrogant, overbearing, extravagant, and licentious displace calamity unto themselves. No doubt this is the constant pattern of things.

Pliancy and visibly effected weakness thus become correctives for power's tendency to become too strong, to grow inflexible and break. "Great Achievement Seems Deficient" expresses it somewhat more simply: "Tranquillity conquers rash activity; cold conquers heat. The clear and tranquil are a corrective for All under Heaven."

The Role of the Sage

The military discussions above have already previewed how the *Tao Te Ching's* activist strain contradicts its core teachings on inactivity. While embracing the *Tao Te Ching's* teachings and espousing noncontention, nonaction, and harmonizing with the Tao, Wang Chen tends to conceptualize solutions from within a Confucian, or at least bureaucratic, perspective. Therefore, he perceives a need for Sages, especially in the role of rulers, who appropriately initiate affairs. Occasionally there are direct clashes, such as statements not to undertake military affairs, and behests, in accord with the *Tao Te Ching's* verses, to be timely, to move early. The contradictions may simply be apparent, ultimately resolvable within the context of the Tao through actionless action—that is, nonselfish, noninterfering action. Nonetheless, the threads merit brief contemplation, even at the risk of overemphasizing or obscuring very real distinctions and contradictions.

Before we ponder these questions, another problem takes precedence: according to Wang Chen and the *Tao Te Ching,* what constitutes being "actionless"? The details of the widely divergent possible answers can be left to the various texts, commentaries, and numerous annotated translations readily available; the critical issue is simply how to define and translate the Chinese term *wu wei.* Literally, it means "without action" (or perhaps "inaction") rather than "nonaction," as often rendered. (In theory, "nonaction"—or literally, "not acting"—would be *pu wei,* although contextual employment rapidly blurs precise distinctions.) As we state in our commentary to "Do Not Esteem Worthies," throughout the *Tao Te Ching, wu wei* clearly encompasses a range of meanings. Sometimes it is identical to totally not acting, and sometimes it functions as a relative indicator with circumscribed referents; in aggregate, it connotes not taking violent or unnatural action, not initiating action contrary to the Tao, and similarly constrained understandings. Wang Chen frequently comprehends it as synonymous with not undertaking disharmonious, forceful actions that result in misery and harm, especially military endeavors. The actions of minimalist government, to the extent that they do not negatively impact the people while cohering with the seasons and satisfying other parameters of the people's welfare, are thus functionally active but defined as inactive and actionless from Wang's perspective, in accord with the Tao's example (see such chapters as "Tao Gave Them Birth" and "The Great Tao Overflows"):

> *The Tao gave them birth;*
> *Te nurtured them;*
> *Things shaped them;*
> *Power completed them.*
> *For this reason, the myriad things all revere Tao and*
>   *honor Te.*
> *Tao being revered and Te honored,*
> *Unmandated, has always been naturally so.*
> *Thus, Tao gives birth to them;*
> *Virtue nurtures them,*
> *Grows them and rears them,*
> *Completes them and matures them,*
> *Nourishes them and sustains them.*
> *It nurtures but does not possess,*
> *Acts but does not rely,*
> *Sustains but does not control.*
> *This is what is meant by Dankly Mysterious Virtue.*
> . . .
> *The Great Tao overflows,*
> *So can be on the left and right.*
> *The myriad things rely on it for birth and are not declined.*

It achieves success but does not claim possession.
It sustains and nurtures the myriad things without
*   acting as their master;*
Eternally without desire, it can be termed small.
The myriad things return to it, yet it doesn't act as their
*   master,*
So can be termed great.
To the very end, it doesn't regard itself as great,
So can achieve greatness.

Wang Chen's commentary to the "The Great Tao Over-flows" explicates the Sage's role:

This chapter states that the Great Tao overflowingly fills All under Heaven. That it can be on the left and right means that the myriad things all follow it, there is nowhere that it is not present. In this way, the myriad things are able to rely upon it to be born and flourish, but the Tao still declines any gratitude for its beneficence. "It achieves success but does not claim possession" refers to the Sage who accords with the Tao in patterning things, applying unconscious love, and covering them with unemotional nurturing. Thus, he does not act as the master of the myriad things and is naturally and always free of desire. How can this be named small? Moreover, the myriad things all return there. The Sage governs them with the purely unselfish Tao, so again does not claim to be acting as master of the myriad things. How can this not be termed great? Accordingly, it is clear that the Sage, by never acting great, can achieve greatness.

The *Tao Te Ching*'s second chapter, "All under Heaven Know," summarily depicts the Sage's role and activities, his stance toward the results of his efforts:

For this reason, the Sage dwells in actionless affairs,
Implements unspoken instructions.
The myriad things that arise there are not declined.

He nurtures but does not possess;
He acts but does not rely.
His achievements complete,
He does not dwell in them.
Only because he does not dwell in them
Do they not depart.

The Sage (ruler) thus maintains a shadowy existence, never exploiting his power nor claiming the credit and benefits deriving from his achievements. This doesn't mean that he lacks strength or fails to employ it but simply that he acts without flaunting it. Accordingly, his posture is epitomized by the core lines of "With Government, Order the State":

Thus, the Sage says:
I am actionless, so the people are transformed of themselves.
I love tranquillity, so the people become upright by
*   themselves.*
I mount no affairs, so the people become rich by themselves.
I am desireless, so the people become simplified by themselves.

Wang not only perceives the absence of military affairs embodied in these verses, as is his penchant, but also notes a distanced, upright stance of tranquillity:

The Sage says, "I am actionless, so the people are transformed of themselves." This means that if he doesn't undertake military affairs, the people will be settled and transformed. "I mount no affairs, so the people become rich by themselves" points out that in the absence of taxes and impositions, the people will be ordered and daily grow richer. "I love tranquillity, so the people become upright by themselves" asserts that by going back to the root and returning to one's fate, the people will become upright by themselves. "I am desireless, so the people become simplified by themselves" says that if they don't pursue the ruler's tastes and desires, the people will become simple by themselves.

Verses such as these in turn give rise to the pivotal question of the Sage's nature and character. Is he an ordinary human who has surpassed the mundane through self-cultivation and self-effort, through realization and penetration of the Tao? Or is he some sort of transcendent being—just an unattainable figment for contemplation, for coalescing operative characteristics that rulers, and perhaps even individuals, should emulate? Although, in Wang's thought, *Sage* is frequently a cognomen for "astute ruler" (especially in antiquity), he does venture a definition in "The Tao That Can Be Spoken Of":

> Those who, through embodying the ch'i of yin and yang, are born, dwell within the three realms of Heaven, Earth, and Man, and are more numinous than the myriad things are termed the most numinous. One who is more numinous than the most numinous is termed a Sage. Acting on behalf of Heaven and Earth, the Sage patterns the myriad things. Accordingly, he relies upon words to establish the Tao and relies upon the Tao to control names. . . . The Tao of the Sage is to act on behalf of Heaven in patterning things so that each one has its nature and fate rectified, truly another dark mystery. Thus, it states, "more abstruse than the mysterious." For this reason, Lao-tzu makes it clear that, except by proceeding through this door, how can kings govern All under Heaven, give peace to the many states, and order the regiments and brigades?

Wang thus conceives the Sage as an active agent, though hardly one in the mundane sense, who acts through patterning in harmony with the Tao rather than through creating or forging. He therefore hopes that kings and other rulers, in their role as Sage leaders, will embrace the *Tao Te Ching*'s lessons, as dark and abstruse as they may appear, and thereby benefit all the people under Heaven.

Although the Tao is frequently characterized as nebulous and amorphous, it clearly functions as the ultimate force in the universe, acting without being acted upon, inactive yet all-accomplishing and all-encompassing, as stated in "Tao Eternally Actionless":

Tao is eternal and actionless,
But there is nothing not done.
If lords and kings could cleave to it,
The myriad things would be transformed by themselves.

Wang's commentary points out that through penetrating the Tao and embracing its patterns, Sage rulers will become empowered and the world will be transformed fully in accord with Tao:

> The Tao patterns on the natural, so the harmonizing unification of Heaven and Earth, yin and yang, occurs without any action ever being spoken of. Thus, Lao-tzu speaks of its being "actionless." It extends to the four seasons revolving and the hundred things maturing, so the chapter adds, "nothing is not done." . . . Accordingly, the *Tao Te Ching* says that if kings and lords can merely preserve the Tao, things will all be transformed by themselves.

While extensive discussion is thus devoted to the nature of the Tao and its actionless yet all-accomplishing character, according to bold statements found in "Sparse Words Are Natural," the Tao cannot be successfully contravened and should therefore be accorded with:

Thus, one who accords with the Tao
Shares in Tao.
One who accords with Virtue
Shares in Virtue.
One who fails to accord with Tao and Virtue
Shares in loss.
One who accords with Tao,
The Tao similarly delights in gaining.
One who accords with Virtue,

Virtue similarly delights in gaining.
One who accords with loss,
Loss also takes pleasure in gaining.

Wang Chen's reaction to "The Tao That Can Be Spoken Of" is equally applicable here: "If those fellows who love shortcuts do not respect the Tao, they will certainly suffer the regret of having their actions overturned. Even more so will those who contravene the easy for the constricted yet hope to be lucky!"

Completing a somewhat meandering circle, the Sage's activism again looms in a verse from "Credible Words Are Not Beautiful," which clearly states, "The Tao of Heaven is to benefit, not harm; the Tao of the Sage is to act, not contend." Wang Chen's analysis reconciles these contradictory impulses to actionlessness and activism by envisioning the Sage as also arbitrating and implementing essentially conventional virtues and thereby achieving even an end to conflict:

This chapter, which summarizes the five thousand words that Lao-tzu personally wrote for transmission down through interminable ages and generations, clearly illuminates the sun and moon, the harmonizing Virtue of Heaven and Earth, and how the Vast Tao, preceding Heaven, gave birth to yin and yang. The Sage takes Earth as his model to determine the relative good points of Virtue and benevolence and discuss the weightiness and lightness of the rites and righteousness, and thus rejects thin floweriness to dwell in thick substantiality. . . . The chapter subsequently says, "The Tao of Heaven is to benefit, not harm." So in the end, Lao-tzu wants to emphasize that the Sage imitates the Great Virtue of Heaven and Earth in assisting the patterns of unfolding life. Thus, the chapter reiterates, "The Tao of the Sage is to act, not contend."

Now the Sage values actionlessness, so why is it said here that he acts but does not contend? I believe that this chapter constitutes the ultimate one among the other eighty and that this single sentence is similarly the ultimate one among his five thousand words. Therefore, we know that Lao-tzu's quintessential meaning lies here. The reason he doesn't discuss action and actionlessness but directly speaks about acting is that he wants rulers to act actionlessly. Moreover, he wants them to have nothing undone. His meaning is clear. When a family is not contentious, fighting and quarreling cease. When a state is not contentious, deployment for warfare ceases. When All under Heaven are not contentious, punitive campaigns cease. When fighting and quarreling cease in the family, military deployment ceases in the states, and punitive expeditions cease throughout the realm, the Sage's principles will be realized. Thus, the *Tao Te Ching* states, "The Tao of the Sage is to act, not contend." This is what he means.

Wang Chen's conclusions well cohere with his assertion regarding "Looked at but Unseen" that "actionlessness similarly applies to not mounting any military affairs."

In his commentary to "Regulating the Earthly Soul to Embrace Unity," Wang envisions this activity in even more positive, manifest modes:

> "In loving the people and governing the state, can you be actionless" means that anyone who would govern a state should first love the people, while one who would love the people should first be actionless. "Being actionless" is synonymous with not undertaking military affairs because martial activities cause the greatest harm. In order to love the people, one should first eliminate any harm, which means that military affairs should not be undertaken. . . . the Sage accords with the Tao of Heaven in order to nurture the myriad things without dwelling in his achievements, behavior that the *Tao Te Ching* identifies as the Virtue of Heaven.

As the *Tao Te Ching* states in "The Highest Good Is Like Water," "Only by not contending will there be no rancor."

Positive Measures

"Governing a Great State" likens rulership and administration to poaching small fish—a saying conventionally understood as meaning that one should leave them essentially undisturbed. Nonetheless, various verses of the *Tao Te Ching,* particularly the *Te Ching* section, advocate active government measures that forcefully stray from the simple minimalist position, no doubt because of the era's requirements and the deficient virtue of the rulers themselves. For example, "All under Heaven Term Me Vast" notes three previously unmentioned qualities of rulership requisite to engaging in warfare:

> *I have three treasures that I grasp and preserve.*
> *The first is called solicitude;*
> *The second is called frugality;*
> *The third is called not daring to precede the world.*
> *Because of solicitude, there can be courage;*
> *Because of frugality, there can be expansiveness;*
> *Because of not daring to precede the world, one can be the*
>   *leader of implements.*
> *Now abandoning solicitude yet being courageous,*
> *Abandoning frugality yet being expansive,*
> *Abandoning being last yet being first,*
> *Would be fatal!*
> *Solicitude yields victory in warfare and solidity in defense.*
> *When Heaven is about to rescue someone,*
> *It protects him with solicitude.*

Against a background of Chinese military thought that much pondered issues of motivation and control, Wang's commentary naturally focuses upon the psychodynamics of gaining the people's allegiance and thereby eliciting, even compelling, courageous behavior:

> "Because of solicitude, there can be courage" means that a single man's [the ruler's] solicitude can gain the death-defying strength of All under Heaven. If this cannot be deemed courage, what can? "Because of frugality, there can be expansiveness" means that a single man's frugality and parsimony

can acquire all the riches under Heaven. If such possession isn't expansive, what is?

Accordingly, the Three August Ones employed solicitude and frugality to conquer the Nine Li; the Five Emperors employed them to expel the four evil chiefs. King T'ang of the Shang and King Wu of the Chou employed them, and their armies conquered All under Heaven. Kings Ch'eng and K'ang of the Chou and Emperors Wen and Ching of the Han employed them, and their punishments and fines were emplaced. But Chieh of the Hsia and Chou of the Shang abandoned them, and their states were extinguished. Kings Yu and Li of the Western Chou abandoned them and perished. Ch'in Shih-huang neglected them, and his son was torn apart. Hsiang Yü abandoned them and his limbs were scattered. Han Wu-ti abandoned them and lost half the realm. Ts'ao Ts'ao abandoned them, and the states of Wu and Shu divided the empire into thirds.

Thus, the *Tao Te Ching* speaks about "abandoning solicitude yet being courageous, abandoning frugality yet being expansive." "Abandoning solicitude" means eliminating loving solicitude for other men. Since people will no longer repay the ruler with death-defying strength, his singular ardent courage must withstand the empire's enmity. How can he then implement his own courage and daring?

"Abandoning frugality" refers to not knowing to be frugal and parsimonious but instead imposing heavy impositions, building extravagant palaces, and augmenting the army. When both the state's wealth and food stocks are exhausted, how will the ruler be sufficient?

Moreover, the *Tao Te Ching* advises that "putting yourself behind, you will be first" and adds that "if you want to precede men, you must put yourself behind them." For this reason, the Sage never dares to precede any under Heaven, yet in the end precedes All under Heaven. This is illustrated by the beneficial examples of all those from the Yellow Emperor down through Emperors Wen and Ching, and further attested by [the ill fate of] all those who abandoned [this principle], from Kings Chieh and Chou down through Ts'ao Ts'ao.

Accordingly, the *Tao Te Ching* concludes, "Now solicitude yields victory in warfare and solidity in defense. When Heaven is about to rescue someone, it protects him with solicitude."

Moreover, as discussed in the section on disorder and its correctives, according to the program espoused in "Do Not Esteem Worthies," the government should act to implement policies to simplify and diminish the people's desires:

> *For these reasons, the Sage's administration*
> *Makes their minds vacuous but satiates their bellies,*
> *Weakens their intentions but strengthens their bones.*
> *He constautly causes the people to have neither knowledge*
> * nor desire,*
> *Ensures the wise dare not act.*
> *Acting through actionlessness,*
> *Nothing will be unordered.*

Clearly the verses are advocating more than simply having the ruler avoid stimulating the people's desires by not valuing objects or expressing preferences. Although "With Government, Order the State" curiously speaks about actively repressing the people with simplicity, in Wang Chen's interpretation, "All under Heaven Know" focuses on nonaction as being inactive in the onerous practices of government:

> When kings do not act out of happiness and anger, their punishments and rewards will not be excessive, nor will metal weapons and leather armor arise. When they are actionless in what they exact, their taxes and impositions will not be heavy, what must be offered not troublesome. When they do not act out of love and hate, their employing and dismissing will certainly be appropriate, the worthy and unworthy distinguished. When they are inactive with respect to their close servants, their attendants will all be upright men. When they are inactive over territory, their weapons and armor will not go forth, their officers and troops will not labor. When they are inactive with regard to the hundred surnames, then All

under Heaven will be tranquil. The beauty and advantages of being actionless are truly thus!

While "Looked at but Unseen" unhesitatingly advises, "Take hold of the ancient Tao in order to govern contemporary beings," the *Tao Te Ching*'s most blatant activism is embedded in two consecutive chapters, "Act Actionlessly" and "The Tranquil Is Easily Grasped," which stress the need to initiate action at the earliest possible moment. The crucial verses of the former, supplemented with key lines from Wang's commentary, unfold the dictum preserved in "The Highest Good Is Like Water" that asserts, "in movement, focus on timeliness":

> *Act actionlessly,*
> *Undertake insubstantial affairs,*
> *Taste the tasteless.*
> *Increase the small,*
> *Make the few numerous.*
> *Plan against the difficult while it remains easy;*
> *Act upon the great while it is still minute.*
> *The realm's difficult affairs invariably commence with*
>   *the easy;*
> *The realm's great affairs inevitably arise from the minute.*
> *For this reason, the Sage never acts against the great,*
> *So can achieve greatness.*

Rulers who realize the Tao of true kingship begin by standing upright, folding their hands, and letting their robes hang down. Thus, the *Tao Te Ching* states, "act actionlessly." They de-emphasize the martial and do not contend, so it says they "undertake insubstantial affairs." They embrace the Tao and are spiritual, so it says, "taste the tasteless." . . .

"The realm's difficult affairs invariably commence with the easy" means that if the ruler slights affairs, misfortune and difficulty will certainly be spawned amid them. "The realm's great affairs inevitably arise from the minute" says that by not ignoring minor actions, in the end the ruler will accumulate great Virtue. Accordingly, the Sage takes precautions against the subtle before it becomes obvious and accumulates the small in order to complete the great. If he wants to act when something has already become obvious and great, he will not succeed. Thus, the *Tao Te Ching* states, "For this reason, the Sage never acts against the great, so can achieve greatness." . . . Moreover, the Tao of focusing upon the easy is easily followed, but the error of slighting the easy gives birth to difficulty. "For this reason, the Sage still takes them as difficult." Only through such extreme attentiveness and caution can be always avoid difficulty among the myriad affairs and subtle moments. Thus, the *Tao Te Ching* concludes, "to the end [he] suffers no hardship."

"The Tranquil Is Easily Grasped" equally enjoins acting at the earliest possible opportunity, at the incipient moment of change, to preclude disaster and misfortune, and initiating affairs with the subtly minute:

> *The tranquil is easily grasped;*
> *What yet lacks signs is easily plotted against.*
> *The brittle is easily split;*
> *The minute is easily scattered.*
> *Act upon them before they attain being;*
> *Control them before they become chaotic.*
> *Trees that require both arms to embrace*
> *Are born from insignificant saplings.*
> *A nine-story tower commences with a little*
>   *accumulated earth.*
> *A journey of a thousand kilometers begins beneath one's feet.*
> *One who acts on things defeats them;*
> *One who holds things loses them.*
> *Being actionless, the Sage suffers no defeats;*
> *Never grasping, suffers no losses.*
> *In undertaking affairs, people constantly thwart them-*
>   *selves on the verge of success.*
> *Being as attentive at the end as the beginning, there will*
>   *be no thwarted affairs.*

Wang's commentary again expands the theme of prescient action, a course that he does not regard as contravening the Tao of developing affairs or precluding military actions necessary to thwart evil while it remains tractable:

This entire chapter states that success and failure lie with men, that there is a Tao for beginning and ending. Accordingly, the Sage does not dare wantonly act just to seek the swift completion of things. Therefore, when secure, he thinks of danger, which is why the chapter says, "easily grasped." Since he does not contravene what precedes Heaven, it states [that such affairs are] "easily plotted against." If evildoers suddenly appear to foment difficulty, you must take advantage of their brittle beginnings to destroy them. Since you will then easily grapple with slender, minute beginnings, you will certainly scatter them without difficulty. Thus, it says, "act on them before they attain being; control them before they become chaotic." This is foresight and prescience. Before events sprout or show any signs, you want to act on them for fear that it will be difficult to plan against them when they are flourishing and overflowing. Moreover, great trees are given birth from insignificant saplings, high towers arise from over-turning a basket of earth, and a distant journey commences from where you are. These three make it clear that by accumulating the small, one attains the great, that from the near, one reaches the distant, just like patiently following the river's flow to a destination. If you seek things too fervently, you will be entangled by a desire for quickness.

For this reason, military affairs cannot be undertaken; anyone who undertakes them will inevitably defeat himself. Weapons such as staves and halberds cannot be taken up; anyone who brandishes them will lose by himself. Therefore, the Sage has nothing he does, nothing he grasps, so it is clear that he has nothing by which to be defeated, nothing through which to lose. Moreover, in prosecuting their affairs, the people of our age are all filled with doubt and prefer shortcuts when approaching the road. In mobilizing the army and defending the state, many are those who thwart themselves on the verge of success. In every case, they lose the foundation and tip, confuse beginning and end.

Thus it is said, "Being as attentive at the end as the beginning, there will be no thwarted affairs." Since the Sage desires what people do not want, the chapter also advises, "do not value products difficult to obtain." He studies what other people do not study, so it says he "reverts the people's transgressions." Lao-tzu probably wants [rulers] to supplement and assist the myriad things, ensure that they naturally mature and attain completion, but at the same time not dare to act presumptuously or manifest themselves, which would be called "taking action." Thus, he concludes the chapter by advising that the Sage ruler "sustains the naturalness of the myriad things but does not dare act."

Clearly, at least in Wang Chen's view, ending warfare requires a cosmologically derived, metaphysically anchored activism undertaken by a virtually transcendent Sage ruler who selflessly participates in the workings of the Tao and refrains from implementing measures inimical to the people.

TAO
CHING

1

The Tao That
Can be Spoken of

The Tao that can be spoken of is not the ineffable Tao.
The name that can be named is not an ineffable name.
The nameless is the beginning of Heaven and Earth;
The named is the mother of the myriad things.
Thus, cleave to nonbeing in order to observe its etherealities;
Cleave to being in order to observe its manifestations.
These two emerge together but are differently named;
Together they are referred to as the Dankly Mysterious.
More abstruse than the mysterious,
The gate to a myriad etherealities.

WANG   Those who, through embodying the ch'i of yin and yang, are born, dwell within the three realms of Heaven, Earth, and Man, and are more numinous than the myriad things are termed the most numinous. One who is more numinous than the most numinous is termed a Sage. Acting on behalf of Heaven and Earth, the Sage patterns the myriad things. Accordingly, he relies upon words to establish the Tao and relies upon the Tao to control names. But this differs from the true and invariant Origin. Thus, the *Tao Te Ching* says it can be spoken of. Since it is the mother of the myriad things, the chapter then states it can be named. Moreover, the Tao of Heaven and Earth lacks any traces that can be sought out, so it says, "cleave to nonbeing in order to observe its etherealities." When the Sage acts, there are things that can be observed, so it says, "cleave to being in order to observe its manifestations." "Observing" is like showing.

Moreover, in their functioning, Ch'ien [Heaven] and K'un [Earth] enter being through nonbeing. Thus, even though "they emerge together, they are differently named." The patterns of change and transformation return to nonbeing through being. Therefore, "together they are referred to as the Dankly Mysterious." Within the Tao of Heaven and Earth, the four seasons evolve, the hundred things are born. This is one dark mystery. The Tao of the Sage is to act on behalf of Heaven in patterning things so that each one has its nature and fate rectified, truly another dark mystery. Thus, it states, "more abstruse than the mysterious." For this reason, Lao-tzu makes it clear that except by proceeding through this door, how can kings govern All under Heaven, give peace to the many states, and order the regiments and brigades? Thus, the chapter speaks of "the gate to a myriad etherealities."

I humbly believe that the five thousand words of the Emperor of the Dank Mysterious Origination [Lao-tzu] will be transmitted for a million years, inexhaustibly profiting mankind just as Heaven and Earth over-spread and sustain, just like the radiance of the sun and moon shining down. Therefore, when a king truly understands the *Tao Te Ching*, he can gain All under Heaven; when a feudal lord realizes its teachings, he can pacify numerous states; when a high minister understands it, he can accomplish great achievements; and when officers and common men obtain it, they can know whence to return.

If those fellows who love shortcuts do not respect the Tao, they will certainly suffer the regret of having their actions overturned. Even more so will those who contravene the easy for the constricted yet hope to be lucky! Subtle, subtle to the extreme of being unutterable. Thus, the *Tao Te Ching* commences with the pronouncement that "the Tao [that can be spoken of] is not the ineffable Tao" to point out that different roads lead to the same end and concludes by noting it is "the gate to the myriad etherealities" to make clear that its hundred ruminations are all summarized in the first chapter. Truly excellent.

SAWYER   The very first lines of the *Tao Te Ching* immediately establish the transcendent nature of the Tao, revealing the visible, phenomenal world—all that is conceptualized and named—as merely derivative. Rather than finding this problematic, Wang Chen embraces the distinction because his vision pertains to the world of men and political action, however subsequently couched in terms of constraint and actionlessness. While not ignoring the metaphysical and cosmological issues raised by the *Tao Te Ching*, Wang focuses upon the Sage as an active agent, though hardly one in the mundane sense. The Sage acts through patterning, through being in harmony with the Tao, rather than by creating or forging. Wang therefore hopes that kings and other rulers, in their role as Sage leaders, will learn and embrace the lessons revealed and embodied by the *Tao Te Ching*—as dark and abstruse as they may appear—and thereby benefit all the people under Heaven.

The immediate consequence of penetrating the Tao and embracing its patterns is empowerment in the ordinary world of political realities and violent entities rather than in some transcendent, ethereal realm. Thus, the Sage ruler, liberated by his knowledge, can gain ascendancy over other states and still bring peace and harmony to all. (Wang Chen's comments, however, indicate that he presupposes the privilege of inherited position and never advocates employing the Tao to foment revolution and seize the realm.) Particularly important is the idea that contravening the Tao results in reversal and defeat, leading to "the regret of having one's actions overturned." Conversely, since according with the Tao means harmonizing with the flux of events, it represents the easy course that should unquestionably be followed. As Sun-tzu teaches in the *Art of War*, exploiting hard-won, well-planned advantages of position strikes the average onlooker as easy, so commanders who manage to achieve it are not viewed as having done anything unusual. Such is the power of the easy.

While the *Tao Te Ching*'s eighty-one chapters variously define and characterize the Tao, over the centuries questions have arisen whether the concept of nonbeing is appropriate to the original text. Many commentators and translators understand the second pair of lines as "Non-being names the beginning of Heaven and Earth." Wang Chen, however, was imbued with concepts of government and administration and perhaps subconsciously influenced by the Confucian doctrine of the rectification of names (wherein names are to be appropriate and reality should conform and be conformed to names). Thus, he apparently understands these lines as rendered, "The nameless is the beginning of Heaven and Earth; the named is the mother of the myriad things."

Furthermore, the term *hsüan,* here translated as "dankly mysterious," has a complex history. In Wang Chen's time, it was identified with *hsüan hsüeh,* the study of abstruseness and the ineffable Tao. It is generally understood as being a sort of deep black color marked by an underlying redness, a term describing the depths of a moonless black sky and therefore laden with heavy connotations of dark profundity, obscurity, and mystery. Because it is often conceived of as "glistening," as having an inherent texture of wetness, the translation of "dank" rather than simply dark or black seems appropriate.

2

All Under
Heaven Know

All under Heaven know the beautiful as beauty, so there
is ugliness;

All under Heaven know goodness as the good, so there is
   the not good.
Therefore, being and nonbeing mutually produce each other;
Difficult and easy complete each other;
Long and short shape each other;
High and low contrast each other;
Notes and echoes harmonize with each other;
Front and rear follow each other.
For this reason, the Sage dwells in actionless affairs,
Implements unspoken instructions.
The myriad things that arise there are not declined.
He nurtures but does not possess;
He acts but does not rely.
His achievements complete,
He does not dwell in them.
Only because he does not dwell in them
Do they not depart.

WANG   The *Tao Te Ching* speaks of beauty in contrast to ugliness. When all the people under Heaven "know the beautiful
as beauty," they will have long recognized ugliness. When all
the people under Heaven "know goodness as the good," they
will have long known the ungood. Thus, the text subsequently
states, "Being and nonbeing mutually produce each other; difficult and easy complete each other; long and short shape each
other; high and low contrast with each other; notes and echoes
harmonize with each other; front and rear follow each other."

As soon as things have names and people have emotions,
right and wrong, other and self already exist in their midst.
When right and wrong, other and self exist in their midst, love
and hate will arise and attack each other. When love and hate
arise and attack each other, warfare will flourish. However,
combatants do not invariably employ shields and halberds,
hatchets and axes. Ordinary men confront each other with
their hands and feet, insects and animals with their claws and
teeth, and birds with their beaks and talons. All of them are
disciples of combat. But when it comes to kings and nobles'

taking action, there isn't one who doesn't employ metal [weapons] and leather [armor]. No calamity exceeds this!

Through de-emphasizing the martial and cultivating the civil, benefits are nourished and harm eliminated. Actionlessly, [the Sage's] instructions are thus already implemented. Moreover, the Sage does not speak, so the chapter asserts that "the Sage dwells in actionless affairs [and] implements unspoken instructions." His affairs are actionless because he wants to submerge himself yet achieve results, to secretly bespread his Virtue and cause the common people to unconsciously employ it every day. This is what is meant by actionless. Similarly, his teachings are unspoken because he wants to rectify himself and lead the people by example without having the consequences accrue to him or becoming entrapped. When the ancients spoke of "being actionless" [wu-wei], they didn't go beyond this meaning.

When kings do not act out of happiness and anger, their punishments and rewards will not be excessive, nor will metal weapons and leather armor arise. When they are actionless in what they exact, their taxes and impositions will not be heavy, what must be offered not troublesome. When they do not act out of love and hate, their employing and dismissing will certainly be appropriate, the worthy and unworthy distinguished. When they are inactive with respect to their close servants, their attendants will all be upright men. When they are inactive over territory, their weapons and armor will not go forth, their officers and troops will not labor. When they are inactive with regard to the hundred surnames, then All under Heaven will be tranquil. The beauty and advantages of being actionless are truly thus!

Moreover, "the myriad things that arise there are not declined" means that superior and inferior all realize their natural divisions; none speak of declining. "He nurtures but does not possess," for his beneficence acts, but he doesn't rely on it. His Virtue, standing alone, transforms things, but he doesn't dwell in the achievements. He doesn't presume upon his strength but preserves himself through deference. Therefore, his undertakings are simple and easy, and long do not depart from his body. Thus, the *Tao Te Ching* states, "Only because he does not dwell in them do they not depart."

SAWYER   This chapter is among the *Tao Te Ching*'s most famous: the first two lines alone are quoted innumerable times throughout the centuries, in almost every imaginable context. The verses characterize the relative, mutually defining nature of such dichotomized but dynamically related concepts as good and evil, beauty and ugliness. Moreover, they immediately furnish Wang Chen with a psychological explanation for the presence and instigation of human conflict. Although Wang Chen certainly was severely troubled by the dire effects of warfare and extensively pondered its nature and origins, nothing in the chapter's verses seems likely to have prompted his directed, if tangential, mediations upon them. Perhaps he was aware of Mo-tzu's insight that warfare stems from selfish partiality, even though Mo-tzu lacked credibility in the T'ang dynasty, having been ridiculed and derided from Mencius onward for his advocacy of "universal love" and the ending of selfish distinctions. Or perhaps Wang Chen is merely reflecting the sense that conflict is innate to man found in the classic military writings and several other Warring States philosophical works, such as the *Huai Nan-tzu*.

The famous concept of *wu wei*, of being actionless (or "inactive"), first appears here, and Wang Chen immediately defines it as virtually invisible, intangible action that affects the people without their being conscious of it. (Chapter 4, "The Tao Is Vacuous," further expands the concept, and it reappears throughout the *Tao Te Ching* and Wang Chen's commentaries.) Similarly, the Sage's teachings are unspoken because they are indirect and personally embodied, although other interpretations, such as Han Fei-tzu's well-known explication, hold that the Sage merely allows his subordinates to act appropriately, perhaps simply balking the implementation of inimical plans and detrimental measures.

Even more important, the ruler (or Sage, the two generally being synonymous in Wang's elucidations) doesn't exploit his power or claim the credit and benefits of achievement, preferring a shadowy existence. (As "Those beneath the Ultimate Know" asserts, the best rulers are barely known to exist.) Remarkably, not exploiting his power doesn't mean that he lacks strength or doesn't employ it, but rather that he doesn't flaunt or exploit it, simply acting then moving on. Perhaps this is best imagized by water, since the *Tao Te Ching* constant employs it as an analogy for pliancy and weakness. Water bends and shapes itself according to the terrain's configuration and the contours of objects but, in sufficient quantity and in motion, can crush any obstacle. It is this latent power that allows its efficaciousness, just as the ruler's position provides a point for initiating activity, especially "actionless activity." This is a fundamental assumption for Wang Chen, who never envisions the Sage sitting in a field meditating upon Virtue—a mere caricature of the Confucian Sage—but wielding the actual power of hierarchical position, as reflected in the last paragraph of his commentary.

Finally, the need for rulers to unemotionally maintain their tranquillity, to be free from desires and emotional perturbations, is visible in Wang's expansion of the chapter's implicit opening theme. Not only will the Sage ruler's self-effacing visage offer no target for rancor (as discussed throughout the text and embodied in the idea of not manifesting himself), but his impartiality and lack of perceptible emotion will ensure that his subordinates remain upright, a view perhaps derived from Han Fei-tzu.

3

Do Not
Esteem Worthies

Do not esteem Worthies
To keep the people from being contentious.
Do not value products difficult to obtain
To keep the people from committing robbery.
Do not display what is desirable
To keep the people's minds from being perturbed.
For these reasons, the Sage's administration
Makes their minds vacuous but satiates their bellies,
Weakens their intentions but strengthens their bones.
He constantly causes the people to have neither knowledge
  nor desire,
Ensures the wise dare not act.
Acting through actionlessness,
Nothing will be unordered.

WANG   It is the Sage's principle never to boast of his excellence nor manifest his strength. When superiors appropriate this style, thereby affecting and transforming their subordinates, all those below will end their boasting and esteem compliance. Clearly this does not mean that rulers avoid employing the Worthy and capable to keep the people from becoming contentious. Moreover, the legendary Sage Rulers, Five Emperors, early kings, and hegemons without exception all esteemed the three affairs [of serving Heaven and Earth and governing men] above and respected the hundred officials below, regarding the harmonious assistance of their court ministers, chancellors, and inner palace women as valued resources. Does this suggest they didn't esteem the worthy? Certainly not!

Moreover, "products difficult to obtain" are always unusual items from distant regions. If the ruler unrestrainedly esteems them, the people will supply and transport them endlessly. When they then start to seek them out and seize them from each other, if this isn't robbery, what is? When robbers and brigands begin to flourish, weapons and armor will appear.

Furthermore, everyone wants precious items and beautiful women, but the Sage, penetrating to the principles of things, doesn't allow them to perturb his inner self, to throw his mind into chaos. Accordingly, the Sage "makes their minds vacuous," eliminating the dross and stopping conception. He "satiates their bellies" so that they cherish loyalty and embrace sincerity. He "weakens their intentions" so that they are humbly compliant and externally inoffensive. He "strengthens their bones" so that they are solid and secure and internally prepared. "He constantly causes the people to have neither knowledge nor desire," leading by example in order to rectify them. He "ensures the wise dare not act." Accordingly, the *Tao Te Ching* subsequently speaks about being inactive to directly warn rulers not to undertake military affairs and warfare. As the *Analects* states, "What did Emperor Shun do? Making himself reverent, he correctly faced south, that's all." If every ruler could attain Shun's Virtue, how would All under Heaven not be ordered? Thus, the chapter concludes, "Acting through actionlessness, nothing will be unordered."

SAWYER The chapter begins with a clear injunction against esteeming Worthies that essentially translates the preceding chapter's insights into values and dichotomies. From within his informed vision, Wang Chen nonetheless equates it with simply not honoring or valuing Worthies while still employing their surpassing abilities. In this way, Wang can resolve a troubling contradiction and embrace a program of sagely government with Confucian characteristics marked by circumscribed yet beneficial activity, effective yet unobtrusive.

Accordingly, the final paragraph outlines the actions a Sage should undertake to simplify the people and satisfy their basic wants: he must ensure that they become disinterested in knowledge and projects, stimuli and externals, in accord with the basic premise that stimuli must be consciously reduced to prevent people from developing desires and invariably engaging in conflict, theft, disorder, and even warfare. Although these measures will realize the vision revealed in "A Small State with Few People," a certain degree of tension derives from such "activist" programs. This tension, which somewhat contradicts the overall tenor of the *Tao Te Ching*, is resolvable only in the context of a unique definition of actionlessness.

In theory, the people's desires can be substantially minimized by eliminating all those values derived from the ruler's example, just as Shun, the great Sage Emperor much idolized by the Confucians, reputedly did. (Note that Wang Chen cites the very founding text of Confucianism, the *Analects,* in this regard and will subsequently integrate brief passages from other Confucian classics in his overview of the government as benignly active, despite concurrently citing *Tao Te Ching* verses to the contrary.) In light of the root cause of conflict's being perceived as lying in the clash of desires—or as Hsün-tzu observed, unlimited desires directed toward a limited number of goods—the chapter's emphasis on the pernicious effects of products difficult to obtain becomes comprehensible. Moreover, it constitutes a theme that clearly recurs in several chapters and is echoed in others.

"Do Not Esteem Worthies" also brings into severe relief the problem of defining and translating the term *wu wei.* Literally, it means "without action" (or perhaps "inaction") rather than "nonaction," as often rendered. (Nonaction, or literally "not acting," would be *pu wei,* although such distinctions are hardly definitive, being extensively blurred through contextual employment.) Throughout the *Tao Te Ching, wu wei* clearly encompasses a range of meanings: sometimes it is identical to not acting at all; sometimes it functions as a relative indicator with circumscribed referents, in aggregate connoting not taking violent or unnatural action, not initiating action contrary to the Tao, and similarly constrained, if not contorted, understandings. Wang Chen frequently comprehends it as not undertaking forceful, disharmonious actions that result in misery and harm, particularly unnecessary military endeavors. To the extent that the actions of minimalist government do not negatively impact the people while cohering with the seasons and other parameters of the people's welfare, those actions are thus functionally active but defined as inactive, as actionless, from Wang's perspective.

4

The Tao
Is Vacuous

The Tao is vacuous,
Its employment inexhaustible.
Abysmal-like,
It seems to be the ancestor of the myriad things.
It dulls the sharp,
Dampens fervor,
Resolves confusion,
Harmonizes the scintillating,
Unifies the dust.
Darkly, as if existent,
I do not know whose child it may be,
It is like the imperial ancestor.

WANG This chapter states that when the ruler embodies the Tao and employs his mind, he will be free from profligate intentions. If he is compelled to always be profoundly clear and tranquil like the progenitive ancestor of the myriad things, he will naturally dull the sharpness of blades and resolve confusion, as described. He will thus be able to harmonize his scintillating radiance and diminish his strict awesomeness. Unifying the dusty and heterogeneous, he will embrace the fetid ch'i of the world. Here Lao-tzu sighs because this would be a ruler who has realized the Tao, one able to preserve his perfected Virtue. Thus, he exclaims, "I do not know whose child [he] may be; [he] is like an imperial ancestor." This means the Tao is like the precursor of the Heavenly Emperor.

SAWYER This laconic chapter further characterizes the Tao as vacuous and therefore capable of resolving or bridging extremes, of effecting the reversion of situations of noncentrality or disharmoniousness. Wang Chen immediately perceives an identification between its vacuity and the rulers who embody it, who are free of destabilizing tendencies (and temptations) and therefore suffer no impediments to their realization and expression of Virtue. (The descriptive lines from "dulls the sharp" to "unifies the dust"—often translated as "unites with the dust"—which reappear several times in later chapters and in Wang's commentaries, have been variously interpreted over the centuries, with disagreement particularly arising over their concrete implications.)

5

Heaven
and Earth Are
Not Benevolent

Heaven and Earth are not benevolent
But treat the myriad things like straw dogs.
The Sage is not benevolent
But treats the hundred surnames as straw dogs.
The space of Heaven and Earth is truly like a bellows!
Vacuous and inexhaustible,
Active but increasingly expansive.
Verbosity is frequently impoverished;
It is better to preserve vacuity.

WANG   This chapter speaks about not being benevolent, just as the *Te Ching* [the second part of the *Tao Te Ching*] speaks about not being Virtuous. It says that the Tao of Heaven and the king's Tao are alike, equally bespreading benevolence and beneficence and therefore able to benefit All under Heaven with attractive profits. It does not discuss who benefits nor hold them responsible for repaying the attainment of being.

When the king does not hold people responsible, punishments and fines are naturally not employed. When punishments and fines are not employed, weapons and armor are not flourished. When weapons and armor are not flourished, All under Heaven are naturally free of inimical affairs. Thus, the *Tao Te Ching* states, "the space of Heaven and Earth is truly like a bellows." This means that the monarch is able to harmonize original ch'i and responsively pattern the myriad changes just like using a bellows, to the very end of his rule unwearied by constant vexation. Moreover, when people do not speak, it means that they must have attained vacuity. Therefore, the Sage dwells in actionless affairs and implements unspoken teachings. Thus, the chapter states, "Verbosity is frequently impoverished; it is better to preserve vacuity." Isn't this what Lao-tzu intends?

SAWYER   The fact that language and words, seen here in the extreme of verbosity, are irrelevant to, and even hinder, the nature and true project of the Tao is perhaps disproportionately important to Wang Chen. No doubt he has in mind the first chapter's opening sentences and the words of "The Knowledgeable Do Not Speak": "The knowledgeable do not speak; speakers do not know." However, his commentary fundamentally envisions the Sage as active (in the sense of being solicitous, as discussed in "All under Heaven Term Me Vast") without being prejudicial. (Rulers are similarly active in patterning change, as previously asserted, rather than creating it.) The Sage's actions equally benefit everyone rather than being what might be termed a hypocritical, insincere manifestation of benevolence debased through being directed toward specific individuals rather than humanity at large. Whereas the *Tao Te Ching*'s authors decry the mere shadow of benevolence, misconstruing it for Confucius's defining vision of this great virtue, Wang Chen reconciles their disparate perspectives by making benevolence critical to the Sage's administration and thereby recovering its original universality.

In a remarkable paragraph, Wang Chen then ignores the rather perfunctory, even baleful, treatment accorded "straw dogs" to focus on the idea that (after the Sage ruler sets an appropriate example and implements unspoken teachings) the people should not be held responsible for their actions or, even more astounding, their offenses. In his view, such liberality will prove decisive in ending human conflict and, by extension on an unknown basis, warfare. Clearly Wang's approach requires a degree of blind faith because the methods or basis by which a nonpunitive approach to criminal acts will yield world disarmament is rather mysterious. However, the "chain arguments" evident in the chapter's verses lead seductively, through repetitive cadence, to the focal objective of his commentary.

6

The Valley Spirit Does Not Die

The valley spirit does not die.
Accordingly, it is referred to as the Dankly Mysterious
  Feminine.
The gate to the Dankly Mysterious Feminine is termed the
  root of Heaven and Earth.
Silkily ethereal, extant-like,
It is effortlessly employed.

WANG   Valleys nurture while being empty and vacuous. This means that the spirit's ch'i roams and breathes amid the vacuous emptiness and thus achieves enduring existence. Dankly Mysterious Heaven acts as the nose; feminine Earth acts as the mouth. Heaven is rooted in purity, Earth rooted in tranquillity. Accordingly, when a ruler can long adhere to the clear, tranquil Tao in governing the realm's states, he will naturally be unencumbered by such affairs as movement and employment, by labor and effort. Thus, the chapter concludes that "it is effortlessly employed."

SAWYER   Human experience of the unique mood of valleys, deriving their spiritual power from a combination of vista and containment, no doubt prompted this *Tao Te Ching* meditation upon their emptiness and, by implication, receptive capacity. Although the underlying Chinese character for valley (*ku*) is sometimes understood as connoting the presence of a stream or river, Wang Chen opts to focus upon the valley spirit itself and its relationship to ch'i, the vital pneuma of life and man's very breath that plays a pivotal conceptual role in later chapters. In traditional China, valleys often caught the poetic imagination, and while recluses were largely identified with mountain heights soaring above the fetid world below, some opted for bamboo groves, others—such as the elusive Kuei Ku-tzu, Master of Demon Valley—for valleys.

Wang Chen envisions the valley's vacuity—a defining characteristic throughout the *Tao Te Ching*—as the very ground of purity and tranquillity, perhaps in consequence of three lines found in "Know the Masculine": "Be a valley to All under Heaven. By acting as a valley to All under Heaven, eternal Virtue will always be sufficient." Furthermore, he goes on to immediately translate vacuity into the political realm by slightly reorienting the meaning to characterize Heaven as Dankly Mysterious and shift Earth to constitute the truly feminine rather than having them both rooted in the feminine, the nonbeing from which the *Tao Te Ching* asserts they were engendered. (Although "Realizing the Pinnacle of Vacuity" depicts vacuity's importance, and "The Tao Is Vacuous" mandates it as the very nature of the Tao, the wheels and vessels imagized in "Thirty Spokes Collectively Form a Hub" are more striking and famous.)

7

Heaven Persists;
Earth Endures

Heaven persists; Earth endures.
The way Heaven and Earth are able to persist and endure
Is that they do not live for themselves.
Therefore, they are able to long live.
Accordingly, the Sage de-emphasizes his body, but it takes
*   precedence;*
He externalizes himself, but his body continues to exist.
Isn't this being without selfishness?
Therefore, he is able to complete his personal aims.

WANG   Heaven is pure and unceasingly active, Earth settled
and inexhaustibly tranquil, because they both accord with naturally occurring transformation. They are not opinionated, do
not boast of their achievements, nor augment their being. Unfolding yang and bespreading yin, never acting as masters, they
are able to long endure. For this reason, the Sage is able to imitate the Virtue of Heaven and Earth, purity and tranquillity,
emptiness and vacuity. Because he dares not precede Heaven's
activity, he is able to long be first. Moreover, "externalizing
himself" means he neither boasts nor esteems his body. Therefore, worry and misfortune cannot affect him, allowing his
body to long exist. As the *Tao Te Ching* exclaims [in "Be Startled at Favor and Disgrace"], "If we did not have bodies, what
misery would we have?" Isn't this what the passage means?
    Now if the ruler conquers himself, adheres to the li [the
rites, rituals, and essential forms of human behavior], and
compels All under Heaven to embrace benevolence, he will
gain the willing allegiance of millions, barbarians will bow in

submission, and shields and halberds will naturally be put aside. His ancestral temple will be secure and tranquil. Thus, the chapter concludes, "Isn't this being without selfishness? Therefore, he is able to complete his personal aims."

SAWYER   In this chapter, one of the *Tao Te Ching*'s clearest, the advocacy of rulers' deliberately creating selfless images through the performance of beneficial actions betrays a rather utilitarian orientation. However, in Wang Chen's understanding, through such selfless benevolence, monarchs can achieve the ultimate aim of subduing the world with Virtue and achieve universal peace and tranquillity, not to mention personal security. Remarkably, Wang includes the performance of the li—much excoriated in later chapters, including "Superior Virtue Is Not Virtuous"—as essential to attaining rulership and one of the necessary underpinnings of civilization. His reasoning, in accordance with orthodox theory developed by the Confucian ritual classic known as the *Li Chi*, was that they externally structure society and ensure order while being internally appropriated and absorbed to constrain, yet express, necessary human emotions.

Wang's conclusion essentially reprises the vaunted theory that "Virtue attracts and subdues," vehemently advocated, although certainly not originally formulated, by the pedantic Confucian Sage Mencius. In this view, "erroneous" historical records to the contrary, the most sacred early dynasties were not established through horrific bloody battles but simply through the power of Virtue to shame enemies into submission. Wang Chen largely accepts this view, citing and grounding his comments upon it repeatedly throughout the book. However, in a larger context, it might easily be seen as self-defeating, as well as a major factor contributing to imperial China's ongoing weakness in the face of barbarians. After all, once this view had been espoused, what minister could imply that his ruler lacked surpassing Virtue and advocate the need to develop strong, aggressive military forces? (Note that the problem of true evil in its various threatening embodiments is just posited away. By fiat, evil wilts in the face of true Virtue rather than simply destroying the virtuous. No alternative is admissible.)

Long before Wang Chen's era, the li had come to structure and constitute the very social fabric, prescribing behavior, attitudes, and roles for key human events and family activities, including sacrifices of remembrance, funerals, and weddings. Although they were originally the province of Confucians alone, after being entrenched for more than a thousand years, the li defined civilized orthodoxy, the socialized practices not just of gentlemen (as in the Warring States period) but of society at large, and were deemed essential to being human.

8

The Highest Good Is Like Water

The highest good is like water.
Water excels in benefiting the myriad things without
  contending with them.
It dwells in places men abhor
And so approaches the Tao.
In dwelling, focus on terrain;
In mind, focus on profundity;
In associates, focus on benevolence;
In speech, focus on sincerity;
In administration, focus on governing;
In affairs, focus on capability;
In movement, focus on timeliness.

Only by not contending
Will there be no rancor.

WANG   This chapter, which particularly discusses the essentials of directing the army, is most profound. Now the truly excellent army may be compared with water. Overflowing water produces the disaster of inundation and erosion, disordered armies the calamity of distress. When controlled, water irrigates and nurtures the myriad things while allowing passage for boats with oars. When well disciplined, the army settles the common people and protects the state. A disciplined army that can imitate the noncontentiousness of water and also occupy detested terrain without encroaching upon enemy territory or causing harm will approach the Tao. For this reason, in moving and halting, the army must select and occupy advantageous terrain. The text therefore advises, "In dwelling, focus on terrain." The commanding general's mind must remain profoundly clear and deeply tranquil. Thus, it states, "In mind, focus on profundity." Because many aspects of the army are baleful and harmful, the chapter admonishes, "In associations, focus on benevolence." Now whenever the army's organization is lost, chaos results, so it states, "In administration, focus on order." The army esteems excellence and subtlety in planning, so the chapter advises, "In affairs, focus on capability." Mobilizing the army, ordering the regiments, responding to the enemy, and fending off disaster all require according with the time. Therefore, the chapter concludes, "In movement, focus on timeliness."

Even though the *Tao Te Ching* thus explicates seven Virtues that focus upon noncontention, it emphasizes this thrust by saying, "only by not contending will there be no rancor." I believe that Lao-tzu truly wanted to instruct and encourage rulers of his era neither to contend above nor engage in conflict below. Now actionlessness [*wu-wei*] is the source for ceasing hostilities; noncontention, the foundation for remitting warfare. If kings and feudal lords could clearly perceive the source and comprehensively observe the foundation, it might simply be said that they will cease fighting, that metal weapons and leather armor will lie idle. Moreover, I constantly review the *Tao Te Ching*'s five thousand words. Every time I seek out their fundamental substance and mysterious instructions, carefully investigating the underlying principles, inaction always takes priority, while noncontention is the chief teaching.

Now human nature cannot avoid strife; only Sages can be free from conflict. Furthermore, the disciples of combat are legion. Whenever I examine the causes of strife, I find that they all originate in being thoughtless, neglecting the li [rites, rituals, and forms of social behavior] and the laws, not being fearful, and not exercising forbearance. Therefore, the chaotic and contrary invariably fight, the resolute and strong invariably fight, the brutal and overbearing invariably fight, the enraged invariably fight, the extravagant and profligate invariably fight, the braggarts and boastful invariably fight, those who would conqueror invariably fight, the contrary and perverse invariably fight, the ambitious invariably fight, the courageous and fierce invariably fight, love and hate invariably fight, the purely licentious invariably fight, and the favored and favorites invariably fight. If a king is marked by any one of these, armies will be raised within the four seas; if a feudal lord is marked by any one of these, armies will certainly clash within his state; if a high official is marked by any of one of these, brigands will bring chaos and defeat to his family; if a common man is marked by any one of these, harm will befall him personally. For this reason, any king who knows the Tao for appointing officials and bringing security to the people must first eliminate these diseases. If he brings it about that there is no contention, warfare can be extinguished. When warfare can be extinguished, weapons will naturally be put away. Therefore, the crux lies in not being contentious.

When armies fight for a city, the slain will fill the city; when they struggle for territory, the dead will fill the fields. The *Analects* states, "The *chün-tzu* [perfected man] does not contend." Moreover, it says, "He does not compete within his class." When he contends, the army will do so even more. How can the king have anything for which he insistently contends? Thus, the final chapter of the *Te Ching* states, "The Tao of Heaven is to benefit, not harm; the Tao of the Sage is to act, not contend." This is what is meant by "knowing the meaning of completing the end."

SAWYER   "The Highest Good Is Like Water" provides an impetus for Wang Chen to meditate upon the nature of the army and translate the chapter's general admonitions (which are marked by an inherently active character rather than nihilism, withdrawal, and negativity) into concrete injunctions for the military. It is a matter of faith, or at least advocated belief, that these constitute the way of noncontention. Wang immediately extrapolates this belief into his fundamental tenet that the cessation of warfare is grounded in noncontention, the latter in turn synonymous with *wu wei*, or actionlessness. However, even more important is his expansion of the view that strife is (paradoxically) inherent to human nature. It erupts whenever the forms governing the social and political realm—in particular, the laws and the li—are neglected, allowing minor selfish acts to irritate others and more pernicious offenses to result in bloodshed.

Wang's analysis of the psychodynamics of warfare leads him to conceive active measures that, properly harmonized and free of selfish intent, are essentially actionlessness yet end contentiousness. (Surprisingly, it is not the fundamental Confucian virtue of benevolence that is advocated, nor even the common Taoist techniques of weakness, yielding, and deference, but simple social constraints that here comprise both the spirit and letter of the chapter itself.) He buttresses his argument by once again appealing to the *Analects* for a famous passage on noncontention. However, although the passage was attributed to Confucius himself, it should be noted that Confucius was known for his terrifying visage when donning his armor in a righteous cause and that he never advocated mere pacifism.

The opening verses about water's benefiting without contending emphasize the positive aspects to the exclusion of its destructive power. However, in his commentary to "The Pliant and Weak under Heaven," Wang Chen notes that water can overcome wood, earth, metal, and all other obstacles, such as by boring holes in them. The Chinese military theorists, including Sun-tzu, often appealed to the unopposable power of onrushing water to illustrate the nature of strategic power. In fact, rivers and streams were frequently diverted to act as assault weapons against fortifications and entrenched positions, as well as to flood encampments and inundate terrain that must be denied the enemy.

9

Holding and Filling

Holding and filling is not as good as desisting.
Things forged to sharpness cannot long be preserved.
When gold and jade fill a hall,
No one will be able to retain them.
The rich and noble who turn arrogant
Bring calamity upon themselves.
Retiring when success is achieved and fame attained
Is the Tao of Heaven.

WANG   Human nature relies upon weapons. Thus, when an ordinary fellow carries a sharp three-foot sword or brandishes a dagger several inches long, he may even succeed in insulting the Son of Heaven or coercing the feudal lords into sanctioning visible alliances and accepting clandestine orders. How much more so anyone who occupies the ultimate position of imperial power and possesses a million-man army? Being the solely honored "single man," managing the myriad things below, the ruler knows that holding fullness is not easy, forging sharpness truly difficult. Thus, the *Tao Te Ching* states, "When gold and jade fill a hall, no one will be able to retain them. The rich and noble who turn arrogant bring calamity upon themselves." Thus, Lao-tzu here again uses the gold and jade so prized by his contemporaries to admonish them in the hope that they might be frugal in their employment and maintain an apprehensive attitude. Moreover, he particularly warns kings and feudal lords to preserve their humbleness and vacuity, to reject extravagance and excess, so as to avoid bringing calamity upon themselves.

The final line states, "Retiring when success is achieved and fame attained is the Tao of Heaven." When Lao-tzu speaks about withdrawing, it doesn't invariably mean that a person must abandon his position but rather that he should not possess the achievements. Thus [in "All under Heaven Know"], the *Tao Te Ching* states, "Only because he does not dwell in them do they not depart." Isn't this what he means?

SAWYER   Wang Chen seizes upon the second line's analogy of edged blades to meditate upon the raw power of weapons not only to wound but also to threaten. His statement about the ability of an ordinary fellow to coerce emperors and feudal lords by brandishing a mere dagger reflects several actual examples from China's turbulent Spring and Autumn and Warring States periods. In at least three famous instances, courageous warriors such as Ts'ao Mei furtively gained access to enemy commanders and managed to extract important concessions at knifepoint. Moreover, those concessions were subsequently honored because their powerful victims felt that repudiating them, although contextually justified, would prove detrimental to their own Virtuous images and the cause of righteousness.

The chapter's verses characterize opulence and ostentation as precarious, likely to collapse and rebound because extremes are inherently unstable, as "Reversal Is the Movement of the Tao" postulates. Moreover, visible displays of wealth, manifestations of "products difficult to obtain," can only encourage the activities of robbers and thieves and, in Wang's linked sequence, stimulate social disorder and the consequent imposition of repressive punitive measures. The *Tao Te Ching*'s pervading spirit of self-preservation, visible here, makes it incumbent to maintain a low profile, at least in turbulent and lawless societies. (The *Tao Te Ching*'s authors were undoubtedly not oblivious to wealth's innate awesomeness and consequent deterrent power but probably assumed it would more likely provoke enmity than cower others into submission, would stimulate inimical emotions and untoward acts rather than deter.)

However, Wang Chen interprets retreat, the primary measure advocated by the chapter's concluding lines for ensuring self-preservation when success has been achieved, in an essentially Neo-Taoist fashion. The successful ruler or Sage does not copy the example of those famous eccentrics and legendary military heroes who withdrew to become recluses. Instead, he need only distance himself from the image of achievement, abjure boasting, forsake any claims of achievement and success, and abandon control of the fruits of his efforts. As the *Tao Te Ching*'s final chapter observes, "Sages do not accumulate, so they think they have an abundance when what they have given to men is much greater."

10

Regulating the Earthly Soul to Embrace Unity

In regulating your Earthly soul to embrace unity,
Can you avoid estrangement?
In concentrating your ch'i to attain pliancy,
Can you be an infant?
In cleansing and purifying your dankly mysterious insight,
Can you be free from imperfections?
In loving the people and governing the state,
Can you be actionless?
In the opening and closing of Heaven's Gate,
Can you be feminine?
When your perceptive insight penetrates to the four quarters,
Can you be without knowledge?
In producing and rearing,
Nurture but do not possess,
Act but do not rely,
Sustain but do not control.
This is what is meant by Dankly Mysterious Virtue.

WANG   The Earthly soul is the substance of yin; unity is the essence of yang. This means that the ruler of men should always embrace and preserve unified *ch'i* that he concentrates to be pliant and harmonious, making it like the Virtue and goodness of an infant. In "cleansing and purifying one's dankly mysterious insight," Lao-tzu wants the ruler to wash his mind's reflectivity so that his intentions will be free from flaws and contamination. "In loving the people and governing the state, can you be actionless?" means that anyone who would govern a state should first love the people, while one who would love the people should first be actionless. "Being actionless" is synonymous with not undertaking military affairs because martial activities cause the greatest harm. In order to love the people, one should first eliminate any harm, which means that military affairs should not be undertaken.

"Heaven's Gate" refers to the nose and breath. Breathing should be silkily light, always quiet and regular, ensuring that it attains naturalness. "Perceptive insight" refers to seeing and hearing that should circulate and fully penetrate in all directions, always seemingly without any knowledge.

Up to this point, the chapter has been speaking about controlling oneself and ordering the state, the Tao of undiscriminating love. However, in the final section—"In producing and rearing, nurture but do not possess, act but do not rely, sustain but do not control. This is what is meant by Dankly Mysterious Virtue"—the Sage accords with the Tao of Heaven in order to nurture the myriad things without dwelling in his achievements, behavior that the *Tao Te Ching* identifies as the Virtue of Heaven. "Dankly Mysterious" is synonymous with "Heaven."

SAWYER   Not only does "Regulating the Earthly Soul to Embrace Unity" focus on personal cultivation, as Wang Chen notes; it is also (in the opinion of many commentators) the first *Tao Te Ching* chapter to explicitly invoke yogic practices to explain its insights. (The actual meaning and intent, beyond Wang's comments, have spawned intense debate, both contemporary and historic. Other chapters with yogic echoes and implications include "The Knowledgeable Do Not Speak" and "Governing the People and Serving Heaven.") However, most of the verses are directed to the general practice of self-cultivation, with one interjection on governing the state: "Can you be actionless?"

For Wang Chen, loving the people—a fundamental principle found not only in Confucianism but also in most of the classic military writings—immediately translates into concrete measures designed to nurture their welfare by first eliminating harm. For example, the *Six Secret Teachings* states: "Sparing the people from death, eliminating the hardships of the people, relieving the misfortunes of the people, and sustaining the people in their extremities is Virtue. Wherever there is Virtue, All under Heaven will give their allegiance."

Moreover, the chapter extrapolates the consequences of individual spiritual self-cultivation to the infinite universe whose activity the Sage participates in through actualizing his nurturing and engendering powers. Without denigrating the metaphysical dimension, this means, in mundane terms, according with the seasons while encouraging the principle of growth, never hindering or obstructing while accepting the cyclic nature of things, including death (and subsequent rebirth) as life cycles onward.

11
Thirty Spokes Collectively Form a Hub

Thirty spokes collectively form a hub,
But through nonbeing, the chariot can be employed.
Clay is thrown to make a vessel,

But through nonbeing, the vessel is useful.
Doors and windows are chiseled for a room,
But though nonbeing, the room has use.
Thus through being, there is benefit;
Through nonbeing, use.

WANG   These three—chariots, vessels, and rooms—all become useful through nonbeing. They rely on being but employ nonbeing, so Lao-tzu adduces them as evidence. What about this? Through nonbeing, the five weapons similarly have their martial employment. Moreover, bows and arrows need not harm anyone before being advantageously employed to overawe All under Heaven. Thus, those who understand the army regard preparation as being, cessation as nonbeing, and thus exploit the army's nonemployment. "Through nonbeing, there is use" is thus clear!

SAWYER   Another widely known and commonly quoted *Tao Te Ching* verse, the idea and image of "emptiness" empowering the wheel and bowl's utility much caught the historical imagination. Accordingly, most translations in fact render *wu*, "nonbeing" in the verses above, as "emptiness." However, Wang's commentary focuses upon *wu* with reference to activity, defining the absence or cessation of military activities as "nonbeing" and their employment as "being" thus requiring the translation of "nonbeing" rather than "emptiness." In so doing, he raises the concept of deterrence—the inherent threat that weapons can provide previously imagized by the warrior brandishing a dagger—and their effectiveness in coercing desired responses, including promises of allied support or reticence in engaging in battle, attacks, and aggression. Clearly Wang Chen never naively advises abandoning the army to rely upon an enemy's goodwill but rather assumes that proper preparation (coupled with Sagely rule) can deter incursions and prevent warfare.

Two concepts prove illuminating in this regard. First, the Chinese character for "martial" (*wu*) is actually composed of two individual characters, both classifiers in themselves, one for "halberd," the other for "halting" or "stopping." These two characters were commonly broken out to interpret *wu*, or "martial," as meaning that halberds (and by implication, weapons in general) are being employed to "stop" warfare rather than facilitate it.

Second, the early *Ssu-ma Fa*, a classic military text dating from the fifth or fourth century that advocates restraint as necessary to the conduct of righteous warfare, stressed that one of the few justifications for initiating combat was to end warfare. In a passage not dissimilar to realist aspects of the *Tao Te Ching*, it states "Authority comes from warfare, not from harmony among men. For this reason, if one must kill people to give peace to the people, then killing is permissible. If one must attack a state out of love for their people, then attacking it is permissible. If one must stop war with war, although it is war it is permissible." Moreover, Mencius, well known for his advocacy of the theory of unopposable Virtue, not only countenanced but even advocated punitive expeditions and campaigns of rectification against evil rulers and perverse tyrants. Conversely, despite its strong humanistic orientation, the *Ssu-ma Fa* conveys a prophetic warning about the nature of warfare: "Those who are enthralled with warfare are doomed to perish; those who forget warfare are similarly doomed to perish."

Finally, one of the key theoretical thrusts marking Chinese warfare from Sun-tzu onward has been achieving victory as economically as possible, preferably without even engaging the enemy. Realizing this idealized objective requires intelligence operations, deceptive measures, and the creation of such insurmountable advantage that the army's strategic power simply overwhelms the enemy, essentially cowing soldiers into submission. Although in practice, especially during the imperial period, this theoretical approach was largely ignored, often allowing steppe peoples to realize easy conquests, the principle was well understood and much advocated.

12

The Five Colors
Compel Humans

The five colors cause human eyes to go blind;
The five notes cause human ears to go deaf;
The five flavors cause human mouths to err;
Racing horses and hunting cause human minds to go mad.
Products difficult to obtain cause human activities to be
 hindered.
For this reason, the Sage acts for the belly and not the eyes,
So he rejects that and takes this.

WANG　　The five colors nourish the eyes but when looked at excessively result in blindness. The fives notes nourish the ears but when listened to excessively cause deafness. The five flavors nourish the mouth but when consumed excessively cause it to err. Thus, in governing, sagacious kings always reverse excesses among the masses in order to preserve their bodies and tranquilize their spirits.

Now the monarch's mind takes astute perceptivity as its foundation and clear tranquility as its root. If, in hunting, he pursues animals across the open plains and races his chariot over mountain peaks, his six dragons running so swiftly that ten thousand cavalrymen cannot catch him; contends with birds of prey to be first; matches courage with bears; exhausts the days and months, causing the companies and regiments to become disordered; and gallops about so that he forgets to return, hunting and killing without restraint, unchanged in wind and rain, while the palace remains empty, this is referred to as going mad. Accordingly, in "Weightiness Is the Root of

Lightness" the *Tao Te Ching* says, "How is it that the ruler of ten thousand chariots casts himself away in the realm?" Is this what Lao-tzu meant?

Moreover, when rulers value "products difficult to obtain," thieves and brigands will be spawned. When thieves and brigands appear, armies will arise. There is no greater harm than armies being mobilized. This will "cause human activities to be hindered." Certainly this is true. For this reason the Sage acts for the belly, esteeming tolerance and emotionlessness. He doesn't act for the eyes, disdaining the desires prompted by perceptual encounters. Thus, it says he "rejects that and takes this."

SAWYER   Commencing with several well-known lines, this *Tao Te Ching* chapter psychologically justifies policies directed toward satisfying basic human needs rather than encouraging or even allowing the pursuit of those phenomenal desires that debilitate the body and mind. Furthermore, they immediately prompt Wang Chen to reiterate his view that "products difficult to obtain" foster the development of social disorder—a view that essentially becomes a choruslike refrain, which he chants at every opportune moment, no doubt evidence of his fervid belief. In consequence, he also condemns visible excesses in rulers, especially activities enjoyed outside the court, including hunting. Although, in the ancient period, hunting had comprised an essential part of military training, by the T'ang, it merely disrupted the services of a human army. Apart from being wasteful and destabilizing the government, such profligate activities set a detrimental example of extravagance, encourage the abandonment of agriculture, and directly interfere with the people's livelihood, much as succinctly depicted in "The People's Hunger."

In contrast, the Sage's dedication to keeping life simple by satisfying the people's most basic needs and wants reappears in the well-known eightieth chapter, "A Small State with Few People," which paints an idyllic portrait of village life inhabited by a satisfied populace oblivious even to nearby settlements.

13

Be Startled
at Favor
and Disgrace

"Be startled at favor and disgrace;
Esteem great misfortune like your body."
What does "be startled at favor and disgrace" mean?
Favor elevates, disgrace deprecates.
Gaining them one should be startled;
Losing them one should be startled.
This is what is meant by being startled by favor and
disgrace.
What does "esteem great misfortune like your body" mean?
The reason we have great misery is that we have bodies.
If we did not have bodies, what misery would we have?
Thus, one who values his body when acting on behalf of the
realm
Apparently can be temporarily entrusted with All under
Heaven;
One who loves his body when acting on behalf of the realm
Apparently can be fully entrusted with All under Heaven.

WANG   All the kings who succeeded in preserving their positions were favored by Heaven, while the enfeoffed feudal lords similarly all enjoyed the king's favor. Now through favor, men become honored and through honor, become arrogant. Through arrogance, they commit offenses and, through offenses, suffer disgrace. For this reason, the Sage maintains an attitude of being startled whenever he gains or loses anything.

Moreover, when kings and feudal lords are incapable of honoring those below them, of humbling themselves and respecting men, but are instead enthralled with warfare, rely upon armies, exploit victories, and slight enemies, disaster and misfortune invariably strike. Thus, anyone who has a body will be troubled by favor and disgrace, but if he externalizes his body, won't he succeed in preserving it? For this reason, one who values his body can be temporarily entrusted with All under Heaven; one who loves his body can permanently be entrusted with All under Heaven. Thus, [in "People Do Not Dread Awesomeness,"] the *Tao Te Ching* states, "The Sage knows himself but does not manifest himself, loves himself but does not exalt himself." Isn't this what Lao-tzu means?

SAWYER   The verses encourage people to radically alter the way they perceive and experience events, shifting from immersion and lack of awareness to alertness and a sense of astonishment at unfolding developments. The underlying impetus is toward valuing the body—synonymous with life itself—rather than sensory experience, material things, and achievements. One who is so focused, so oriented, will then be unwilling to risk harm or undertake sweeping projects that might entail violent repercussions and may therefore be safely entrusted with governing the realm. After all, what qualifies someone to be a ruler or king? His wisdom, his acts, or his values? Since humanity has long been saddled with rulers not of their choosing (not to mention tyrants and evil despots), in political cultures such as traditional China, the people could survive only by persuading the monarch to adopt policies of conscious restraint.

Wang Chen emphasizes the tendency of power to corrupt and high position to spawn arrogance not only here but also in "Life of the People," in which he asserts that a disinterested ruler commanding an arrogant general invariably provides a prescription for defeat. The military writers similarly bemoaned the pernicious effects of arrogance and made its detection and exploitation (through manipulating and frustrating enemy commanders) a basic tactic. Conversely, mobilizing the army out of anger and arrogance was much decried and warned against, as previously noted.

Wang's last paragraph also echoes a belief found in the military writings: numerous victories, while marking a successful general, inevitably doom the state to defeat. For example, the great general Wu Ch'i is recorded as saying:

> Being victorious in battle is easy, but preserving the results of victory is difficult. Thus, it is said that among the states under Heaven that engage in warfare, those who garner five victories will meet with disaster; those with four victories will be exhausted; those with three victories will become hegemons; those with two victories will be kings; and those with one victory will become emperors. For this reason, those who have conquered the world through numerous victories are extremely rare, while those who have perished are many.

Thus, everyone from Sun-tzu on condemned prolonged warfare for debilitating the state and causing untold suffering, as well as allowing potential enemies to exploit the resulting exhaustion and collapse.

14

Looked
at but Unseen

What is looked at but unseen is called indistinct.
What is listened to but unheard is called imperceptible.

What is touched but not felt is subtle.
These three cannot be probed to their extremity;
They are confusedly termed the One.
Above the One is not dazzling,
Below not murky.
Continuous and tangled,
Unnameable,
It reverts to not being an object.
For this reason it is called the shape without shape,
The image without form,
And therefore termed the nebulous jumble.
Meeting it, you do not see its head;
Following it, do not perceive the rear.
Take hold of the ancient Tao in order to govern
  contemporary beings.
Being capable of knowing the ancient beginning is
  referred to as
Penetrating the core of Tao.

WANG   "Indistinct" here means level and easy, what is termed the Tao of Heaven. Thus it is looked at but not seen. "Imperceptible" means complying with and going against, what is termed the Tao of Earth. Thus, it can be listened to but not heard. "Subtle" means essential and ethereal, what is termed the Tao of Man. Therefore, it can be touched but *not* felt.

Although Heaven is pure, radiant, and constantly moving, it never acts to be scintillatingly pure because it is self-manifest. Although Earth is quiet and tranquil, extensive and thick, it similarly does not act to be dark and obscure because it is itself abysmal. Even though people are born incessantly, in the end they do not make distinctions because they themselves are respected. Thus, the verses state "Above the One is not dazzling, below not murky. Continuous and tangled, it is unnameable." For this reason, when spread out and arrayed, they compose the three realms of Heaven, Earth, and Man, but when gathered and muddled, comprise solitary Virtue. Thus, the *Tao Te Ching* states, "It reverts to not being an object. For this reason, it is called the shape without shape, the image without form, and therefore termed the nebulous jumble."

Previously the text also said that the myriad things enter being through nonbeing and follow being to return to nonbeing. Existence being obscure and nonexistence jumbled, Lao-tzu thus speaks of a nebulous jumble. Moreover, "Meeting it, you do not see its head; following it, do not perceive the rear" means that from the three, it reverts to One, without beginning, without end, and from the One forms the three, without end, without beginning. Therefore, Lao-tzu would have monarchs employ this ancient Tao of actionlessness to govern the contemporary realm of named things. Actionlessness similarly applies to not mounting any military affairs, while the named refers to military and state tasks. Thus, one who can know the meaning of original, unadorned simplicity can implement the warp and woof of the Tao.

SAWYER   Although Wang's commentary concludes with his refrain on eschewing military activities, this *Tao Te Ching* chapter is devoted to characterizing the imperceptible and introducing the metaphysical concept of the One, which, in turn, stimulated much debate over the centuries as to its relationship with the Tao. However, the final verses conclude with an interesting, so-called typically Chinese appeal to the values and practices of the past by saying, "Take hold of the ancient Tao in order to govern contemporary beings."

The characterizations found in the first three lines are in fact more abstruse and indistinct than apparent in the translation because the three descriptive characters all fundamentally entail a sense of amorphousness and imperceptibility. A certain degree of arbitrariness is thus unavoidably introduced, not only in the translation but also (perhaps deliberately) by the *Tao Te Ching*'s authors in striving to imaginatively convey the nature of the ineffable, although not imponderable, through a series of sensory nondescriptions.

15

Those in Antiquity
Who Excelled
as Officers

Those in antiquity who excelled as officers
Were subtle, ethereal, dankly mysterious, and penetrating,
Profound beyond recognition.
Only because they were beyond recognition
Do I laboriously characterize their appearance:
Hesitant as if crossing a river in winter,
Apprehensive as if afraid of their four neighbors,
Dignified like a guest,
Evanescent like ice soon to disperse,
Sincere like unsullied simplicity,
Expansive like a valley,
Turbid like muddy water.
Who can gradually clarify the muddy through tranquillity?
Who can gradually bring life to the settled through
 prolonged movement?
One who cleaves to this Tao does not desire fullness,
For only by not being full can he exhaust himself without
 further completion.

WANG   "Those in antiquity who excelled as officers" refers
to those superior officers known as Sages and Worthies who
occupied royal positions. "Subtle, ethereal, dankly mysterious,
and penetrating" all being aspects of the Tao's employment,
they cannot really be grasped. This means that when Sages and
Worthies govern armies and states, without exception they are

fearful and respectful, just as if approaching the depths of an abyss or treading on thin ice. In demeanor and intent they always seem "hesitant as if crossing a river in winter, apprehensive as if afraid of their four neighbors." This speaks about their extreme caution. As for being "dignified like a guest," in "Those Who Employ the Military Have a Saying" the *Tao Te Ching* states "Those who employ the military have a saying, 'I dare not act as the host but act as the guest, dare not advance an inch but withdraw a foot.'" Truly so.

"Evanescent like ice soon to disperse" says that in uniting and dispersing, stretching and contracting, the Sage is never obstructed. Sincerity and simplicity refer to plain substance; expansive valleys signify the deep and extensive. Now when things have long been muddy, they gradually clear; when long still, they gradually come to life—both in accord with natural patterns. If one asks who can be quiescent and active at appropriate times, the answer is only Sages and Worthies. Thus, the chapter states that "one who cleaves to this Tao does not desire fullness," meaning that kings and feudal lords who preserve the Tao do not want to become excessive and arrogant. Thus, Lao-tzu says, "only by not being full can he exhaust himself without further completion." This means that anyone able to adhere to the Tao and thereby accord with the end without bragging or glory always seems as if exhausted, so there are no traces of establishing further completion.

SAWYER This chapter and Wang's commentary both being remarkably clear, we might take note of the attitude espoused in the military writings toward martial enterprises. (The concept of the guest and host in martial theory, cited by the *Tao Te Ching* more fully in the verses of "Those Who Employ the Military Have a Saying," are further discussed there. Here, however, Wang Chen has apparently misinterpreted the *Tao Te Ching*'s intent in raising the circumscribed behavior of a guest in no doubt formal circumstances as simply an image for cautiousness and constraint.) From Sun-tzu onward, the undertaking of military activities was, at least theoretically, founded on careful calculation and planning and stressed

I observe their return.
Now the many and various things
All revert back to their roots.
Returning to the root is called tranquillity
And known as reverting to one's fate.
Reverting to one's fate is called constancy.
Knowing constancy is termed enlightenment;
Not knowing constancy wantonly spawns disaster.
One who knows constancy is encompassing;
Encompassing, he is impartial.
Impartial, he is regal.
Regal, he is like Heaven;
Heavenly, he is like the Tao.
Being like the Tao he endures,
To the end his body unendangered.

WANG   Now the Tao of Heaven is ever to be purely vacuous, the extreme ultimate [T'ai Chi], unselfish in its overspreading nurturing. The Tao of Earth is to be constantly submerged in tranquillity, expansively generous, and unselfish in sustaining. Yin and yang each realize their norms; therefore, all men and the myriad things succeed in exhausting the patterns of their being. Thus, the *Tao Te Ching* states that "the myriad things arise together." Those who return see the heart of Heaven and Earth, so it adds, "I observe their return." "The many and various things" means all living beings. Their principles having been fulfilled, all living beings "revert back to their roots" in order to preserve their tranquillity.

This being so, "Reverting to one's roots is termed tranquillity. Tranquillity is called returning to one's fate. Reverting to one's fate is called constancy." This states that none of the myriad things suffers any significant harm; each succeeds in reverting to its nature and fate in order to adequately accord with the natural divisions, what can be termed gaining the truly constant Tao. Therefore, when the Sage is able to know this truly constant Tao, he will comprehend everything within the four regions without any doubts or delusions. A monarch incapable of knowing the truly constant Tao—who indulges his tastes and desires, wantonly initiates inauspicious activities, mobilizes the shields and halberds, and circulates his poisonous venoms— will certainly be repaid with calamity and disaster. Thus, the *Tao Te Ching* says he "wantonly spawns disaster." Moreover, "one who knows constancy is encompassing" speaks of those kings and feudal lords capable of encompassing men and nourishing the masses, for they can be said to be the most impartial, free of any self-interest. Being free of any self-interest, the Tao of kingship will manifest itself. Being manifest by itself, the ruler's Virtue will imitate Heaven. When it imitates Heaven he can, in company with Heaven, attain the Tao. When he attains the Tao, he will naturally persist and endure, thereby living a thousand years without ever suffering the calamity of being endangered.

SAWYER   In his commentary Wang Chen intermixes the metaphysical with the mundane, facilely proceeding just as do the chapter's chain sequences from vacuity being the nature of the Tao to knowledge of the Tao being the key to earthly success. In his view, knowledge underlies the very possibility of effective government, whereas ignorance coupled with unrestrained desire produces only warfare and disaster. Thus, his interpretation once again focuses upon rulership that sustains its people and projects without manifesting itself, that encompasses without prejudice or partial inclinations, being modeled on (the positive aspects of) Heaven and Earth. Wang's views are somewhat astonishing because the *Tao Te Ching* generally views knowledge and wisdom as impediments and therefore advocates casting them out, keeping the people ignorant (as in "In Antiquity Those Who Excelled in the Tao" and "Eliminate Learning and There Will Be No Worry"). However, in order to succeed, rulers must encompass the Tao's transcendent wisdom while preserving their unemotional stance and avoiding artifice.

17

Those Beneath the Ultimate Know

Those beneath the ultimate know it exists;
The penultimate attracts them and their praise.
The next they fear,
While the lowest they detest.
When sincerity is insufficient,
It will be untrusted.
How anxiously they value words.
Achievements successful and affairs complete,
The hundred surnames all view it as naturally stemming
*   from their efforts.*

WANG   When the Great Tao was implemented in remote antiquity, the highest Virtue was not regarded as Virtue. Therefore, the people below knew only that there was a ruler above them, nothing more. They were employed every day but simply didn't know it.

By middle antiquity, benevolence and virtue were simultaneously bespread. Benefits and beneficence reached them daily, so the people loved the ruler and gave him their allegiance. Since they praised his attractiveness, his activities gradually became apparent.

Kings subsequently governed with righteousness, inflicting punishments and imposing fines for minor offenses, wielding shields and armor for major ones, so the people feared them.

Next in order came those who governed with the li [rites, rituals, and forms of socialized behavior], but the li grew vexatious and brought confusion to sincerity. Death cheated life, so the people reviled the ruler. Moreover, people do not trust sincerity that does not proceed from the inner heart. Language was embellished in the quest for mutual deception, and some people valued words alone. How tragic!

For this reason, the king ought to complete tasks he does not dwell in, cleave to undefeatable affairs, and cause the people to be ignorant of his imperial power. This would then be viewed by everyone as naturally stemming from their efforts. Excellent.

SAWYER Chapters such as this one, which clearly describe the project of government, visibly contradict claims that the *Tao Te Ching* is merely a book about self-cultivation and spiritual freedom. The verses themselves simply elucidate three types of administration, each characterized by its discernible impact on the people's psyche. The ultimate or ideal form is virtually invisible, clearly the government of a Sage under whom the people are obviously happy, whereas rulers marked by diminishing virtue cause increasingly greater rancor and annoyance in the people's lives. In contrast, the Sage's government remains so unintrusive that people feel things are merely taking their natural course, that all positive and beneficial results stem from their own efforts alone rather than the ruler's actions.

Wang Chen envisions the chapter as depicting a decline, a devolution from virtuous, minimal rule to brutally oppressive governments marked by harsh punishments, onerous taxes, and unendurable labor services. Traditional Chinese thought strongly embraced the idea of a golden antiquity. Although this idea was variously conceived from the different perspectives of Confucianism, Taoism, and Legalism, there was general agreement about projecting minimalist but virtuous activities onto the Sage Emperors and cultural innovators while decrying ever-increasing activity thereafter. The *Tao Te Ching* itself contains one such sharp portrait at the core of "Superior Virtue Is Not Virtuous" as well as a summary prefiguring in the chapter that follows here, "The Great Tao Abandoned."

Somewhat puzzling, however, for an avowed (or at least nominal) Confucian is Wang's placing of government by the li—the much-esteemed Confucian forms of behavior, including the rites—below righteousness, with its concomitant punishments. In the normal Confucian view, the li, being founded on shame, represent a higher, volitional moral stage. They are embraced and internalized as part of human acculturation and emotional development and include customary usage and practice. When they fail, punishments arise to coerce those without conscience to conform to society's dictates.

(In a sense, a society marked by accepted, well-defined standards of behavior—rites, rituals, and norms—can paradoxically be viewed as the intellectually most liberated because it obviates creatively responding to constantly varying situations. External performance proceeds automatically, so internal life can range far askew. However, this was not a traditional Chinese perspective even though many raised their voice against the vexatious nature of mindless rules particularly, as Wang notes, when the internal substance and understanding of the li were lost.)

18
The Great
Tao Abandoned

The Great Tao being abandoned,
There is benevolence and righteousness.

Knowledge and wisdom coming forth,
There is great artifice.
The six human relations being disharmonious,
There is filiality and parental love.
The state being confused and turbulent,
There are loyal ministers.

WANG   After the Great Tao became hidden, the virtues of benevolence and righteousness were practiced. Subsequently, skillful knowledge, minor wisdom, and great artifice were born. Filiality and parental love come out of disharmony while loyal ministers are born amid murky confusion. This is also what is meant in "All under Heaven Know" by beauty and ugliness giving form to each other.

SAWYER   This chapter essentially continues the last one. It rather remarkably portrays the historical devolution from naturally being in harmony with the Tao—an intuitive, directly apperceptive stage of human culture—through the promulgation of the primary Confucian virtues of benevolence and righteousness, and finally ordinary wisdom (rather than surpassing knowledge of the Tao). When spontaneous human emotions and natural relationships deteriorate, concepts of virtue are advocated and imposed. Such concepts are accompanied by the conscious practice of formal, though artificial, relationships marked by rigorously specified degrees of cordiality and treatment based upon familial degree. As the chapter notes, virtues stand out sharply against such decline and disorder, prompting Wang Chen to cite "All under Heaven Know" to account for the dynamics of their starkness. Moreover, "The Great Tao Abandoned" briefly encapsulates the much longer, multi-item devolutionary sequence that unfolds in "Superior Virtue Is Not Virtuous."

Several of the military writings incorporate similar views, especially *Huang Shih-kung's Three Strategies* which makes devolution its fundamental assumption and premises its very division of strategic methods and principles upon their applicability for different moral ages. The initial passages of its "Middle Strategy" unfold the sequence:

> Now the Three August Ones never spoke, but their transformations flowed throughout the Four Seas. Thus, the world had no one to whom to attribute the accomplishments.
>
> The Emperors embodied Heaven and took Earth as their model. They spoke and issued orders, and the world attained Great Peace. Ruler and minister yielded the credit for this to each other, while all within the Four Seas were transformed without the common people's being conscious of how the changes came about. Therefore, in employing subordinates, they did not rely on the forms of propriety or rewards. There was the beauty of accomplishments and no harm.
>
> Kings governed men by means of the Tao, causing their hearts to be compliant and their wills to be submissive, while also establishing restrictive measures and making preparations against decline. All the feudal lords within the Four Seas assembled at their courts, and the duty of kingship was not neglected. Even though they made military preparations, they never suffered the misfortune of warfare. Rulers did not doubt their subordinates, while subordinates had faith in their rulers. The state was settled, the ruler secure, and bureaucrats could resign with righteousness, so they also were able to have beauty without harm.
>
> The Hegemons governed their officers by virtue of authority, bonding them through trust, motivating them with rewards. When that trust declined, the officers grew distant, and when rewards became inadequate, they would not submit to orders.

19

Eliminate Sagacity, Abandon Wisdom

Eliminate sagacity, abandon wisdom,
The people will benefit a hundredfold.
Eliminate benevolence, abandon righteousness,
The people will revert to filiality and parental love.
Eliminate skill, abandon profit,
Robbers and brigands will be no more.
As civilizing influences, these three being inadequate,
Cause the people to have something to which they adhere.
Display simplicity;
Embrace the unadorned.
Diminish yourself;
Minimize your desires.

WANG This chapter advocates eliminating visible sagacity and abandoning boastful, deceptive wisdom, for then the people will receive great benefits said by the chapter to be "a hundredfold." Moreover, benevolence stems from inhumanity, righteousness from unrighteousness. If you eliminate wanton benevolence and cunning righteousness and ensure [that] relatives naturally unite in harmony, filiality and parental love will be restored. Furthermore, if you eliminate licentious artifice and abandon selfish profit, weapons and armor will not be flourished. When weapons and armor are not flourished, robbers and brigands will not arise. Because Lao-tzu still feared that later ages would not understand such direct words, perhaps even take them to have an opposite meaning, he added, "As civilizing influences, these three being inadequate, cause the people to have something to which they adhere. Display simplicity; embrace the unadorned; Diminish yourself; minimize your desires."

"Displaying simplicity" refers to the external appearance of uncultivated substance, "embracing the unadorned" to one's true and substantial thoughts. Moreover, the great outlines of human nature are preserved in thought and desire, so they can be constrained but cannot be eliminated. Thus, Lao-tzu encourages kings and feudal lords to minimize them. By minimizing them, the state will receive blessings and the people enjoy benefits.

SAWYER   This chapter continues the focal thought of the previous two, as well as prefiguring the next, in emphasizing the decline in Virtue over the millennia—the movement from harmony, simplicity, and according with the Tao to concepts, artifice, and degenerate behavior. Rectifying this disease requires reversing the deterioration, eliminating righteous concepts and conscious practice in favor of simplicity and harmony. Unfortunately, even in Wang Chen's commentary, there is a lack of concrete measures for effecting this reversal, beyond the Sage ruler's being visibly inactive, impartial, and in harmony with the workings of the Tao. However, Wang does emphasize that human desires cannot be completely eliminated and should therefore be channeled and minimized (no doubt through the measures elaborated in the earlier chapters, especially eliminating the rare and unusual, the objects that might stimulate desire), thereby ending the natural progression toward competition, violence, and warfare. Moreover, this approach is pervaded by a strong sentiment for eliminating wisdom—understood, of course, as the wisdom that results from learning, not from knowledge of the Tao—in concord with the opening verse of the next chapter and the sentiments expressed in chapters such as "Those Who Study Daily Increase" and "In Antiquity, Those Who Excelled in the Tao."

The contemplation and appropriation of simplicity is another recurring theme in the *Tao Te Ching*, one found in "Know the Masculine," "Tao Eternal, Unnamed," and especially "Tao Eternally Actionless," which discusses its power.

20

Eliminate Learning and There Will Be No Worry

Eliminate learning and there will be no worry.
How different are "yes sir" and "yeah"?
How different are good and evil?
What the people fear must be feared.
It's vast and barren, not yet exhausted!
The masses mill around as if participating in a great
   sacrificial feast,
Like clambering up a tower in spring;
I alone remain at leisure without a trace,
Like a baby not yet a child,
Languid as if with nowhere to return.
The masses all have more than enough;
I alone seem to be lacking.
I have the mind of a stupid man, murky and turbid.
The common man is lucid and bright;
I alone am dusky and dim.
The common man anxiously probes;
I alone am melancholy,
Placid like the sea, wafted about endlessly.
The masses of men all have attainments;
I alone am obstinate and uncouth.
I alone differ from other men,
Esteeming nurture at the mother.

WANG   If you eliminate accretional learning there will be no worry. The difference between "yes sir" and "yeah," between "good and evil," is extremely close. The chapter adds a further admonition by asking why people are not respectful but instead love arrogance, why they reject good and instead perform evil. Aren't they extremely deluded? Thus, Lao-tzu asserts that "what the people fear must be feared."

Now the masses milling about are deeply immersed in their tastes and desires, just as if hungering for the delicacies of a great sacrificial feast or clambering up a sunny tower in the spring, indulging their natures without surfeit. For this reason, Lao-tzu says, "I alone remain at leisure," quiet and silent like a baby who doesn't yet know anything, or again like someone riding a chariot far out, without anywhere to stop. These are intended to show the appearance of humility and humbleness, of retiring and yielding, of not imitating the masses of men in their boasting and ostentation, their speaking of how their wisdom and knowledge are more than adequate. Thus, he subsequently says, "I alone seem to be lacking. I have the mind of a stupid man."

Does this mean that he has the mind of a stupid man? No, it doesn't. "I alone am dusky and dim," "melancholy," oblivious, and forgetful like obscure loneliness, with nowhere to stop, "alone obstinate and uncouth," "alone differ from other men, esteeming nurture at the mother." Now nurturing entails submission while the mother is the Tao. Lao-tzu probably wanted to encourage rulers to submit themselves to the Tao and dwell in actionless affairs because weapons and armor would then naturally be put away, and All under Heaven would enjoy peace.

SAWYER   Remarkably, "Eliminate Learning and There Will Be No Worry" opens by reiterating the idea that wisdom should be cast out, though phrased specifically in terms of "learning," meaning the accretional products of study, particularly Confucian study. Wang Chen naturally construes this as meaning that the wise man, the Sage, isn't really stupid and doesn't actually abandon his learning about the Tao but should be differentiated from the common man who pursues second-ary, exploitive knowledge. (In doing so, he touches upon, but does not recognize, the great difficulty and paradox of acquired transcendent wisdom—knowledge that provides the vehicle for freedom but yet must be consciously pursued despite being es-chewed. The Sage's superiority derives from wisdom, even when the essence of his quest is forgetful freedom.)

Wang Chen's commentary also incorporates two themati-cally laden images prominent in the *Tao Te Ching:* the inno-cent, completely natural infant (seen especially in "Abundantly Embodying Virtue") and the common man, who, being an enthusiastic victim of his desires, willingly immerses himself in their pursuit. His observations echo the thrust of "The Five Colors Compel Humans," which summarily asserts that the pursuit and enjoyment of sensory pleasures debilitate the body and perturb the mind. Since the crucial project of ending war-fare never ventures far from his mind, Wang Chen caps his dis-cussion by interpreting the final line—"Esteeming nurture at the mother"—as asserting that maternal submission inherently obviates conflict.

21

Vast Encompassing Virtue

Vast encompassing Virtue
Stems solely from the Tao.
As a thing existent,

Tao is nebulous and jumbled.
Jumbled, nebulous, in its midst there are images;
Nebulous, jumbled, in its midst there are things;
Indistinct, dark, in its midst there is essence.
Its essence extremely pure,
Amid it there is sincerity.
From antiquity to today,
Its name has never been abandoned.
Through it, one scrutinizes the myriad beginnings.
How do I know the shape of the myriad beginnings?
From this.

WANG   "Vast" means extensive. Thus, in speaking about the shape and characteristics of Great Virtue, the chapter is referring to Heaven and Earth. Heaven and Earth are born through the Tao; they receive the Tao and transform. Thus, the *Tao Te Ching* says "Stems solely from the Tao." "As a thing existent, Tao is nebulous and jumbled. Jumbled, nebulous, in its midst there are images" elucidates the image of ch'i at the ultimate origin entering existence from nonexistence. "Nebulous, jumbled, in its midst there are things" speaks about what is termed the ch'i of the ultimate beginning achieving shape through existence. "Indistinct, dark, in its midst there is essence" means that through the intercourse of male and female the myriad things are transformed to life. Even amid such indistinct darkness, it never loses its sincerity. Thus, the *Tao Te Ching* states, "From antiquity to the present its name has never been abandoned." Lao-tzu also says that when the myriad things were first born, they all proceeded from out of the nebulous and jumbled, indistinct and dark. Therefore, he adds, "How do I know the shape of the myriad beginnings? From this."

SAWYER   As is well known, the *Tao Te Ching* contains several cosmogenic sequences, which differ in generative priority and succession. Sometimes nonbeing or the Tao constitutes the ultimate origin; other times the One, which should be derivative, assumes chronological precedence. "Vast Encompassing Virtue" speaks of nothing before the Tao itself, which is again characterized as beyond conception—vague, jumbled, indistinct—all terms to convey a sense of the transcendently elusive yet amorphously immanent portrayed in "Looked at but Unseen."

However, Wang Chen's commentary introduces the additional element of ch'i, no doubt because of its fundamental importance in the metaphysical and protoscientific thinking of his time, some twelve to fourteen hundred years after the compilation of the *Tao Te Ching* but before Sung dynasty Neo-Confucians defined ch'i and principle to be the two critical determinants of the myriad things. Although Wang Chen frequently conceives his commentary in terms of ch'i, it appears only sparsely in the *Tao Te Ching* itself, sometimes inserted in generative sequences, at other times connoting the ephemeral. The first occurrence may be found in "Regulating the Earthly Soul to Embrace Unity," the remaining two in "Tao Gave Birth to the One" and "Abundantly Embodying Virtue." This chapter so concentrates upon metaphysical issues of the Tao that even Wang Chen fails to derive any martial implications.

22

The Curved
Will be Preserved

The curved will be preserved,
The crooked straight,
The depressed full,

The exhausted hew.
The few will gain;
The many will be deluded.
Accordingly, the Sage embraces the One,
Acting as a model for All under Heaven.
He doesn't manifest himself, so is luminous;
Doesn't justify himself, so is illustrious;
Doesn't boast, so has achievements;
Is not self-confident, so long persists.
Only because he does not compete,
No one under Heaven can contend with him.
Was the ancient saying
"The curved will be preserved"
Empty words?
Sincerely preserve and abide in it.

WANG   The "curved" discussed in this chapter refers to being pliant and bending, not to the disciples of crooked force and perversion. The first six pronouncements are all straightforward even though appearing opposite in intent.

"Accordingly, the Sage embraces the One." Only by embracing the curved, the Tao of completion, can the Sage be a model for All under Heaven. Moreover, the four lines starting with "doesn't manifest himself" all elucidate the Tao of not competing. Thus, the chapter states, "Only because he does not compete, no one under Heaven can contend with him." Since no one under Heaven can contend with him, combat between armies will naturally cease. Thus, Lao-tzu asks, "Was the ancient saying 'The curved will be preserved' empty words?" Truly, he took the curved to be the Tao for preservation, abiding in it to be rooted in true tranquillity. Making this foremost in the Tao for controlling the army and governing the state is acting ethereally!

SAWYER   In elucidating the inescapable reversals that prompt the wise to vigorously adopt a self-effacing stance and cleave to innocuousness, the chapter's verses resound almost biblically. Wang Chen naturally emphasizes the aspect of noncompetition—really, nonassertion—paradoxically perceiving a path to ultimate victory. Although, as previously discussed, noncompetition is a well-known trait of the Confucian perfected man, or *chün-tzu*, it is not because he is pliant and yielding like water that he does not compete. Rather, it is because noncompetition is part of his essential distanced stance of self-cultivation and virtuous superiority. The behavioral manifestations may appear identical, but their motivation and resolution radically diverge.

The military writings espouse a somewhat similar, though differently oriented, idea in the concept of attaining victory without combat, of subjugating one's enemies without the clash of blades. Over the ages, strategists pondered a number of distinct options for achieving this objective: overawing the enemy, whether through righteousness, spirit, or strategic power; manipulating and debilitating the enemy until they become too exhausted and therefore lack any alternative to withdrawing, tantamount to surrender; and simply refusing battle, thereby frustrating the enemy's purposes and preserving the army intact. In the countless engagements that wracked China over the centuries, these strategies were often successfully implemented. However, under dire circumstances—such as massive enemy assaults on population centers—even Sun-tzu's idea of not engaging except on one's own terms was sometimes found wanting. (Sun-tzu would counsel launching indirect attacks against the enemy's critical points to draw them off, threatening or even seizing "what they love," but without mobile forces and sufficient opportunity, this might not be possible.) Wang Chen frequently asserts that when someone refuses to compete, no one can compete with him, a view that undeniably evinces a certain intuitive cogency and inherent veracity. For ordinary people trapped in mundane reality, however, such merely semantic victories might only entail death.

The views expressed here by Wang Chen and the *Tao Te Ching* fundamentally presuppose the existence and indirect exercise of vast, surpassing power on the part of the Sage ruler. Not surprisingly, this is possible because he participates—both metaphysically and actually, through temporal power—in the activity of the universe. He structures its flow while ever maintaining an unobtrusive profile to avoid stirring rancor and annoyance, the latter a refrain found in several chapters. His stance, behavior, and course therefore differ dramatically from the options available to ordinary men, who lack transcendent attainments or awesome position and are therefore compelled to remain humble out of powerlessness.

23

Sparse Words
Are Natural

Sparse words are natural.
Thus violent winds do not outlast the morning,
Nor pounding rain persist a day.
Who renders it so?
Heaven and Earth.
If Heaven and Earth are still unable to prolong them,
How much less so Man?
Thus, one who accords with the Tao
Shares in Tao.
One who accords with Virtue
Shares in Virtue.
One who fails to accord with Tao and Virtue
Shares in loss.
One who accords with Tao,
The Tao similarly delights in gaining.
One who accords with Virtue,

Virtue similarly delights in gaining.
One who accords with loss,
Loss also takes pleasure in gaining.
When sincerity is insufficient,
It is untrusted.

WANG   "Sparse words" connote actionlessness, the absence of undertakings. Lao-tzu simply wants to have rulers economize their words and minimize their affairs, thereby according with the natural Tao. Moreover, in governing their states and controlling their armies, he wants them to eschew vexatious and oppressive measures. Therefore, he raises the analogy of violent winds and pounding rain to make it clear.

Now whenever one accords with Tao and Virtue, affairs proceed smoothly. However, according with loss [neglecting the Tao] similarly results in loss because one's days of delusion will assuredly be long. Compliance and neglect thus each result in appropriate consequences, but as people do not know about this loss, Lao-tzu adds, "loss also gains him."

"Inadequate sincerity" refers to the inadequate trust of the lower ranks, similarly stemming from their superiors not being trustworthy.

SAWYER   Another of the *Tao Te Ching*'s relatively clear chapters, "Sparse Words Are Natural," discusses the virtues of according with the Tao and avoiding explosive, self-debilitating extremes (imagized by violent winds and heavy rains) to attain security and prolong life. Wang Chen draws the appropriate abstract conclusion—"Whenever one accords with Tao and Virtue affairs proceed smoothly"—but fails to discuses any concrete implications: How does one perceive the Tao, know what accords with it and what opposes it? Is the Tao particularistic or universal, immanent everywhere or nowhere, locally determined or a sort of cosmic flux? Why can't it simply be ignored, violated, and contravened? Although no answers are forthcoming, whether for the ordinary man or for highly visible rulers, wisdom certainly lies in maintaining a low profile that will not irritate others, a practice Wang Chen repeatedly advises.

24

Those on Tiptoe
Do Not Stand

Those on tiptoe do not stand;
Those striding do not walk.
One who manifests himself is not enlightened;
One who justifies himself is not illustrious;
One who boasts lacks achievements;
One who is arrogant does not long persist.
In the scope of the Tao
They are called leftover food and redundant actions.
Since there are things that detest them,
Those who attain the Tao do not dwell in them.

WANG Men who are up on their toes or stride widely never manage to stand properly or be stable when walking. This discusses how the disciples of fierce wrangling raise troops and agitate the masses, none of them ever realizing the central, correct Tao. How much more so [is this true of] those who manifest their enlightenment, praise their own illustriousness, boast of their achievements, and display their persistence. Thus, Lao-tzu mentions leftover, contaminated food and redundant, ugly actions as things that all men detest, so how would someone who has attained the Tao be able to dwell in them?

SAWYER "Those on Tiptoe Do Not Stand" continues the previous chapter's themes and admonitions, advocating a low, unabrasive profile to avoid personal catastrophe because, although unstated, reversal is the movement of the Tao. Wang's interpretation is somewhat startling since it implies that violence is less pernicious than arrogance.

25

There is Something Turbidly Complete

There is something turbidly complete,
Spawned before Heaven and Earth.
Silent and still,
Solitary and unchanging,
Everywhere active, unimperiled.
It can act as the mother of All under Heaven.
I do not know its name but designate it as Tao.
If I am forced to characterize it,
It is called great.
Being great, it goes beyond;
Going beyond, it is distant;
Being distant, it then reverts.
Thus the Tao is great;
Heaven is great;
Earth is great;
The king is also great.
In the cosmos these are the four greats;
The king dwells among them.
Man models on Earth;
Earth models on Heaven;
Heaven models on Tao;
Tao models on the natural.

WANG   This chapter is the ultimate discussion of how the Tao embodies shapeless shapes, imageless images, nameless names, and nonexistent things. Thus, Lao-tzu states, "If I am forced to characterize it, it is called great."

Now "great" refers to being inexhaustible, unbounded. Moreover, among the multitudinous directions, there isn't anywhere that the expansive, great Tao does not go. This "going" is like dispersing [going beyond]. Endlessly dispersing, it must go far. When it goes far and reaches the pinnacle, it invariably returns, so this is termed "reversion." This states that the Tao is active and present everywhere and thus acts as the mother of All under Heaven. The mother is the ancestor of the Tao, while the ancestor is the One. Thus [in "Those in Antiquity Who Realized the One,"] the *Tao Te Ching* states, "Kings and lords realized the One and thereby exemplified truth for All under Heaven." This is what is meant by saying that one who can rectify the masses can be king. For this reason the three realms of Heaven, Earth, and Man model on each other in order to attain the Tao. The Tao models on naturalness, so if the king models on naturalness, he will be able to complete his affairs.

SAWYER   This chapter might well be read in conjunction with "Looked at but Unseen," "Vast Encompassing Virtue," "Tao Eternal, Unnamed," "The Great Tao Overflows," and "When Superior Officers Hear about the Tao," all of which speak about the Tao even though it remains transcendent and nameless, just as the very first lines of the entire *Tao Te Ching* assert. Wang's commentary focuses upon the Tao itself, invoking ideas about "shapeless shapes" found in "Looked at but Unseen" while merely touching upon the monarch's existence and activity without noting his integral relationship with Tao, Heaven, and Earth. Clearly anchored in cosmic dimensions, the king is thus validated as highly capable of achieving goodness for the people rather than deprecated as the useless appurtenance that anarchistic readings of the *Tao Te Ching* would envision.

26

Weightiness Is the Root of Lightness

Weightiness is the root of lightness;
Tranquillity the ruler of rashness.
For this reason, despite traveling the whole day,
The Sage does not depart from the baggage train;
Even though there are voluptuous vistas to observe,
He placidly dwells in the transcendent.
How is it that the ruler of ten thousand chariots casts
*   himself away in the realm?*
When he is frivolous, his ministers are lost;
When rash, his rulership is lost.

WANG   When the perfected man [*chün-tzu*] is not weighty, he will not be awesome. Moreover, tranquillity is the fundamental nature of benevolence.

In antiquity, the term *chün-tzu* always designated the Son of Heaven and the feudal lords. "Traveling the whole day" means that when the ruler travels throughout the day, he must use the proper imperial carriage and ensconce himself amid the baggage train in order to take precautions against the unexpected. The baggage [or escort] train provides the means for mounting temporary defensive fortifications.

This chapter also says that although the monarch dwells in a detached palace, transcendingly remote, how can he act lightly when bearing the heavy responsibility for ten thousand chariots? The passage thus strongly warns against such negligent practices as going out in disguise and secretly traveling about with a single chariot or horse, acting foolishly and thereby losing one's rulership. If the rites and rituals are hastily performed, his ministers will neglect their affairs. How can the obligation of serving the ruler not be respected? Thus, Lao-tzu concludes, "When he is frivolous, his ministers are lost; when rash, his rulership is lost." Doesn't this state it?

SAWYER In "Realizing the Pinnacle of Vacuity," Wang Chen previously warned against the ruler's mindless pursuit of pleasure destabilizing his realm, a recurrent theme that concludes this chapter's verses. Having no doubt cast his eye over the historical records, Wang is prompted to further decry the habit of rulers going out in disguise and thereby jeopardizing the monarchy and the state's power. His comments throughout the book, mirroring concerns embodied in the *Tao Te Ching*'s verses, portray government as a serious, austere matter, one that should be pursued with strictness, severity, and humility, always keeping the people's welfare foremost.

27

Those Who Excel in Moving Have No Tracks

Those who excel in moving have neither tracks nor traces;
Those who excel in speaking, no blemishes or defects.

Those who excel at calculating use no tallies or counters.
Those who excel at closing have no locks yet cannot be
*   opened;*
Those who excel at knots use no ropes yet cannot be untied.
For this reason, the Sage always excels at rescuing people
So there are no rejected people.
He always excels at rescuing things
So there are no discarded things.
This is termed accepting enlightenment.
Those who excel are teachers for the incompetent;
The incompetent are resources for the competent.
Do not esteem teachers nor love resources;
Even wisdom is a great delusion.
This is termed essential ethereality.

WANG   One who has "neither tracks nor traces" moves
without movement. "No blemishes or defects" signifies
cleaving to the middle. "Uses no tallies or counters" means
that he will invariably be victorious in battle. "Cannot be
opened" means his defenses must be solid. "Cannot be untied" means there are no beginnings or ends. Excelling in
these five, the Sage secretly plans and clandestinely acts. He
doesn't expose his ability, exhibit himself, manifest his traces,
or reveal his shape. He always wants to effect the army's demobilization before the moment of action, end warfare before conflict begins. Accordingly, the state never has any
rejected people; the people, no discarded things. These are
both attained through accepting and employing the ethereal
Tao of enlightened sagacity. Moreover, the Sage does not establish Virtue among men, nor display benevolence among
things, but merely causes the hundred surnames to be unconsciously employed every day. This similarly means he does not
esteem teachers or human resources. However, as Lao-tzu
still feared the masses of men would not awaken to these
principles or would even regard them as a great delusion, he
profoundly discussed these mysterious instructions, sincerely
making them "essential ethereality."

SAWYER A sense that the truly accomplished who transcend normal attainments have invisibly penetrated the Tao of some specific realm or activity has always pervaded Chinese culture, particularly the martial arts. Thus, even though the connection seems highly tangential, it is not surprising that Wang Chen fastens onto the chapter's first few lines to explicate military matters. In this context, the chapter's reference to tallies is particularly interesting because they were extensively employed in prebattle calculations for determining a net assessment and the probability of victory as early as the Spring and Autumn period, based upon the *Art of War*. In his initial chapter, Sun-tzu said:

> Before the engagement, one who determines in the ancestral temple that he will be victorious has found that the majority of factors are in his favor. Before the engagement, one who determines in the ancestral temple that he will not be victorious has found few factors are in his favor. If one who finds that the majority of factors favor him will be victorious while one who has found few factors favor him will be defeated, what about someone who finds no factors in his favor? If I observe it from this perspective, victory and defeat will be apparent.

The chapter's last three lines are generally understood not as an injunction, as Wang interprets them, but as:

> *Anyone who doesn't esteem the teacher nor love the resources,*
> *Although wise, is greatly deluded.*
> *This is termed essential ethereality.*

28
Know the Masculine

Know the masculine, cleave to the feminine;
Be a watery ravine to All under Heaven.
By acting as a watery ravine to All under Heaven,
Eternal Virtue will never be estranged,
And you will revert back to being a child.
Know the white, cleave to the black;
Be a model for All under Heaven.
By acting as a model for All under Heaven,
Eternal Virtue will never err,
And you will revert back to the unbounded.
Know glory, cleave to disgrace;
Be a valley to All under Heaven.
By acting as a valley to All under Heaven,
Eternal Virtue will always be sufficient,
And you will revert back to simplicity.
When simplicity is dispersed, it creates vessels.
When the Sage employs them, they make office chiefs.
Thus great administration does not cut.

WANG   Now anyone ruling men already has heroic talent,
strategic ability, robust demeanor, and fierce spirit [ch'i].
Moreover, since [rulers] dwell in the realm's most honored
position at the pinnacle of millions, are protected by six
armies, and attended by the hundred officials, even without
being evil they will be severe, even without getting angry will
be awesome. Thus, Lao-tzu wants them to constantly cleave
to feminine tranquillity, being just like a watery ravine to All
under Heaven, because watery ravines are void, empty, and
receptive, terrain that stores illness and accepts contamination.
In this way their Virtue will never depart from their bodies.

"Revert back to being a child" speaks about the ruler cleaving to the Tao and embodying Virtue so that his nature remains like a child's. When the truly constant has not yet dispersed, it prevents crooked and artful beginnings from being able to enter the boundaries of his mind. Moreover, even though the ruler knows the bright, white, dazzling, and pure, Lao-tzu wants to ensure he always cleaves to the dark and silent Tao because he can then "be a model for All under Heaven." In this way his Virtue will be free of error and he will return to the pinnacle of central uprightness.

Glory and disgrace are things that follow upon each other. When the ruler is able to know this—so that when glory suddenly comes, he already thinks of the misery and disgrace that will attack in its train—he will "be a valley for All under Heaven." Valleys and watery ravines have the same significance. Accordingly, his Tao and Virtue will always be sufficient for him "to revert back to simplicity." Simplicity is the material substance of primal ch'i. Thus when the Sage disperses simplicity, it creates vessels; when he measures and employs men, they make bureau chiefs.

"Great administration" refers to governing all the states under Heaven. How would anyone who governs All under Heaven have fragmented and disjointed affairs? Thus, Lao-tzu says, "great administration does not cut."

SAWYER   Throughout his commentary, Wang Chen criticizes the tendency of rulers to become immersed in glory and opulence, to abuse their powers and then suffer reversal as well as bring calamity upon the people. Accordingly, he stresses the need to cleave to the dark, silent, and lowly, just as the *Tao Te Ching* verses advise. However, this is premised upon monarchs' having attained great achievements; correspondingly negative measures redress the imbalance and maintain Virtue.

Wang's second thrust stresses precaution and preparation because (as he states in his commentary to "The Government Is Morosely Quiet") "it is simple human nature to be elated about immanent good fortune; few trouble themselves over incipient misfortune. In the midst of calamity people constantly think about good fortune, but when enjoying good fortune, no one takes precaution against misfortune." This echoes the military theorists who ruefully observed that commanders tend to ignore even clearly foreshadowed doom, to be enamored only with the prospects of victory. This tendency prompted Sun-tzu to comment, "The wise must contemplate the intermixture of gain and loss. If they discern advantage in difficult situations, their efforts can be trusted. If they discern harm in prospective advantage, difficulties can be resolved."

Tao Te Ching chapters frequently employ images of valleys for their spiritual aspects and depths of presence as well as the undeniable tendency of all moving things, including water, to accumulate at the bottom. (Such images can be seen, for example, especially in "The Valley Spirit Does Not Die" and also in "Those in Antiquity Who Excelled as Officers" and are manifest as the underlying spirit in "Great States Defer to the Flow.") Through modeling upon their ability to be below, to accept rather than protrude and reject, the Sage and those aspiring to his surpassing attainments naturally come to be powerful yet retain their Virtue and simplicity.

29

About to Seize All Under Heaven

Those about to seize All under Heaven and act upon it
I perceive will not succeed.
All under Heaven is a Spiritual vessel.

It cannot be acted upon;
It cannot be held.
Those who would act on it, defeat it;
Who would hold it, lose it.
Thus among things,
Some move, some follow;
Some snort, some blow.
Some are strong, some emaciated;
Some sustain, some overthrow.
For this reason, the Sage rejects extremes,
Casts out extravagance,
And abandons excess.

WANG   In this chapter, Lao-tzu particularly discusses men who have no hope: "Those about to seize All under Heaven and act upon it I perceive will not succeed." "To act on it" refers to mobilizing the army and flourishing weapons. Thus, he says that "All under Heaven is a Spiritual vessel; it cannot be acted upon." "Cannot be acted upon" means that shields and halberds cannot be employed to capture it; anyone who proceeds in this fashion will certainly be defeated. Even someone who temporarily gains hold of it will still quickly turn about and lose it.

"Thus, among things, some move, some follow; some snort, some blow. Some are strong, some emaciated; some sustain, some overthrow." Calamity and good fortune rely upon them all. "For this reason, the Sage rejects extremes, casts out extravagance, and abandons excess." Wanting to establish himself in the middle of the Tao, he earnestly cleaves to it. This is the very pinnacle of precaution.

SAWYER   Although Wang Chen concludes with a minor blandishment about caution, the fundamental insight advanced by both his commentary and the verses themselves is the virtual impossibility of seizing the world through force of arms or, more accurately, seizing and then maintaining control over it, as the next chapter will reveal. (Unstated here, but visible in Wang's commentaries throughout, is the idea that when the people do not willingly give their allegiance, they remain beyond control.)

The chapter itself seems to have been assembled from two thematically different parts, because the first half abjures the use of force to impose one's will, whereas the second comprises a meditation upon the *Tao Te Ching*'s frequently revisited postulate on the instability of extremes (summarily expressed in "Reversal Is the Movement of the Tao"). Moreover, as many commentators have pointed out, in recommending that people cleave to centrality, to the middle point, it remarkably mirrors the core doctrine of one of Confucianism's most sacred texts, the *Chung Yung,* known in the West as *The Doctrine of the Mean.*

30

Assisting the Ruler with the Tao

One who assists the ruler with the Tao
Does not coerce the realm with weapons.
Such affairs easily rebound.
Wherever the army has encamped,
Thorny brambles will grow.
After large armies have flourished,
There will certainly be baleful years.
One who excels rests in the results, that's all,
Not daring to exploit his strength.
He attains without bragging;

He attains without boasting;
He attains without becoming arrogant.
He attains because he has no alternative;
He attains but does not manifest his might.
When things are strong, they grow old.
This is termed contrary to Tao.
What is contrary to Tao early perishes.

WANG   This whole chapter specifically admonishes generals, chancellors, and ministers who would assist their rulers by saying, "One who assists the ruler with the Tao does not coerce the realm with weapons, for such affairs easily rebound." In explication, I would like to raise a few examples, men such as Li Ssu, Chao Kao, Pai Ch'i, and Meng T'ien. None of them assisted their rulers in accord with the Tao but directly, through martial strength, were brutal and strong. They bit off and swallowed up territory, seized and struck, burned the *Book of Odes* and *Book of Documents,* buried Confucian scholars, and slaughtered more than four hundred thousand troops from Chao. Wherever they encamped, they ravaged and massacred, causing nothing to be left behind. The first Ch'in emperor, although alone in imperial power, looked down upon the realm like a great bird of prey but still wasn't satisfied in his heart. Even when Heaven's emolument was exhausted [and his dynasty collapsed], the poisonous remnants still resulted in mutual destruction and harm. In no time at all, the earth itself was cracked and rotting. For this reason, Hu Hai was slain at Wang-yi, Tzu Ying was macerated at Hsien-yang, Fu Su died along the Great Wall, Li Ssu and his son were exterminated at Yün-yang, Pai Ch'i was forced to commit suicide at Tu-yu, and Chao Kao suffered execution in the inner palace. These are all affairs that rebounded.

Furthermore, "Wherever the army has encamped, thorny brambles will grow. After large armies have flourished there will certainly be baleful years." In addition, the daily expenses for mobilizing an army of one hundred thousand will be a thousand catties of gold. When an army of a hundred thousand is in the field, a million men will wander the roads. Add to this the murderous spirit, impulse to harm, and drought and pestilence that follow, no disaster exceeds this. Thus one who excels at being a general should decisively achieve his objectives and desist, never daring to exploit his strength.

"He attains without bragging; he attains without becoming arrogant. . . . He attains because he has no alternative." This is what is meant by achieving one's objective but not exploiting strength. "Having no alternative" is the essential Tao of the Sage's employment of the military. Thus, it is appropriate that he should be decisive and implement the Tao of not exploiting his power, not boast about his achievements, and not take pleasure in killing men. Placidity is uppermost; even victory is not glorified. This is the meaning of achieving results and not exploiting strength.

"When things are strong, they grow old." This refers to the army becoming curved [fatigued]. What is termed "early perishing" speaks about armies that lack the Tao. They should be halted early on and never again advanced for employment. If Li Ssu and Pai Ch'i had been compelled early on to plan their withdrawal and standing down, how would they ever have suffered the calamity of incinerating themselves?

SAWYER   "Assisting the Ruler with the Tao" is one of the crucial antiwar chapters of the *Tao Te Ching*, one whose verses—particularly "wherever the army has encamped thorny brambles will grow"—clearly reflect the vast carnage occurring during the Warring States period, when the book was no doubt compiled. Consequently, the writers caution advisers (and thereby monarchs and feudal lords) not to employ force to gain control of the realm, thus continuing the previous chapter's mournful admonitions. Wang Chen then expands this theme with examples who figured prominently in China's sorrowful military history, including the first imperial emperor, Ch'in Shih-huang, whose astonishing tomb has ironically become famous for its large terra-cotta army, a symbol of martial prowess carried to its final extreme. (Had Wang Chen been writing today, no doubt Hitler and Mao

Tze-tung would number among his illustrative examples. However, neither he nor the *Tao Te Ching* take note of, or adequately account for, the conspicuous, long-lived success many tyrants achieved through force of arms.)

Although intensely decrying the misery inflicted by warfare, in adding the phrase "having no alternative," the *Tao Te Ching* still (however grudgingly) recognizes a need may exist for employing the army and accordingly counsels how to avoid the inevitable repercussions. The commander "who excels rests in the results, that's all." Wang (in consonance with assertions found throughout the classic military writings) appropriately adds the thought that the commander should act decisively and then embrace a low profile rather than exploit his strength and accomplishments. His view is actually somewhat remarkable because Sun-tzu vehemently condemned generals who fail to exploit victories for being "wasteful and tarrying," inasmuch as warfare, being the greatest affair of state, must be economical and efficient. Although Wang may simply be referring to the act of boasting and coercing, more interesting is his emphasis upon maintaining a mournful attitude, never rejoicing even over victory, because men have been killed and sorrow is requisite, as the very next chapter advises.

Two other points bear note. First, the *Tao Te Ching* observes that "after large armies have flourished, there will certainly be baleful years." No doubt this is because of the staggering damage caused by their simple physical presence and activities such as plundering and foraging, combined with destructive effects upon the terrain and critical infrastructure, including dikes, bridges, terraces, and roads, even prior to the advent of explosives. However, Wang Chen interprets the lines in terms of economic factors, citing Sun-tzu's late Spring and Autumn calculation about the expense of mobilizing a hundred thousand men. Unexpectedly, Sun-tzu was perhaps the first to emphasize warfare's astoundingly negative impact upon a state's resources and economy, contrary to the fervently advocated view that conquest brings wealth, land, people, and profits. (The quest for empire was hardly confined to the West!) Unfortunately, China's tenuous geopolitical history bears stark witness to the *Tao Te Ching*'s perspicacity, because millions repeatedly perished in dynastic upheavals, millenarian revolts, and foreign incursions. Not only were soldiers slain in combat itself, but millions of the general populace also perished as famine followed the destruction of fields and earthworks, pestilence ravaged the countryside, and economies fell below sustainment levels.

Second, the image of the infant, pliant and flexible, lies behind the concluding lines, for old age is associated with stiffness and rigidity. Moreover, in the *Tao Te Ching*'s elucidation of the Tao, the hard and firm easily break; the strong and rigid rapidly grow old. ("Wanting to Reduce Something" applies this principle, and "Abundantly Embodying Virtue" ponders the fate of the "old.") Even if they are victorious, armies long exposed to the hardships of campaign have their spirits broken and bodies fatigued and quickly become exhausted. If they lack justification and strong motivation, they sink into hopelessness even more quickly and perish without a trace.

31

Superlative Weapons

Superlative weapons being inauspicious implements,
There are things that detest them.
Thus, those who attain the Tao do not dwell among them.
In normal affairs, the perfected man honors the left,
But when employing the army honors the right.

Weapons are inauspicious implements,
Not the instruments of the perfected man.
But when he has no alternative but to employ them,
He esteems calmness and equanimity.
Victories achieved are not glorified,
For glorifying them is to take pleasure in killing men.
One who takes pleasure in killing men
Cannot achieve his ambitions under Heaven.
Auspicious affairs esteem the left;
Inauspicious affairs esteem the right.
Subordinate generals occupy the left;
Commanding generals the right.
This states that one treats military affairs as rites of
   mourning.
After killing masses of the enemy's men,
Weep for them with grief and sorrow.
After being victorious in battle,
Implement the rites of mourning.

WANG   "Weapons" include such things as swords, halberds,
and spears. "Superlative" means excellent. In speaking of implements, Lao-tzu means these weapons. The chapter thus says
that these polished and decorated hides, these marvelous, sharp
weapons are actually not good implements. Moreover, left and
yang are [normally considered] auspicious; right and yin, baleful. When the perfected man [*chün-tzu*] absolutely cannot avoid
employing them, he should "esteem calmness and equanimity."
"Calmness" means being settled and tranquil; "equanimity"
means acting without relish. This says that even when deployed
forces score a victory, the commander should remain placid and
not relish it, "not glorify it." One who glorifies victory delights
in killing men. Moreover, all those killed are actually one's own
men. How can anyone take pleasure in killing his own men?
Even when warfare is necessary, how can any king who takes
pleasure in killing "achieve his ambitions under Heaven"?

Moreover, in antiquity, "after killing great masses of the enemy's men, they wept for them with grief and sorrow. After
being victorious in battle, they implemented the rites of

mourning." Since those killed were all their own men, how could they not hold the rites of mourning for them? Later ages were not thus. Campaign armies were generally successful half the time, so when a general managed to score a victory, he would immediately record the affair prominently on a great silk roll, amplifying the engagement so that ten enemy soldiers became a hundred, a hundred a thousand, and every thousand ten thousand, wanting to bolster his achievement. Some men, knowing of these deceptions, exploited them to establish their own awesomeness. This caused people to be annoyed at their prominence and the spirits to be angry in the realm of darkness. Thus, the chapter asserts that "they could not achieve their ambitions under Heaven." How could a general who acts like this be said to assist the ruler with the Tao?

SAWYER   Apart from expanding the theme of the last chapter on the balefulness of warfare and the need to embrace sorrow rather than rejoice after conquests, "Superlative Weapons" opens with another famous line, one both quoted and misquoted whenever anyone wished to oppose any and all military activities: "Superlative weapons being inauspicious implements, there are things that detest them." Although often over-looked by cultural proponents at the expense of the martial, the *Tao Te Ching*'s authors clearly recognized the potential need for employing force at times. This stands forth clearly in the chapter's prefatory statement, "when he has no alternative but to employ them." (The appearance of the perfected man as an active agent of government may be a grudging acknowledgment that so-called ethically empowered figures rather than Taoist Sages controlled governments, or the term *chün-tzu* may simply be a reference to an ordinary ruler, as Wang Chen notes in another commentary.)

Wang also appropriately explicates the chapter's clear pronouncements on the attitudes that should accompany any martial activities. The cause of postbattle sorrow is not just the loss of one's own men but the deaths of all men, for to the Sage, partiality is anathema; the enemy's men are viewed as one's own in the wider sense of the world and universal rule. (Unmentioned, but no doubt underlying, is the psychological concept of transitioning and decompressing. This involved eroding the warrior mentality by returning soldiers to civilian life through appropriate ceremonies—in this case, the rites of mourning to emphasize the gravity and pain of the experience—as the early military classic known as the *Ssu-ma Fa* advocates.) Furthermore, when forced to grapple with the reality of evil, the ruler or commander should maintain his equanimity, the detached emotional uninvolvement that will not only preclude rash errors but also (according to Wang Chen) prevent antagonizing men and spirits through displaying inappropriate exhilaration at the conquest. (Wang's comment on the tendency to amplify achievements also bears noting.)

32

Tao Eternal, Unnamed

The Tao is eternally unnamed.
Simplicity, although small,
Cannot be subjugated by any under Heaven.
With any monarch who cleaves to it,
The myriad things willingly cast their lot.
Heaven and Earth mutually unite to send down sweet dew,
Which the people, uncommanded, share equally.
At the beginning, when things were ordered,
There were names.
Names already being extant,

They similarly knew to stop.
One who knows where to stop
Will not be imperiled.
Tao's imminence under Heaven
Is like valley streams joining the great rivers and oceans.

WANG   Simplicity is the Tao's substance. As there isn't anywhere that its ethereal minuteness is not present, it is called "small." This means that if monarchs can cleave to the subtle, ethereal Tao and constantly be actionless, clear, and tranquil, the myriad things will willingly be submissive. Moreover, Heaven and Earth, *yin* and *yang* will naturally harmonize and unite, and sweet dew and seasonal rains will similarly fall to moisten those below. Lao-tzu thus says that without being commanded, everyone will gain equally. For this reason, they ordered things at the beginning, creating names for the myriad things. Once things are named, ruler and minister, above and below, the myriad things and all affairs, without exception, know where to stop. Rulers know to stop at benevolence, ministers at loyalty, sons at filiality, friends at sincerity, and husbands and wives at righteousness. Those who wield shields and halberds know to stop with cessation; those who impose taxes and impositions, with the minimum. Knowing where to stop, they all manage to avoid danger and destruction. This may be compared with "Tao's immanence under Heaven." When employed to govern, "it's like valley streams joining the great rivers and oceans." This says that their response [to the terrain] and movement to accumulate, to return to the ancestor, continues day and night, never ceasing for a moment.

SAWYER   Between opening and closing with observations about the Tao, the chapter focuses upon the world of manifest things, the realm of names existent and people active. The image of simplicity, first seen in "Eliminate Sagacity, Abandon Wisdom" and further unveiled here as powerful, recurs as a recommended paradigm for monarchs. Combining these two, Wang Chen makes the implications incumbent for nurturing and fulfilling human relationships within the social and political hierarchy. He also raises the core Confucian virtues of benevolence and righteousness as appropriate for human society, even though those virtues are sometimes (at least in their debased, hypocritical form) excoriated by the *Tao Te Ching* itself. The idea that voluntary self-restraint will facilitate self-preservation, expressed as "one who knows where to stop will not be imperiled," reappears throughout the *Tao Te Ching* in a number of variants, such as the next chapter's "Those who know sufficiency are rich." The same idea enters ordinary language in the commonly quoted form, "If you know the point of sufficiency, you will enjoy enduring pleasure."

The final verse, "Tao's imminence under Heaven is like valley streams joining the great rivers and oceans," offers a portrait of naturalness as the various waters, of themselves, move toward the seas and thereby conveys a sense of the Tao's ubiquitous presence. However, there is another dimension to the premise, one of active conquest through deference, that allows the oceans to conquer the rivers, as unfolded in the initial verse of "How Rivers and Seas Can Be Kings of the Hundred Valley Streams." Whether this obverse aspect implies the Tao as conquering, as mandated by the reversal of extremes, might well be pondered.

33

Knowing
Men Is Wisdom

Those who know men are wise;
Who know themselves are enlightened.

Those who conquer others have power;
Who conquer themselves are strong.
Those who know sufficiency are rich;
Who act boldly are willful.
Those who do not lose their places will endure;
Who die without vanishing attain longevity.

WANG   Now if you estimate a man's shallowness and depth, listen to his speech, and observe his behavior, how can a man conceal himself? This merely means that wisdom is this sort of knowing, so the chapter says, "Those who know men are wise." Only after attaining a clarified mind and achieving inner illumination free of oneself and others do people know themselves. If this isn't enlightenment, what can be? Mencius, being called someone who knew himself, thus illustrates the difficulty of self-knowledge.

Now before Ch'in attained hegemony, it usurped the title of emperor, and before Hsiang Yü's strength justified it, he styled himself hegemon. Accordingly, when Ch'in seized hold of All under Heaven and Ch'u subjugated and swallowed up the feudal lords, the six states shrank back. The threatening clamor caused everyone's armies to scatter and disperse. Such cases can truly be termed being powerful enough to conquer others. However, in the end, those powerful enough to conquer others have always been themselves conquered.

In contrast, shouldn't the Chou house, marked by their loyal, generous Virtue, be termed men who conquered themselves? Tan-fu, their progenitor, avoided the barbarians because he loved the people, so his followers were like the crowds in a marketplace. King Wu [at the Chou dynasty's inception] inspected the weapons and bound the troops with an oath, and their secret allies arrived on time. Accordingly, the Chou attacked their former masters, the Shang, and with one battle settled everything. Even during the reigns of the Chou's last perverse remnants, the powerful feudal lords still dared not act as masters of the realm, so the position of central authority over all within the four seas was vacant for forty or fifty years. Shouldn't this be termed conquering oneself?

Thus, it is said, "One who would achieve hegemony or kingship must be victorious." To be victorious, one must be strong. To be strong, one must be able to employ the strength of men. To employ the strength of men, one must gain their hearts. To be able to gain their hearts, one must realize himself. One who is able to realize himself will certainly be pliant and weak. Thus, when the strong and great realize the Tao, they conquer without warfare; when the small and weak attain the Tao, they are successful without combat.

The richness of knowing sufficiency, of goods and wealth beyond counting, is the Tao of Man. Strengthening one's own will, continuously without cessation, is the Tao of Heaven. If one who excels at cleaving to the Tao without losing his position doesn't endure, who will? One who is as cautious at the end as the beginning will suffer no failures. If that doesn't connote longevity, what does?

SAWYER   "Knowing men" has been a great theme and significant factor in Chinese culture for more than two millennia, having suddenly become important late in the Spring and Autumn period and critical in the Warring States. The ability to recognize hidden talent, whatever its nature and dimensions, frequently led to a life-defining relationship between the "knower" and the "known." In order to repay his benefactor, the latter often undertook heroic actions that required his unique, perhaps generally disparaged skills, including theft, assassination, and seduction.

However, in the Warring States period, considerable debate also arose as to whether the minds and motives of other men might truly be known. (Wang Chen's first paragraph on man's essential transparency largely echoes well-known Confucian pronouncements.) A series of active tests, such as getting the person drunk or tempting him with women and wealth, was therefore evolved to fathom character. Thus, the chapter's first line is frequently understood as "Knowing men is wisdom; knowing yourself, enlightened."

The Chinese military classics, as part of their absolute emphasis on plotting and calculation, stressed the need for information about the enemy—even if gathered through the much-deprecated employment of spies—and oneself, prompting Sun-tzu to say, "One who knows the enemy and knows himself will not be endangered in a hundred engagements. One who does not know the enemy but knows himself will sometimes be victorious, sometimes meet with defeat. One who knows neither the enemy nor himself will invariably be defeated in every engagement."

The chapter's fourth line is equally integral to traditional Chinese thought and the martial sphere. The development of self-discipline, while popularly seen as contrary to the Tao, engenders real power according to the *Tao Te Ching*'s definition of strength. Such strength is another manifestation of simplicity, the ability not to be enamored by desire, proceed to extremes, boast or manifest oneself, or generally be seduced by the values of a turbid world. Wang's commentary politicizes this concept of self-conquest, but the essential idea that unobtrusive yet beneficial government attracts the allegiance of the people, the foundation of true strength, certainly underpins it. Those who garner sufficient strength naturally prove overwhelmingly attractive and become virtually unopposable.

34

The Great
Tao Overflows

The Great Tao overflows,
So can be on the left and right.

The myriad things rely on it for birth and are not declined.
It achieves success but does not claim possession.
It sustains and nurtures the myriad things without act-
ing as their master.
Eternally without desire, it can be termed small.
The myriad things return to it, yet it doesn't act as their
master,
So can be termed great.
To the very end, it doesn't regard itself as great,
So can achieve greatness.

WANG   This chapter states that the Great Tao overflowingly fills All under Heaven. That it can be on the left and
right means that the myriad things all follow it; there is
nowhere that it is not present. In this way, the myriad things
are able to rely upon it to be born and flourish, but the Tao
still declines any gratitude for its beneficence. "It achieves
success but does not claim possession" refers to the Sage who
accords with the Tao in patterning things, applying unconscious love and covering them with unemotional nurturing.
Thus, he does not act as the master of the myriad things and
is naturally and always free of desire. How can this be named
small? Moreover, the myriad things all return there. The Sage
governs them with the purely unselfish Tao, so again does
not claim to be acting as master of the myriad things. How
can this not be termed great? Accordingly, it is clear that the
Sage, by never acting great, can achieve greatness.

SAWYER   The characteristics of the Tao enumerated by the
verses—primarily its pervasive immanence and its trait of acting without claiming possession or mastery—recur throughout the *Tao Te Ching*, particularly finding expression in "Tao
Gave Them Birth." However, perhaps inspired by the verses
in "All under Heaven Know," "The Tao of Heaven," and
"Regulating the Earthly Soul to Embrace Unity," Wang
Chen shifts the reference from the Tao to the phenomenal
world of men and action by particularizing the Tao in the
Sage and envisioning him achieving greatness.

35

Grasp the
Great Emblem

Grasp the Great Emblem;
All under Heaven will go there.
Going they are unharmed,
Settling in unperturbed tranquillity.
For music and fragrant foods,
Passing guests will stop;
Words spoken about the Tao
Are placid and flavorless.
Looked at, it is insufficient to be seen;
Listened to, it is insufficient to be heard;
But employed, is insufficient to ever exhaust!

WANG   Heaven hangs out emblems, and the Sage models on them. This chapter states that when the king takes hold of the great emblems, never losing their Tao, All under Heaven will go and give their allegiance without exception. If he then nurtures and settles those who go there with Tao and Virtue, bringing it about that they penetrate to tranquillity unharmed, how would this differ from setting out drinks and food, a feast and music, on the open thoroughfare, pleasing and satiating people who pass by?

If the ruler controls and maneuvers the army in accord with the subtle, ethereal Tao—stressing placidity, equanimity, and nonzealousness—he will naturally lack shape and traces, thus causing onlookers and listeners to be unable to hear or see it. Furthermore, the more the Great Tao is practiced, the more inexhaustible and unimpoverished it becomes. Thus, the *Tao*

Te Ching says, "employed, is insufficient to ever exhaust." "Exhaust" here means to use up, to be finished.

SAWYER   The vast amorphousness of the Tao, previously the focus of "Looked at but Unseen," anchors the chapter's meditation, entailing an impossibility of perception that prompts Wang Chen to ponder the shapeless and formless army. In fact, "shapelessness" and "formlessness" are much exploited in Chinese military thought, having already assumed a prominent place in Sun-tzu's initial conceptualizations. For example, in the *Art of War*, Sun-tzu states, "When someone excels in attacking, the enemy does not know where to mount his defense. When someone excels at defense, the enemy does not know where to attack. Subtle! Subtle! It approaches the formless. Spiritual! Spiritual! It attains the soundless. Thus, he can be the enemy's Master of Fate."

Wang Chen introduces an additional element: an army's formlessness (or unfathomability) stems from command and control that is imbued with the subtlety of the Tao, from leaders free of strong emotions and mental perturbations. The result is a commander without visible flaws or traits that might be exploited, producing scenarios such as Sun-tzu describes:

> At the moment the general has designated with them, it will be as if they ascended a height and abandoned their ladders. The general advances with them deep into the territory of the feudal lords and then releases the trigger. He commands them as if racing a herd of sheep: they are driven away, driven back, but no one knows where they are going.

36

Wanting to
Reduce Something

*If you want to reduce something, you must certainly
   stretch it.*
*If you want to weaken something, you must certainly
   strengthen it.*
*If you want to abolish something, you must certainly
   make it flourish.*
*If you want to grasp something, you must certainly give it
   away.*
This is referred to as subtle enlightenment.
The pliant and weak will conquer the hard and strong.
Fish cannot abandon the depths;
*The state's sharp implements cannot be displayed to the
   people.*

WANG   This entire chapter explicates the meaning of
Heaven and Earth, ghosts and spirits, harm and fullness, blessings and humility. It states that anyone who would govern the
state and control the army must certainly contemplate the Tao
of Heaven above and investigate human affairs below. He
should constantly be profoundly circumspect and wary, saying:

> If at present the seasons of Heaven and human affairs
> truly are opening and extending me, are there none who
> will want to reduce and defeat me? If presently they are
> truly strengthening and augmenting me, are there none
> who will want to weaken and diminish me? If presently they
> are truly making me flourish, are there none who will want
> to abandon or cast me away? If presently they are truly

blessing and sustaining me, are there none who will want to constrain and seize me?

Those kings and lords who manage to be wary and cautious from beginning to end in this way may be said to understand the subtle and know the illustrious. Thus, the chapter subsequently states, "The pliant and weak will conquer the hard and strong." This really does not refer to the practitioners of the flexible and soft invariably being able to control and conquer hard and strong enemies but directly points out that kings and lords who already dwell in the hard and firm ought to preserve the intention to conquer through pliancy. For this reason, the humble and lowly, the parsimonious and constrained, will long enjoy their years while the arrogant, overbearing, extravagant, and licentious displace calamity unto themselves. No doubt this is the constant pattern of things.

Fearing people still will not awaken, further down Lao-tzu provides another severe admonition: "Fish cannot abandon the depths." Fish are analogous to the common masses, the depths to the Tao and Virtue. When a king takes charge of the people, he should immerse them in benevolence and longevity. If the fish in the watery depths never suffer the misfortune of the water's drying up or being caught in a net, they will realize security and pleasure. Furthermore, when the Former Kings manifested their scintillating Virtue, they never inspected the army because the army is the state's sharp implement and must not be displayed to the people. However, the army is also something that, although not employed in warfare, should be preserved, never abandoned. Still, it must only be prepared and maintained within, not exhaustively exposed outside, because when externally displayed to the people, the shame of defeat will inevitably follow. Shouldn't one be careful!?

SAWYER Although several of the classic military writers embraced the concept of the "pliant conquering the stiff," especially in the domain of psychological warfare, Wang Chen understands the chapter as admonishing strong, successful rulers to adopt softness and pliancy as their watchword and thereby endure. This stance may be extrapolated to all circumstances in which one's affairs are flourishing because there will always be others beset by desire or enmity who evince little goodwill. However, Wang Chen's pointed denial here of the ability of the weak to overcome the strong contrasts markedly with his views in other chapters, including "Reversal Is the Movement of the Tao," particularly with reference to the power of water.

Over the centuries, commentators have variously interpreted "sharp implements of state" as weapons, authority, and the "handles of power," the latter being synonymous with rewards and punishments. However, since the chapter—one much maligned for its deceitful approach by later Confucians—discusses principles for conquest, either weapons or the most powerful weapon of all, the army itself, must be intended, just as Wang Chen interprets the term. Moreover, Wang emphasizes the idea that the army, even though not employed, should be retained and prepared as a deterrent force and also continues to advocate the importance of benevolence for the people. (Again, this certainly refers not to the mere benevolence of nominal Confucians but to the substantial benevolence of Confucius himself!)

37

Tao Eternally Actionless

Tao is eternal and actionless,

But there is nothing not done.
If lords and kings could cleave to it,
The myriad things would be transformed by themselves.
After they are transformed, should they want to arise,
I will repress them with unnamed simplicity.
Unnamed simplicity similarly has no desire.
When they do not desire and are quiescent,
All under Heaven will correct themselves.

WANG   "Eternal Tao" refers to nameless origination; "Tao is eternal," to named beginning. Originally, at the beginning, when the Tao was undesignated, it acted as progenitor of unified ch'i. Similarly, once named, it became the origination of the myriad things. Moreover, the Tao patterns on the natural, so the harmonizing unification of Heaven and Earth, yin and yang, occurs without any actions ever being spoken of. Thus, Lao-tzu speaks of its being "actionless." It extends to the four seasons revolving and the hundred things maturing, so the chapter adds, "nothing is not done."

Furthermore, because the Tao of Heaven is beneficial, not harmful, monarchs ought to implement it. They should recognize everything that brings harm to All under Heaven and avoid it, know everything that benefits All under Heaven and enact it. Under Heaven, no harm exceeds employing weapons, no benefit surpasses demobilizing the army. Accordingly, the *Tao Te Ching* says that if kings and lords can merely preserve the Tao, things will all be transformed by themselves. When their transformation is complete, any desires that again threaten to arise should be "repressed with unnamed simplicity." Unnamed simplicity similarly takes nondesire as its root. Through tranquillity, one returns to the root. When this return is protracted and one reverts to fate, it may be termed reverting and cleaving to the true and eternal Tao. When someone reverts to the true and eternal Tao, how would the myriad things not follow and be correct? Thus, Lao-tzu says, "All under Heaven will correct themselves." Similarly, ["With Government, Order the State," in referring to the Sage,] states, "I am tranquil, and the people become upright by themselves." Moreover, the *Analects* observes, "If you lead them with uprightness, who will dare not be upright?" Don't they refer to this?

SAWYER   Wang Chen interprets the chapter's pronouncements of the twin recurrent themes of the Tao's eternal nature and simplicity's function in terms of the protoscientific theory that began to evolve about the era of the *Tao Te Ching,* projecting ch'i and yin and yang into ongoing universal processes. However, two of his views diverge somewhat from the *Tao Te Ching*'s original conceptions. First, the Tao of Heaven's actions are solely beneficial, giving Wang transpersonal grounds for condemning man's employment of harmful weapons. Second, uprightness—the same character as for "correct themselves" in the chapter's last line but reflexively applied—will transform the people when tranquilly implemented. (Although a solid Confucian Virtue, uprightness will nonetheless be disparaged in the next chapter.)

Wang's definition of being "actionless" also bears note because it falls into the prominent tradition that holds that wu wei isn't equivalent to no action at all. Instead, it signifies totally natural action that is in harmony with the Tao and universal flux and therefore should not be saddled with the sobriquet of "action." In this conception, only artificial efforts and movements—particularly those that disrupt the harmony and lives of the people while perturbing the mind and debilitating the spirit—should therefore be deemed "actions." (Within this perspective, it requires but a minor step to envision prolonging life and cultivating longevity through appropriate nonartificial measures, including minimizing the desires and maintaining an unobtrusive profile.)

Finally, there is the apparently violent act of repression described in the verse that states, "After they are transformed, should they want to arise, I will repress them with unnamed simplicity." Totally abstract and puzzling as to what it entails, this verse surprisingly betrays a remarkably activist strain much in contrast with the *Tao Te Ching*'s idea of minimal and virtually invisible government. Although somewhat ameliorated by the antecedent "after they are transformed" (no doubt meaning after they have attained their true natures and realized tranquillity), it still evokes a startling scene of amorphous government's beating down the desirous and rebellious with simplicity. (The uncarved block in Arthur Waley's classic version provides another concrete image of this.)

德經 TE CHING

38
Superior Virtue
Is Not Virtuous

Superior Virtue is not virtuous, so is Virtuous.
Inferior Virtue does not lose virtue, so is
 without Virtue.
Superior Virtue is actionless, without external objective;
Inferior Virtue is actionless but has external objectives.
Superior benevolence is implemented but without any
 objective;
Superior righteousness is practiced with an objective.
Superior rites [li] are implemented, but if there is no
 response,
Arms are bared to coerce one.
Thus, only after the Tao has been lost is there Virtue;
Only after Virtue has been lost is there benevolence;
Only after benevolence has been lost is there
 righteousness;
Only after righteousness has been lost is there ritual.
Now ritual is the veneer of loyalty and sincerity, the start
 of chaos.
Precognition is the flower of Tao and the beginning of
 stupidity.
For this reason, the great man dwells in the thick and does
 not reside in the thin,
Occupies the substantial and does not dwell in the
 superficial.
Thus, he rejects that and takes this.

WANG   Superior Virtue, which characterized the era of the
Three August Ones, is of one body with the Tao and cannot

be described. Thus Lao-tzu states it is not virtuous. Inferior Virtue, which employs the Tao, characterized the age of the Five Emperors, when intimacy and love first germinated. Therefore, Lao-tzu says they had Virtue.

Benevolence, righteousness, and the rites [ritual] were all implemented together at the beginning of the era when the Three Kings successfully guarded against calamity and rescued the chaotic. Roughly characterized, the way they governed the states of the realm and themselves was one. Thus, it may be said that the Three August Ones, Five Emperors, and Three Kings acted differently but from the same impulse, reached the same destination but by different roads. Accordingly, when kings employed all five of them—the Tao, Virtue, benevolence, righteousness, and ritual—they were just like the five phases [elements] in being resources for each other. Consequently, lacking any one of them was not acceptable. Lao-tzu cited developments stretching from antiquity to his own time in order to illustrate the ongoing loss of Virtue. Weapons simply lay beside the steps of the August Ones but were initially brandished during the Three Dynasties [Hsia, Shang, and Chou]. Loyalty and sincerity having already grown thin, the rituals of imperial power were emptily practiced, good and evil festered below, and the common people looked with longing to antiquity.

Now when the li [rites and rituals] are lost, there is chaos. One who would resolve this chaos must employ the li. Now the character for "chaos" also has an antique meaning of "to order." This means that the li, synonymous with ordering, are the start of chaos. Lao-tzu probably wanted the kings of his era to abandon the li and implement righteousness, abandon righteousness and achieve benevolence, eliminate benevolence and honor Virtue, and contravene Virtue to attain the Tao. Thus, he says, "For this reason, the great man dwells in the thick and does not reside in the thin; occupies the substantial and does not dwell in the superficial." Accordingly, abandoning that [the thinness of the li and righteousness] and taking this [the thickness of the Tao and Virtue] will furnish an ordering transformation for kings. Isn't this the pinnacle! Thus, he says, "rejects that and takes this."

SAWYER   The chapter is comprised of essentially symmetrical halves that express the same concept in slightly different ways: the devolution from Virtue previously depicted in rather less detail, conceived either historically or atemporally. Each of the first four verses contrasts some natural performance that merits a laudatory name such as "benevolence" with its conscious, and therefore debased, counterpart. The next six lines go on to fundamentally bemoan the sequential, inexorable decline from the Tao through natural Virtue and eventually punishments and arms. (Surprisingly, Wang Chen barely identifies warfare's onset with the realm's movement from Virtue to chaos and thus ignores strong grounds for condemning it and pontificating on its pernicious effects.) Naturally the only viable antidote to devolution is eschewing the artificial in favor of the substantial, casting out the superficial in order to provide a model for all the realm.

With his Confucian background and solid indoctrination in the political and social realities of his era, Wang Chen clearly recognizes this devolutionary trend. Yet he seizes upon the protoscientific concept of the five phases (or elements) to analogously justify not abandoning these (debased) virtues and instead advocates their coordinated implementation. At the same time, he would have monarchs, to the fullest extent possible, revert to the substantiality of the Tao and Virtue, thereby obviating such secondary, conscious (and conscientious) practices. Moreover, any defect or deficiency in benevolence, righteousness, and the li must derive from their artificial, insincere (and therefore insubstantial) practice rather than their nature as conceived by Confucius and implemented by true Sages.

39

Those in Antiquity Who Realized the One

Among those in antiquity who realized the One:
Heaven realized the One and cleared;
Earth realized the One and was tranquil;
The spirits realized the One and became numinous;
Valley streams realized the One and became full;
The myriad things realized the One and were born;
Lords and kings realized the One and thereby exemplified
    truth for All under Heaven;
All achieved through attaining it.
If Heaven lacked the means to clear, it would probably
    crack.
If Earth lacked the means to be tranquil, it would
    probably fissure.
If the spirits lacked the means to be numinous, they would
    probably be deficient.
If valley streams lacked the means to be full, they would
    probably become exhausted.
If the myriad things lacked the means to be born, they
    would probably become extinct.
If lords and kings lacked the means to be noble and high,
    they would probably stumble.
Thus, nobility takes meanness as its basis;

Height takes lowness as its foundation.
For this reason, lords and kings style themselves solitary,
alone, and unnurtured.
Isn't this taking the inferior as a basis? Or not?
Thus, the highest praise lacks praise.
Do not want to tinkle like jade;
Do not want to clunk like stones.

WANG   Only Lao-tzu would comprehensively cite Heaven, Earth, the spirits, valley streams, and even the myriad things in their realization of the One just to admonish monarchs to employ it. Accordingly, he says that if Heaven and Earth did not employ its clarity and tranquillity for their own settled ease, they would have to constantly fear the changes of cracking and fissuring. If the spirits and valleys did not employ its numinousness and fullness for self-reliance, they would have to fear the misery of exhaustion and becoming parched. If the myriad things did not employ its birthing and completion to long sustain themselves, they would have to constantly fear a time of extinction. If lords and kings didn't employ its nobility and high position to strengthen and augment themselves, they would have to constantly fear the disaster of being overturned and stumbling. Thus, the *Tao Te Ching* says, "take meanness as its basis." Isn't this it?

Now anyone who does not take himself to be strong and great will not be contentious. When rulers are not contentious, armies and warfare will cease by themselves. When armies cease by themselves, rulers will long preserve their Heavenly emoluments.

SAWYER   Although the verses extensively describe the cosmic importance and beneficial effects of "realizing the One," the nature of the One and the process for realizing it remain elusive and mysterious, even in the only *Tao Te Ching* chapter that actively discusses it. (In the upcoming "Tao Gave Birth to the One," the One is merely a transition element bridging the generative sequence from the Tao to the myriad things, whereas previous chapters such as "Regulating the Earthly Soul to Embrace Unity" and "The Curved Will Be Preserved" have only indicated the advisability of embracing the One.)

Over the centuries, commentators have extensively but inconclusively speculated upon the role and definition of the One, differing over whether it is simply identical to the Tao. It might be wondered whether it derives from a different tradition altogether, with two different generative concepts—from the Tao or from the One—being cobbled together by the *Tao Te Ching*'s authors. This uncertainty perhaps prompted Wang Chen to reiterate its characteristics preliminary to admonishing monarchs to again cleave to the substantial and maintain a low, unobtrusive profile. Moreover, he perceives an attitude of humility in itself helping to staunch combat and contention because rational men who feel themselves to be insufficiently strong will generally not initiate warfare.

40

Reversal Is the Movement of the Tao

Reversal is the movement of the Tao;
Weakness is the Tao's employment.

The myriad things under Heaven are all given
  birth in being,
But being stems from nonbeing.

WANG This chapter discusses how the myriad things all move forth tangled and intertwined, each and every one of them returning to its roots. Thus, it says, "Reversal is the movement of the Tao." Now ordinary things move through movement; only the Tao's movement occurs in tranquillity. Thus, it states, "Reversal is the movement of the Tao." Reversal is like returning, while returning manifests the heart of Heaven and Earth. Heaven and Earth take tranquillity to be their heart, movement to be their employment. Thus, when they revert from movement, they return to tranquillity. Therefore, the chapter says, "Reversal is the movement of the Tao."

For this reason, the Sage is cautious about his movements, constantly dwells in actionlessness, and deeply penetrates to the idea that returning to the root preserves tranquillity, for then he can know the constant. Only by knowing the constant can he avoid wanton actions. Being able to avoid wanton actions, he can be enlightened.

Moreover, pliancy and weakness are the Tao's employment, which means that the Sage must employ the Tao of pliancy and weakness in order to conquer the strong and brutal throughout the realm. In addition, "things" are like affairs. Now "all the affairs under Heaven are given birth in being, but being stems from nonbeing." Thus, the Sage constantly dwells in actionless affairs and reverts to tranquillity, for then the myriad things will naturally be born and go to completion. He doesn't foolishly say that he acted on them, so the chapter concludes with "being stems from nonbeing."

SAWYER This pithy, twenty-one-character chapter stimulated reams of speculative commentary, and the observation that "Reversal Is the Movement of the Tao" became a slogan frequently heard whenever trends or events precipitously reverted, when the great and shining were suddenly eclipsed. As a watchword, it conveys the insight that extremes are unstable, excesses of any type especially so, and should be guarded against—which is, of course, a constant theme in the *Tao Te Ching* and one of its fundamental tactics for the craft of living. Moreover, the *Tao Te Ching* adopts maintaining minimality as its predominant survival strategy, thereby adumbrating any growth that would lead to excessive achievement. However, because such preventative approaches contravene human inclinations and the irrepressible power of desire, conflict and frustration inevitably arise. (The view of the pliant and weak's being, in some sense, supreme because of their participation in the Tao might well be contrasted with Wang Chen's interpretation in "Wanting to Reduce Something.")

The second couplet grounds Chinese cosmogony and much later philosophy, including interpretations of the *I Ching*. Being itself, rather than being timeless and permanent, stems from nonbeing. Other chapters suggest how the ineffable stirred and the incipient attained form; "Reversal Is the Movement of the Tao" only reveals the root principle. Wang Chen perceives unity in these two couplets, integrating them with a view of the Sage engaged in effortless activity and thus marked and defined by both nonaction and nonpossession, an idea seen in other chapters as well. However, even though these four lines have a certain resonance, they probably originated as distinct sayings in an ancient time, only to become fortuitously juxtaposed here.

41

When Superior Officers Hear About the Tao

When superior officers hear about the Tao,
They exert themselves to practice it.
When ordinary officers hear about the Tao,
It sometimes seems to be present, sometimes absent.
When inferior officers hear about the Tao,
They uproariously laugh at it.
If they didn't laugh,
It would be unworthy of being taken as the Tao.
Thus, the following pronouncements:
* The Tao that enlightens appears dark.*
* The Tao for advancing seems like withdrawing.*
* The Tao of equanimity seems cluttered.*
* Superior Virtue is like a valley.*
* Great whiteness seems smeared.*
* Expansive Virtue seems insufficient;*
* Established Virtue seems sneaky;*
* Substantial Virtue seems vacuous.*
* Great squareness lacks corners;*
* Great vessels are completed late;*
* Great notes sparsely sound;*
* Great emblems lack shape.*
The Tao is concealed and nameless.
Only the Tao excels at bespreading and completing.

WANG   Although Sages and Worthies are marked by degrees, how might the ordinary person know about such distinctions? Lao-tzu therefore roughly divides them into three levels—upper, middle, and lower—to make clear the degree to which they recognize the Tao. Confucius said, "One who hears of the Tao in the morning can die that night," so the superior officer's resolve to exert himself in its practice can be seen. Moreover, because of the distinction of superior and inferior natures, Lao-tzu sarcastically speaks of those for whom it sometimes seems present, sometimes absent.

Just as brief-lived summer bugs doubt discussions about the existence of ice, there are those who hear about the Tao and then laugh uproariously, prompting Lao-tzu to reprise several pronouncements about the Tao. Among them, "The Tao that enlightens appears dark" speaks about Heaven's Virtue, which, although gloriously shining above, always seems obscurely dark. "The Tao of advancing seems like withdrawing" discusses Earth's Virtue, which, even though persistently fulminating below, always seems as if humbly withdrawing. "The Tao of equanimity seems cluttered" refers to the ruler's Virtue, which, even though eminently imposing, models on Heaven and always unites with many categories, never displaying its own distinctiveness.

Because these are so, even a ruler marked by superior Virtue must be as humble as a valley stream and vacuously accept contamination below. Similarly, the truly pure and unsullied ruler must always act as if dwelling amid dust and disgrace. Even though he might be expansive, great, and fully prepared, he must always act as if inadequate. Moreover, even though he wants to establish Virtue among men, he must always fear the people will learn about it. Thus, the *Tao Te Ching* says [established Virtue] "seems sneaky." Even though embodying the Tao's true substance, the Sage always seems to be changing.

"Great squareness lacks corners," preferring to display outstanding angles. "Great vessels are completed late," so do not seek to quickly attain objectives. "Great notes sparsely sound," so they will certainly shake the torpid insects. "Great emblems lack shape," which is the formlessness of the formless.

The Tao originally was nameless, so if you force a name, it is designated as the mother of the myriad things. Everything relies on the natural to be born and raised. Thus, the *Tao Te Ching* says, "it excels at bespreading and completing." Now when the ruler takes hold of Virtue and grasps pliancy, employing the obscure and actionless in this fashion, who under Heaven can contend with him? When there is no one to contend with, weapons and armor will naturally be collected and stored away.

SAWYER Although both the verses and Wang's commentary are remarkably clear, the variations in human ability to understand the Tao and the range of accompanying reactions merit noting. Essentially tautological—since those who laugh clearly do not have the capacity to understand, just as those who do not understand naturally laugh—a degree of intellectual elitism has definitely crept in here, despite frequent *Tao Te Ching* admonitions to abjure wisdom and cleave to simplicity.

The Sage's transcendence clearly derives from his penetration of the Tao and consequent wisdom and knowledge, just as the Tao remains elusively beyond the grasp of most men (contrary to later expansions and religious variations that presume the Tao to be accessible to everyone just because it is the Tao). This impenetrability immediately engenders a hierarchy of knowers and provides an implied justification for the existence of government and functions of administration, for a benevolent, appropriately informed Sage ruler to guide the people amid their inescapable ignorance and keep them simple by reducing tertiary, unnecessary knowledge and desires. Meanwhile, the "wise" (whether Taoist or Confucian Sages, according to Wang Chen's citation) bend themselves to the effort of learning about the Tao and penetrating its essence.

A second theme of interest is the relativity of viewpoint and perception explicitly brought out by Wang Chen's comment (no doubt echoing Chuang-tzu's explorations of relativity, of great and small knowledge) on the inability of short-lived insects to understand discussions about phenomena they have never experienced. Although certainly a partial explanation for misperceiving the Tao, the chapter itself makes it clear that, from an ordinary viewpoint, the Tao—which is, after all, ineffable, amorphous, and transcendent—is inherently deceptive and therefore misleading, as might be expected.

However, a singular insight informs the chapter's enumeration of the Tao's paradoxical characteristics: the achievements and greatness of Tao somehow seem lacking, yet the Tao "excels at bespreading and completing." This surpassing ability prompts Wang Chen to once again envision that in mimicking the Tao so as to be pliant and obscure, the successful ruler will yet be overwhelmingly powerful. The conclusion that no one will contend with him no doubt derives in part from the fact that everyone will rush to give his allegiance and become satisfied and secure, enabling the ruler to effortlessly dominate.

42

Tao Gave Birth to the One

Tao gave birth to the One;
The One gave birth to the two;
The two spawned the three;

The three engendered the myriad things.
The myriad things shoulder yin and embrace yang,
Infusing their ch'i to achieve harmony.
The only things people hate are being orphaned, widowed,
 unnurtured,
But kings and dukes style themselves accordingly.
Thus, some things, being diminished, are augmented;
Some, being augmented, are diminished.
What people teach, I also teach:
"The strong and powerful do not attain a natural death."
I take this as my chief instruction.

WANG   Now as primordial ch'i, the beginning of life, gives birth unceasingly, the myriad things fill up the interstice of Heaven and Earth. Moreover, when the myriad things emerge, they all shoulder yin's severe ch'i on their backs and embrace yang's harmonious core. Those who embody and harmonize them become men and are therefore termed most numinous. Being numinous as well as wise, they can know the meaning of diminishing and augmenting. Rulers call themselves by generally detested terms because they voluntarily accept diminishment in the hope of being thereby augmented. Accordingly, the chapter states, "Thus, some things, being reduced, are augmented; some, being augmented, are reduced." This is what Lao-tzu means.

When Lao-tzu says that he must use the admonitory teachings of others to instruct men, he means that people who don't understand the Tao of augmenting and diminishing simply rely upon troops and love weapons. The brutally strong who slight their enemies will inevitably suffer the humiliation and destruction of defeat, will overturn their armies and bring about the slaughter of their cities. Since it is obvious that they will prematurely lose their lives, he comments, "The strong and powerful do not attain a natural death." Since no calamity greater than this can befall state rulers, Lao-tzu concludes, "I take this as my chief instruction," thereby asserting that no admonition is more important than this.

SAWYER   "Tao Gave Birth to the One" is one of the few crucial chapters that actually depict cosmogenic sequences, although perhaps the most famous, and the only chapter to envision an active role for ch'i. (Despite being prominently mentioned in such early texts as Sun-tzu's *Art of War*, the concept of ch'i required many centuries to fully evolve and acquire all its metaphysical and spiritual implications. Furthermore, the character only occurs two other times in the *Tao Te Ching*, in "Regulating the Earthly Soul to Embrace Unity" and "Abundantly Embodying Virtue," both of which discuss controlling the body's internal ch'i.) Interpretations of the sequence's correlates vary, although the One is often seen as a simple solid, the transcendent ultimate unity known as T'ai Chi (and later also imagized by the famous yin-yang integrated circle), which divides to produce yin and yang themselves. Thereafter, yin and yang interact, creating (in some views) the trigrams that form the foundation for the *I Ching's* sixty-four hexagrams, the patterns for all existence. However, rather than being innate, this interpretation relies heavily on later *I Ching* generative sequence theory and may be partially misdirected or even totally irrelevant.

The thematically disjointed second half of the chapter revisits the *Tao Te Ching* theme that force and hardness inherently entail their own destruction. These verses prompt Wang Chen not just to reiterate the need to avoid military enterprises but also to make the qualified observation that the absence of a proper cautionary attitude fates the powerful to be overturned. The lesson is clear: it is not power that destroys but inflexibility and arrogance in employing it. Moreover, the key to circumventing the inexorable process of reversal is deliberate self-deprecation and humility.

43

The Most
Pliant Under
Heaven

The most pliant under Heaven
Gallop over the firmest under Heaven.
The nonexistent enter where there is no gap.
Accordingly, I know there is advantage to actionlessness.
Unspoken instructions and the advantages of
    actionlessness
Under Heaven are rarely attained.

WANG   "The most pliant" is humble, vacuous, quiet, and
tranquil—what is called "natural ch'i." "The firmest" is
hard, strong, revolving, and moving—what is called "action's disciple." The pliant is quiescent, the firm is active,
while weakness will invariably conquer strength, so the
verses state that [the most pliant] "gallop over the firmest
under Heaven." If the ruler can realize the principle of being actionless through the subtle and mysterious Tao, there
is nowhere he will not enter. Thus, the *Tao Te Ching* states,
"The nonexistent enter where there is no gap." "Actionless
affairs"—also termed pure, quiescent, and most princi-
pled—are synonymous with not undertaking martial activities. Lao-tzu speaks about "unspoken instructions" because
he wants the ruler to rectify himself in order to lead those
below, for then the people will follow without relying upon
his words. As is commonly said, "They do not follow their

commands but follow their actions." Moreover, [in "All under Heaven Know,"] the *Tao Te Ching* notes that [the Sage] "implements unspoken instructions." Truly. But can't the Sage's administration add something to this? To his regret, Lao-tzu realized [that] few of his contemporaries could implement these methods, so he added, "Under Heaven, they are rarely attained."

SAWYER   The chapter's first image is somewhat startling. It is hard to imagine the pliant and weak—normally victorious through sustained but diffuse efforts, through refusing battle, enervating and exhausting the enemy, literally wearing away their strength—"galloping" roughshod over "the firmest." (This principle was previously asserted in "Wanting to Reduce Something" as well.) Moreover, although the nonexistent can obviously penetrate even where there is no gap, armies that would approximate it still suffer from physical dimensions that would presumably thwart their efforts. This can only be considered an example of what might be termed the vaporously abstruse, of an intuitively understood principle that cannot be directly translated into concrete reality and, as the verse states, is "under Heaven . . . rarely attained." However, a sense of the "lesson" still allows it to be applied in the real world, just as Wang Chen conceives in his commentary. (The recurring stress on unspoken teachings, synonymous with leading by example, in both the verses and commentary should be particularly noted.)

44

Fame or the Body, Which Is More Intimate?

Fame or the body, which is more intimate?
The body or goods, which more numerous?
Gain or loss, which more debilitating?
For this reason, extreme love will certainly incur great
  expense;
Abundant storing certainly entail severe loss.
To know sufficiency is to avoid disgrace;
To know stopping is to be unimperiled
And thus able to long endure.

WANG   "Fame" entails salary and position, so those who contend for them forget their bodies. "Goods" refer to material wealth and treasures, so those who covet them slight their own deaths. Even the stupidest person understands that fame is something apart from his body, and his body much greater than mere goods, but in the incipient moment between gain and loss, at the edge of giving and taking, even the reasonably wise are not always able to avoid confusion. Only the Sage is capable of knowing that war can be halted and therefore does not fight for fame; that wealth and material goods can be sufficient and therefore does not harm his body to obtain them; and that by not abundantly storing things away, he will not suffer severe loss. Thus, to the very end of his life, harm, disgrace, and danger cannot touch him personally. Therefore, he can long endure.

SAWYER   The chapter's first three questions, no doubt intended to prompt soul-searching and provoke unexpected intellectual and emotional reactions, prefigure the prominent, recurring teaching of the final three lines, which also essentially conclude "When the Tao Prevails throughout the Realm." As previously enunciated in "Tao Eternal, Unnamed," the key to longevity and constant enjoyment is simply knowing the point of sufficiency. For some, of course, "sufficiency" means rulership over the empire or amassing millions. However, the *Tao Te Ching*'s predominant thrust—not to mention its detailed admonitions to simplify life and reduce desire—is toward minimality and an encompassing spirit that precludes the need to personally possess things, especially as (according to Chuang-tzu) they can only be successfully stored in the wide expanse of the world.

Wang Chen's explication appropriately emphasizes the tenuousness and fragility of human existence, for as the verse implies, the inescapable foundation and premise of life is corporeal existence. When the body is debilitated or racked with pain, wealth, fame, and material goods provide little consolation. This is why "Be Startled at Favor and Disgrace" plaintively observes, "If we did not have bodies, what misery would we have?" and concludes that the realm can be entrusted to any ruler solicitous of his own body. Longevity thus stems not from strange, esoteric practices but from knowing the value of life and stressing the virtues of simplicity and sufficiency. (More radically, but unextrapolated, the desires cannot possess someone who doesn't become a slave to them, who doesn't permit them to rule his actions and life, to perturb his thoughts and tranquillity.)

Traditional China preserves several well-known anecdotes about desire and wealth relevant in this context. In perhaps the most famous, a man obsessed with the color, feel, and glitter of gold was so determined to possess it that he snatched some pieces from an open jeweler's stall in bright daylight amid a crowded marketplace. Naturally he was immediately apprehended by the police, who had been standing about. When asked why he had so foolishly seized the gold with so many people about, knowing that he would certainly suffer severe corporeal punishment or even death, he replied that all he saw was the gold, he never noticed the people! Moreover, Legalist philosophers such as Han Fei-tzu (and many military writers as well) deduced that it is only through man's greed for profits that he can be coerced and cajoled into undertaking miserable, even life-threatening activities, such as rushing into burning buildings and racing forth into battle. Although the compounded threat of punishment was often employed to ensure that the requisite behavior would be elicited, Han Fei-tzu's approach clearly illustrates the application of the chapter's psychodynamics.

45

Great Achievement Seems Deficient

Great achievement seems deficient,
But its employment is unwearying.
Great fullness seems vacuous,
But its employment is inexhaustible.
Great straightness seems curved;
Great artifice seems clumsy;
Great sophistry seems stammering.
Tranquillity conquers rash activity;
Cold conquers heat.

*The clear and tranquil are a corrective for
All under Heaven.*

WANG Even when the Sage occupies the most perfect position of rulership, he still does not boast of his achievements. By always seeming humbly deficient, his employment [of his position] will remain ever free of such worries as exhaustion and defeat. Even when dwelling at the pinnacle of strategic power, he still does not become arrogant about his fullness. By always being humble and vacuous, his employment [of power] forever avoids the distress of exhaustion and hardship. Moreover, he is straightforward with others but curved with himself. Thus, the *Tao Te Ching* says, "seems curved." He conceals clever subtlety and employs substantial simplicity, so it says he "seems clumsy." He circumscribes his language and eliminates eloquence, so it states he "seems to be stammering."

Furthermore, earlier chapters have already detailed the Sage's great return to the foundation of clear, tranquil Virtue. Lao-tzu therefore draws upon the concept of rashness and tranquillity's being mutually defining, cold and heat mutually conquering, for evidence. Clear tranquillity being actionless, the actionless can also be said to be inactive in military affairs. Therefore, they can be the leaders of All under Heaven. [In "With Government, Order the State," the] *Tao Te Ching* further states, "I love tranquillity, and the people become upright by themselves." Previously [in "Tao Eternally Actionless"], it noted that when [rulers] "have no desires and are tranquil, All under Heaven will correct themselves." All of these fall into this category.

SAWYER The chapter opens by arraying a series of misperceptions that stem from the Tao's elusive nature, echoing the verses of "When Superior Officers Hear about the Tao." Wang Chen converts them into a paean to unobtrusive government, concluding with an assertion that inactivity in military affairs, congruent with tranquillity and actionlessness, constitutes one of the chief benefits for the people. His explication that the people embark on self-correction because the ruler effortlessly exemplifies the Tao is therefore highly appropriate. (It should be noted that for "Tranquillity conquers rash activity; cold conquers heat," many versions of the *Tao Te Ching* read, "Rash activity conquers cold; tranquillity conquers heat." Unfortunately, Wang's comments fail to conclusively indicate which edition he relied upon.)

46

When the Tao Prevails Throughout the Realm

When the Tao prevails throughout the realm,
Swift steeds are released to fertilize the fields.
When the Tao does not prevail throughout the realm,
War horses multiply amid the suburbs.
No misfortune is greater than not knowing sufficiency,
No calamity greater than being covetous.
Therefore, the contentment of knowing sufficiency
Is everlasting contentment.

WANG   When swift steeds are released to fertilize fields of thorny brambles, isn't the Tao attained? When war horses multiply amid the many fortresses in the four outer districts, isn't the Tao absent?

When the ruler of men indulges his heart of desire, All under Heaven suffer punishment. When his tastes and desires are awakened but he does not know the boundary of stopping and sufficiency, then All under Heaven suffer misfortune. Moreover, when the ruler of men obtains all that he desires, All under Heaven will inevitably be ensnared in disaster and calamity. When the ruler knows the contentment of being sufficient, who among the people under Heaven will not always be content?

SAWYER   Both the *Tao Te Ching*'s verses and Wang Chen's commentary express the classic Taoist view previously seen in "Fame or the Body, Which Is More Intimate?" here phrased as "the contentment of knowing sufficiency is everlasting contentment." Conversely, the human condition vividly attests to the negative, or yin, face of its absence: "No misfortune is greater than not knowing sufficiency, no calamity greater than being covetous."

When, as Wang Chen and Mencius point out, this affliction consumes a ruler, his extravagance and indulgence produce nothing but widespread misery and poverty. Not only does the monarch thus set a visibly perverse example that encourages the people to pursue material gains and ceaselessly satisfy their desires, but he also deprives them of their wealth, their very means of subsistence, as will be seen in "The People's Hunger." Furthermore, the unconstrained desire for wealth, power, and glory inevitably ends in punishment: military campaigns, warfare, and the conquest and annexation of enemy territories—all activities that require the imposition of additional exactions on a long-suffering populace.

In contrast, when the Tao is attained and the people have ample means for life, weapons are set aside and war horses are released to idly fertilize the fields, evoking an image contrary to that of "Assisting the Ruler with the Tao": "Wherever the army has encamped, thorny brambles will grow." (Wang's commentary thus integrates two disparately focused four-line verses that probably were not originally related.)

47

Without Going
Out the Door,
Know All
Under Heaven

Without going out the door,
Know All under Heaven.
Without peering through the latticed window,
Perceive the Tao of Heaven.
The farther one goes,
The less he knows.
For this reason, the Sage knows without traveling,
Comprehends without perceiving,
Achieves without action.

WANG   The ruler models on Heaven, imitates Earth, respectfully corrects himself, and faces south. Inactive above, he simply relaxes in his robes, nothing more. There is nothing not done below: the officials all preserve the natural; the hundred measures are all correct; the myriad things are all as they should be. Why must he know only after acting, comprehend only after perceiving, achieve only after doing?

SAWYER   The verses express a fundamental Taoist notion that wisdom need not be sought externally but can simply be derived from within. (This should immediately prompt puzzlement about the nature and content of such wisdom, for clearly political facts and military events differ greatly from patterns or principles derived from one's own ruminations and penetration of the Tao.) Wang Chen essentially follows Han Fei-tzu's ideas in his commentary, even though Han's formulation derives its meaning from a greater vision wherein the ruler, through his aloof supervision, allows the well-ordered bureaucratic system to function automatically. Thus, appropriate policies are suggested and implemented while the ruler maintains his actionless tranquillity. However, in doing so, Wang ignores the basic issue of knowledge and intelligence, whereas in Han Fei-tzu's system, since information automatically flows up to the ruler, he need not seek it.

Moreover, across history, many bureaucrats cited this chapter to justify advising the ruler not to commit the state to active intelligence work on the presumption that he is already all-knowing or at least the assumption that he can be. (This is extensively discussed in our book *The Tao of Spycraft*.) Furthermore, with the line "The farther one goes, the less he knows," the chapter evinces the Taoist disinclination to overt study and accretional knowledge that will be clearly enunciated in the next chapter.

Remarkably, the Confucians embraced a somewhat similar view, as seen in Confucius's own explanation of how the Sage Emperors managed to govern the realm without venturing outside their courts: "When you love people, people will love you, but when you hate people, they will hate you. What you know from yourself is the same as what you know from men. What is meant by not venturing beyond the confines of a single room and yet knowing All under Heaven just refers to knowing yourself." Again, the question of the type of knowledge is conveniently ignored, although in Confucius's view, real knowledge consists of knowledge about men, not external incidentals.

48

Those Who Study
Daily Increase

Those who study daily increase,
Who practice the Tao daily diminish.
Diminish and further diminish
In order to attain actionlessness.
Being actionless, there is nothing not done.
Those who would seize All under Heaven
Always do so with the absence of affairs,
For the presence of affairs
Makes it impossible to seize All under Heaven.

WANG   "Study" refers to the transmission and practice of
the rites, laws, governmental measures, and nurturing
statutes of the former kings, so the *Tao Te Ching* characterizes it as daily increase. "Those who practice the Tao" are
those who excel in closing off the seven sensory gates, in conquering and maintaining the three treasures. Thus, the chapter says they "daily diminish."

[As stated in "The Tao of Heaven," the] Tao of Heaven is
to diminish the excessive and supplement the insufficient, so
here the *Tao Te Ching* speaks about diminishing. The Tao of
the Sage is to diminish the excessive and sustain All under
Heaven, so it adds, "further diminishes it." Anyone capable
of employing this Tao will naturally attain to actionlessness
[wu-wei].

Now the Sage minimizes his thoughts and makes his desires
few, de-emphasizes the martial and cultivates the civil, naturally, without anything that might be termed action. Further-

more, the Sage ruler does everything under Heaven known to benefit the people, so the chapter says, "there is nothing not done." In acting as a ruler, the Sage is always actionless and without affairs. [As "The Sage Has No Preset Mind" observes,] "By taking the minds of the hundred surnames as his mind," he can seize the minds of All under Heaven.

When a ruler mounts affairs, he confiscates the people's wealth through military and civil taxes; when he acts, he harms the people's basic nature and their very lives with shields and halberds. Under such conditions, his relatives will be estranged and his troops rebellious, the state extinguished and the people endangered, so how will he be able to seize the minds of All under Heaven? Thus, the *Tao Te Ching* states he will be "incapable of seizing All under Heaven."

SAWYER   The first two lines epitomize the Taoist approach to accretional wisdom as contrasted with the practice of the Tao. Wang Chen's commentary delimits the contents of knowledge somewhat arbitrarily to the especially "artificial" aspects of society and glides over their deprecation in these verses untroubled, despite having previously envisioned these aspects as fundamental to governing. Thereafter, his comments insightfully integrate the two parts of the chapter by providing a solid explanation for garnering the allegiance of All under Heaven through the "actionless" affairs previously well discussed rather than through military measures that will rebound to destroy one's own populace as well as antagonize the realm.

Wang also touches on, but does not explore, the yogic implications of "practicing the Tao," here probably a form of meditative breath control designed to attain stillness and tranquillity. As for the three treasures mentioned in his first paragraph, "All under Heaven Term Me Vast" defines one such set as solicitude, frugality, and "daring to precede the world." Here, however, Wang probably has in mind another, internal set found within the greater context of later Taoist thought: original essence (or endowment), original ch'i, and original spirit.

49

The Sage Has
No Preset Mind

The Sage has no preset mind
But takes the minds of the hundred surnames as his mind.
The good I regard as good,
The ungood I also regard as good,
Making a Virtue of goodness.
The trustworthy I trust,
The untrustworthy I similarly trust,
Making a virtue of trust.
The Sage's presence under Heaven is recessive.
In acting on All under Heaven,
He muddies their minds.
The hundred surnames are all obsessed with their ears
*   and eyes;*
The Sage regards them all as children.

WANG   "The Sage takes the minds of the hundred surnames as his mind" basically means that he follows the desires
of others. "The ungood I also regard as good" can also be
termed instructing them with Tao and Virtue, causing them
to become good. Thus, [in "Tao of the Myriad Things,"] the
Tao Te Ching asks, "How can the not good among the people be rejected?" Truly.

Moreover, "The untrustworthy I similarly trust" says that
when I inadequately trust others, it causes others not to be
trustworthy. Therefore, if I similarly instruct them with Tao
and Virtue, it will make them become trustworthy, "making a
virtue of trust." Furthermore, the crux is doubt and investiga-
tion. In trepidation, the Sage constantly investigates All under

Heaven, never stopping or resting, and muddies their minds, causing them all to reject evil and pursue good. Accordingly, the hundred surnames all reverse their obsessions with their ears and eyes, looking and listening instead to the thoughts and ideas of the Sage, who loves them all like his children. Thus, the *Tao Te Ching* states that he "regards them all as children." Since they are children and he nourishes them all, clearly he acts as their father and mother. Have fathers and mothers ever been willing to harm their children with shields and halberds, punishments and fines? Certainly not.

SAWYER   Clearly the chapter contains some inexplicable contradictions. The first two lines state, "The Sage has no preset mind but takes the minds of the hundred surnames as his mind," yet the chapter essentially concludes by portraying the Sage in an active role: "In acting on All under Heaven, he muddies their minds." Wang imaginatively interprets the latter as "causing them all to reject evil and pursue good," which is a wonderful Neo-Taoist interpretation, a convenient bridge to an image of the Sage as a loving parent and therefore purely benevolent, unmarked by any inclination to, or implementation of, negative corporeal measures. But such an image is hardly consonant with the thrust of "muddying" in the sense of making turbid, undefined, and imprecise and thereby eliminating motivating perturbations from the people's lives. However, the point that benign government leads to harmony and a sense of allegiance, as previously seen, remains incontrovertible.

50

Going
Forth into Life,
Entering Death

In the progress from life to death,
The partisans of life are thirteen,
The partisans of death are thirteen,
And the living who act on deadly terrain are also thirteen.
Why is this?
Because they nurture their lives too abundantly.
You have probably heard that those who excel at taking
*   hold of life,*
When traveling on land, do not encounter rhinoceroses or
*   tigers,*
When entering the army, do not wear weapons or armor.
Rhinoceroses have nowhere to impale their horns,
Tigers nowhere to sink their claws,
Weapons nowhere to engage their blades.
For what reason?
Because they have no deadly terrain within them.

WANG   Actively going forth is life; inactively entering is
death. "Thirteen" refers to the four limbs and nine bodily orifices. The four limbs are the dynamic source of nature and life,
the nine orifices the gates and doors to the tastes and desires.
Movement and tranquillity preserve the dynamic source's
constraints; the gates and doors have appropriate times for
opening and closing. According with them is conducive to
longevity; contravening them leads to death. Nothing sur-

passes nourishment for preserving life, but when nourishment becomes excessive, it reverts to harm. Thus, the *Tao Te Ching* asks, "Why is this? Because they nurture their lives too abundantly." In contrast, "those who excel at taking hold of life" are Sages and Worthies. Lao-tzu was simply being humble in saying, "you have probably heard."

Now the Tao of the Sage is to benefit, not harm, so how could the Sage injure any creature? Thus, even out on the level plains, he neither hunts nor seeks out tigers or rhinoceroses to kill. Even amid the army, he does not wear armor, carry weapons, or strive to slay the enemy. Accordingly, to the very end of his life, he is unworried about being injured by horns and claws, blades and edges because he can unify the radiant, unite with the dust, adjust and nurture his original ch'i, preserve the minutely ethereal Tao, and realize the principle of nurturing life. Therefore, the chapter concludes, "For what reason? Because he has no deadly terrain within him." By employing weapons, subsequent ages placed themselves amid death. Even if someone then sought to avoid death, how could he achieve it?

SAWYER   Traditionally, most commentators (and therefore translators in their wake) have understood the characters here rendered as "thirteen" as referring to a proportion, giving the following:

> *In the progress from life to death,*
> *The partisans of life are three in ten,*
> *The partisans of death are three in ten,*
> *And the living who act on deadly terrain*
>   *are also three in ten.*

However, Wang Chen's self-explanatory elaboration follows Han Fei-tzu's interpretation, coincidentally suggesting that many of his commentaries to other chapters are premised upon a general acceptance of Han Fei-tzu's founding views as they were preserved and filtered through later tradition. (If understood as "three in ten," obviously "one in ten," or one-tenth of the populace, remains unaccounted for—presumably infants and those in accord with the Tao?)

Wang's depiction of human excessiveness in nourishing life—conspicuous consumption, gluttony, and similar images are naturally stirred—accords with the *Tao Te Ching*'s recurrent admonitions against sensory indulgence and the frequently suggested corrective, knowing the point of sufficiency. However, less clear are the implications of the chapter's middle verses, which portray invincible men passing through mortal danger unscathed. Although the *Tao Te Ching*'s abstract, metaphysical explanation—"because they have no deadly terrain within them"—describes the effect noncontention presumably has in dispelling (or simply not evoking) aggression in others, it has historically stimulated many diverse beliefs.

By unifying the myriad things and harmonizing with them, the Sage is seen as escaping conflict and therefore being protected from violent impulses. However, in more general application, this "absence of deadly terrain" implies that ordinary men might somehow cultivate an inherent impenetrability, an imperviousness to weapons, by achieving a state of "no deadly terrain." Many theorists and adepts suggested that this may be done spiritually, through casting out aggressive intentions, but for warriors generally embarked upon the path of death and destruction, who must utilize their anger and emotions (despite the *Tao Te Ching*'s views to the contrary), it came to mean the cultivation of fearlessness, unbending will, and cloaks of invisible ch'i, as well as such hard characteristics as physical toughness.

Religious and mystical practitioners also came to employ mantras, elixirs, and symbols, but the focused view preserved in the military writings essentially finds that spirit is always the dominant factor in combat, that being oblivious to one's life paradoxically results in saving it. This accounts for the terrible power manifested by the swordsman in the market-place—an image raised in several military writings—in comparison with the terrified hordes who scurry about to avoid even the threat of danger. (In contrast, there is also a psychophysiological martial arts concept derived from acupuncture theory that identifies certain susceptible points on the body as "death points," believed to result in delayed death when struck with a skillful, properly focused blow.)

51

Tao Gave
Them Birth

The Tao gave them birth;
Te nurtured them;
Things shaped them;
Power completed them.
For this reason, the myriad things all revere Tao and
*   honor Te.*
Tao being revered and Te honored,
Unmandated, has always been naturally so.
Thus, Tao gives birth to them,
Virtue nurtures them,
Grows them and rears them,
Completes them and matures them,
Nourishes them and sustains them.
It nurtures but does not possess,
Acts but does not rely,
Sustains but does not control.
This is what is meant by Dankly Mysterious Virtue.

WANG   Since the Tao of Heaven unemotionally gives birth and the Te [Virtue] of Earth unemotionally nurtures, things achieve dynamic shape and power gains transformative completion. Therefore, "the myriad things all revere Tao and honor Te." "The Tao being revered and Te honored," everyone will naturally receive his rank and emolument from Heaven, so how can there be an overlord? When kings and lords model upon them, they should give birth, nurture, grow, rear, complete, mature, nourish, and sustain the myriad things without ever missing the appropriate time. However, they still should not possess achievements nor rely on strength, but instead reject mastery, eliminate conflict, and desist from struggling, which can then be said to accord with the Virtue of Heaven. Therefore, the *Tao Te Ching* refers to it as "Dankly Mysterious Virtue."

SAWYER   This chapter suffers from textual corruption and internal repetition, the last half largely mirroring the first in slightly different language, while several verses appear in "All under Heaven Know" and "Regulating the Earthly Soul to Embrace Unity." Moreover, although Wang's title suggests that the Tao will be the thematic subject, the verses actually focus on Virtue, which he identifies with Earth, thereby obviating extensive speculation on the metaphysical and cosmogenic relationship of Te and Tao.

In this conception, Wang sees Earth's nurturing aspect as definitive because it sustains and nourishes without ever exercising control over the myriad species dwelling upon it. Therefore, it provides a model for eliminating conflict and strife. (This is especially true if natural calamities such as earthquakes and floods are conveniently disregarded by attributing them to Heaven, by seeing them as an admonitory response to the ruler's transgressions. Yet increasing the people's afflictions in this manner would seem to be a callous method for coercing imperial compliance!) However, the commentary advances the oft-raised key point that government should concentrate upon benefiting and nourishing the people, thereby ending contention, no doubt on the assumption that their desires will thereby be reduced. Otherwise, the basic problems of life having been resolved, people will simply devote their newfound surplus energy to the pursuit of personal gain and profits.

52

All Under
Heaven Had
a Beginning

All under Heaven had a beginning,
Which acted as their mother.
From knowing the mother, one understands the son.
One who, understanding the son,
Reverts to cleave to the mother
Until the body's destruction will be unimperiled.
One who blocks off the orifices,
Closes the gates,
Until the end of life will be untroubled.
One who opens the orifices,
Pursues affairs,
Until the end of life will be beyond rescue.
Being able to discern the small is called perspicacity;
Preserving the pliant is called strength.
One who employs radiance
And reverts back to perspicacity
Will not inflict misfortune upon himself.
This is termed according with the constant.

WANG   Only when the Tao had been named could it act as
the mother of All under Heaven. The king in his walled city
thus symbolizes her son. "One who, understanding the son, reverts to cleave to the mother" means that the king ought to
cleave to the Tao, sustain things, stop up wisdom, and occlude
brilliance, for then he will never suffer from exertion, bitterness,

danger, or extinction. Moreover, being capable of discerning and impeding the minutest sprouts can be termed "perspicacity." Similarly, being able to cleave to the pliancy and weakness of the Tao will inevitably result in gaining its strength and greatness. "Employing its radiance" speaks about externally flourishing Virtue; "reverting back to perspicacity" refers to internally embodying the Tao. When, in governing the state and controlling the army, things are not harmed, what misfortune will there be? Thus, it says, "accords with the constant." According with something is like minutely using it. This means that kings always should just employ the Tao in minute detail.

SAWYER   This chapter essentially provides a metaphysical linkage and cosmological justification for reverting to the Tao's primary aspects of tranquillity and pliancy. The theme of minimizing sensory input to end distractions and perturbations, already strongly advocated in "The Five Colors Compel Humans" and about to reappear in "The Knowledgeable Do Not Speak," anchors the middle verses and informs the process itself. Since the mindless pursuit of worldly affairs simply leads to self-destruction, Wang Chen advises absorbing the chapter's lessons, which will in turn engender great strength even in worldly affairs. Consequently, when the tranquillity and pliancy of the Tao are employed in government, the ruler will benefit rather than harm the people, and the army, while still extant, will similarly cause no harm. However, this innocuousness no doubt stems from the army's inactivity in a purely deterrent role, although its employment might still be termed actionless if the ruler were to adhere to the Taoist parameters previously raised.

"All under Heaven Had a Beginning," perhaps in consonance with the title's focus on "beginnings," also introduces the idea of "perspicacity"—discerning events just as they commence, perceiving (or perhaps sensing) incipient sprouts even before they become visible. Wang Chen immediately stresses the possibilities for successful action predicated upon such perspicacious wisdom, prefiguring the encouragement to implement measures early on expressed in two upcoming chapters, "Act Actionlessly" and "The Tranquil Is Easily Grasped."

53

If I Minutely

If I were to suddenly have knowledge
And travel along the Great Tao,
Straying from it would be my only fear.
The Great Tao is exceedingly conducive,
But the people love narrow paths.
The court is thoroughly scoured,
The fields extremely weedy,
The granaries very empty.
They wear colorful, embroidered clothes,
Bear sharp weapons,
Surfeit themselves with drink and food,
And have wealth and goods in surplus.
This is termed the boasting of robbers;
It is not the Tao!

WANG   "I" refers to our lords and kings. This says that if lords and kings were suddenly able to realize by themselves how to "travel along the Great Tao," the only thing they would need seriously fear would be straying from it. This means that the Great Tao is level, extremely smooth, and easy, but rather than traveling along it, people just want to hasten along oblique paths in pursuit of lucky profits. Because their desire for speed will invariably fail, the verses deeply advise against it. Moreover, the chapter observes that although the court and offices have been swept clean and scoured, the fields are heavily overgrown, the storehouses and granaries exceedingly empty, but militant ministers and martial generals are unlimited. Whether merited or not, they all wear fine silks and bear weapons such as daggers and swords. Sated with drink and food, they store away the goods and bribes that they rapaciously seize. The people, despite their own insufficiency, still have to support the houses of those who enjoy excess. This truly may be described as the "boasting of robbers and brigands." How could it ever be termed the Great Tao? Thus, Lao-tzu sighed deeply over the distress besetting his degenerative era and created this chapter to caution and upbraid the world about excess.

SAWYER With striking clarity, both the verses and Wang's commentary bemoan the excesses of government perniciously depriving the people of material resources. His commentary also looks forward to a verse characterizing human tendencies found in "The Tao of Heaven," which runs: "The Tao of Heaven reduces the excessive and augments the insufficient, but the Tao of man is not thus, for men reduce the insufficient to support the excessive." Moreover, Wang views the first lines as depicting the correspondingly perverse methods of people who, obsessed by their desires and hopes for profit, seek out the quickest path.

Although the entire chapter would thus seem to characterize modern, postindustrialized countries and their frenzied societies, the apparent widespread contemporary success of profit-driven activities contradicts its spirit and raises questions about its applicability for all but true believers. (It should be noted that among the taxes governments imposed to sustain themselves, the specialized military tax could easily become the most onerous. Not only did it require men to perform often uncompensated service, removing them from the agricultural workforce, but in many eras, it also forced them to supply their own equipment and provisions.)

54

Those Who Excel at Establishing Are Not Pulled Out

Those who excel at establishing are not pulled out,
Who excel at embracing are not cast off,
So their sons and grandsons perpetuate their sacrifices
indefinitely.
When they cultivate it in their person,
Their Virtue will be pure.
When they cultivate it in their family,
Their Virtue will be abundant.
When they cultivate it in their village,
Their Virtue will be extensive.
When they cultivate it in their state,
Their Virtue will flourish.
When they cultivate it in the realm,
Their Virtue will be ubiquitous.
Thus, employ the body to observe bodies;
Employ the village to observe villages;
Employ the family to observe families;
Employ the state to observe states;
Employ the realm to observe All under Heaven.
How do I know All under Heaven is thus?
From this.

WANG   The dynastic founders who arose and became well known because of their Virtue may be said to have excelled at establishing themselves. Once they were established, they could not be pulled out. Similarly, their descendants who preserved their positions through benevolence so that they could not be cast off once they grasped [their positions] excelled at embracing. This chapter makes it clear that they all cultivated Virtue and practiced benevolence in order to perpetuate the good fortune of a myriad of sacrifices. Through the changing ages, none of them employed shields or halberds, power or strength to seize the realm. Thus, [in "Those Who Study Daily Increase,"] the *Tao Te Ching* states, "Those who would seize All under Heaven always do so with the absence of affairs, for the presence of affairs makes it impossible to seize All under Heaven." Moreover, [in "Harmonizing Great Rancor,"] it also says, "The Tao of Heaven has no intimates; it always associates with good men."

Furthermore, beginning in antiquity with the August Ones of Heaven down through the five Sage Emperors, in the most lengthy case, the founders' sons and grandsons continued family rule for some ten thousand years, and in the least, for several thousand years. Even as late as the Three Dynasties [the Hsia, Shang, and Chou], despite the harm inflicted by uncouth kings, the ruling families still achieved eight or nine hundred years before being torn asunder and losing their states. From this perspective, could they have employed shields and halberds, power and strength through the changing ages to seize their positions? Certainly not. Moreover, a poem about King Wen in the *Book of Odes* states, "A model unto his wife, he affected his brothers and thence governed all the families and states." The *Odes* also notes that "King Wen's sons and grandsons, main and collateral lines, lasted a hundred generations." Thus, the *Tao Te Ching* asks, "How do I know All under Heaven is thus? From this." Isn't this what he means?

SAWYER   As many commentators have pointed out, this chapter's spirit and tone, if not its focal message, closely echo the famous *Doctrine of Mean* (*Chung Yung*), one of the famous *Four Books* of Confucianism (with the *Analects, Mencius,* and *Great Learning*) from the Sung dynasty onward. (Naturally the concept of "Virtue" in the two works is strikingly different, although both have transcendent dimensions as well as earthly implications and functions.) The discussion about observing and thus evaluating others in the concluding verses, possibly a remnant from a political or military intelligence context, is somewhat unusual because such comparative reflection is directed toward determining whether someone has attained and embodies Virtue.

Taken in sum, these verses provide Wang Chen with an opportunity to emphasize the role of Virtue—defined in terms of benevolent, nonactive government—in establishing and maintaining the ideal dynasties of antiquity and thereby stress its power in the mundane political world. Virtue is therefore not some irrelevant, impotent quality found among do-gooders but a real, vital force for forming and reforming, contrary to attitudes witnessed today.

55

Abundantly Embodying Virtue

One who abundantly embodies Virtue
Is comparable to an infant.
Poisonous insects do not sting;
Fierce animals do not bite;
Birds of prey do not strike.
His bones are soft, tendons pliant,
But grasp solid.
To be fully aroused,

Unknowing of male and female,
Is the pinnacle of essence.
Wailing throughout the day without becoming hoarse
Is the pinnacle of harmony.
Knowing harmony is called constancy;
Knowing constancy is called enlightenment.
Augmenting life is called auspicious;
Mind manipulating ch'i is called strong.
When things are strong, they grow old;
This is termed contrary to Tao.
What is contrary to Tao early perishes.

WANG   This chapter states that rulers marked by abundant
Virtue invariably preserve their essence and harmonize their
ch'i, just as an infant does. Free from impulses and contemplation, in themselves they are sincere and enlightened. Accordingly, nothing can harm them. "Poisonous insects, fierce
animals, and birds of prey" being analogies for perverse, evil,
violent, and harmful men, even the fierce blades and ven-
omous poisons of such perverse and evil men cannot injure a
ruler marked by abundant Virtue. Moreover, the *Tao Te
Ching* cites the example of infants' wailing without becoming
hoarse as the pinnacle of harmony.

Now when the five constants are fully prepared, it is termed
harmony. Thus, Lao-tzu says that "knowing harmony is
called constancy, knowing constancy called enlightened."
Furthermore, sustaining and augmenting life is termed "auspicious." This means that the ruler should constantly diminish his body and constrain his mind, making them pliant and
weak, loving and compassionate, rather than manipulating his
ch'i or relying upon power for strength. The *Tso Chuan*
states, "A single drumming arouses the ch'i; a second time
and it declines; a third and it is exhausted." This makes it
clear that those who employ their ch'i cannot long endure. In
addition, while the strong are sturdy, the sturdy become old.
The meaning of the phrase "old armies are crooked" similarly
lies in this. Thus, the *Tao Te Ching* advises desisting early and
refraining from employing the army a second time.

SAWYER   Wang Chen envisions this meditation upon the pliancy of original Virtue (or, Te, itself understood as the Tao's embodiment) as applicable to rulers themselves rather than to Sages or adepts who cultivate a life in harmony with the Tao. Accordingly, he depicts the monarch as dwelling well apart from danger and essentially impervious to harm because no one would want to harm such a beneficent, shadowy figure. However, the consistent implementation of what might well be termed yin measures, designed to avoid growing overly strong and prevent any visible manifestation of or reliance upon strength, remains incumbent.

Wang Chen's commentary also introduces the crucial psychological topic of the nature and role of ch'i in combat. The three *Tao Te Ching* lines that read, "Mind manipulating ch'i is called strong. When things are strong, they grow old; this is termed contrary to Tao," reiterate the fundamental view that activities oriented toward strength, here explicated in terms of the will's driving and controlling the body's ch'i, contravene the Tao and are therefore inherently self-destructive. Well aware of this, Wang Chen cites the first known Chinese passage that analyzes the effects and manipulation of ch'i in warfare. His interpretation of this laconic *Tso Chuan* account of a Spring and Autumn battle, itself self-explanatory, is consistent with the classic military writings in concluding that prolonged warfare debilitates the troops and enervates the state both physically and spiritually and should therefore be avoided. Nonetheless, despite fervently condemning weapons, he never categorically rejects the military's employment any more than does the *Tao Te Ching* itself.

The military classics, having been composed in the same milieu and era as the *Tao Te Ching,* generally envision ch'i (spirit, morale, psychic energy) as the decisive component in any conflict. For example, the early *Ssu-ma Fa* asserts, "In battle, one endures with strength and gains victory through ch'i." Sun-tzu's famous *Art of War,* in proposing tactical principles for confronting an enemy, introduces an analogy much cited thereafter:

The ch'i of the Three Armies can be snatched away; the commanding general's mind can be seized. For this reason, in the morning, their ch'i is ardent; during the day, their ch'i becomes indolent; at dusk, their ch'i is exhausted. Thus, one who excels at employing the army avoids their ardent ch'i and strikes when it is indolent or exhausted. This is the way to manipulate ch'i.

Sun Pin's subsequent *Military Methods* devotes a full chapter to it, appropriately entitled "Expanding Ch'i," while the purportedly T'ang dynasty *Question and Replies* points out that Sun-tzu's discussion provides a general characterization of the psychodynamics of spirit, not one simply limited to specific times of day. For martial theorists, ch'i was therefore merely another factor that must be constrained and controlled when exercising command and directing battlefield engagements. They might decry prolonged warfare and frequent combat, but second or third engagements should hardly prove troubling, explaining Wang Chen's somewhat different inference on the question of ch'i.

(The topic of invulnerability, not through strength but through pliancy and weakness, was previously raised in "Going Forth into Life, Entering Death." Here, however, the infant is presumed to be invulnerable, due to the natural protection still provided by as yet uncontaminated original ch'i—a presumption contrary to Western fears that infants' helplessness renders them the most vulnerable of all. In some instinctual sense, this insight about infants' invulnerability seems valid—it may even be a subconscious recognition of the natural immunity they possess until several months of age—especially as infants are often the only survivors in violent catastrophes, such as plane and auto wrecks. However, there is enough real evidence and experience to the contrary to cause puzzlement. Embracing the lessons of this chapter obviously requires an imaginative leap of faith.)

56

The Knowledgeable Do Not Speak

The knowledgeable do not speak;
Speakers do not know.
Block the orifices,
Close the gates,
Dull the sharp,
Resolve confusion,
Harmonize the radiant,
Unite with the dusty.
This is referred to as Dank Unity.
Thus, it cannot be brought near,
Cannot be made distant,
Cannot be profited,
Cannot be harmed,
Cannot be honored,
Cannot be demeaned.
Therefore, it is the most honored under Heaven.

WANG   When the army is employed according to the Tao, the knowledgeable will certainly not speak about the vital points, while those who speak inevitably will not know the crux of affairs. Thus, the *Tao Te Ching* states, "the knowledgeable do not speak; speakers do not know." "Block the orifices, close the gates"—this constitutes the army's profound subtlety. "Dull the sharp, resolve confusion, harmonize the radiant, unite with the dusty"—these comprise the army's very crux. Moreover, because they cannot really be spoken about, they are termed "Dank Unity." Thus, the Sage's army is victorious in battle and solid in defense, so no force under Heaven can match it. Even so, the Sage never dares slight any enemy under Heaven. For this reason, neither the distant nor the nearby can bring it nearer or make it distant; neither the well-intentioned nor the rancorous can benefit or harm it; neither the distinguished nor the common can honor or demean it. Therefore, All under Heaven honor and value it.

SAWYER   Key verses in "The Knowledgeable Do Not Speak" previously appeared in "All under Heaven Had a Beginning" and "The Tao Is Vacuous," naturally suggesting consistent themes. However, quite interestingly, Wang Chen interprets the entire chapter as characterizing necessary army practices, including the maintenance of secrecy and caution. When these traits of Dank Unity mark it, the army itself somehow attains a certain transcendence or immutability, becoming unaffected by the enemy's actions and therefore "victorious in battle and solid in defense." Clearly this ideal enjoyed currency among the military writers as well because they often spoke about the army's being formless and independent, capable of manipulating and compelling others while yet being beyond any enemy's control. Only a formless army can engage the enemy when advantageous and mount a solid defense when desirable. No doubt Wang Chen had these images in mind when reading a chapter that has otherwise inspired commentators to speak about yogic practices and the very transcendence of the ineffable Tao in its various manifestations and unnameable attributes.

57

With Government, Order the State

With government, order the state;
With the unorthodox, employ the military;
Without mounting affairs, seize All under Heaven.
How do I know that this is so?
As follows:
As the realm's prohibitions and interdictions are multiplied,
The people grow increasingly impoverished.
As the people's sharp implements multiply,
The state becomes increasingly muddled.
As human skill and artifice multiply,
Rarities are increasingly brought forth.
As laws and edicts are further publicized,
Robbers and brigands are increasingly numerous.
Thus, the Sage says:
I am actionless, so the people are transformed of themselves.
I love tranquillity, so the people become upright by themselves.
I mount no affairs, so the people become rich by themselves.
I am desireless, so the people become simplified by themselves.

WANG   States are ordered through government. Here "government" means uprightness. When the ruler leads with uprightness, who will dare not be upright? The army is employed through the unorthodox, "unorthodox" signifying a tactical imbalance of power. When a tactical imbalance of power is conjoined with the Tao, how can there be any harm? As for "without mounting any affairs, take All under Heaven," "without affairs" means the absence of affairs involving weapons and armor. Thus, Lao-tzu asks, "How do I know that this is so? As follows." Moreover, he speaks about the realm's prohibitions and interdictions' being multiplied because whenever [the ruler's] fishing and hunting exhaust the marshes and numerous prohibitions are imposed on other sources, the people's material resources will be insufficient and profits will not circulate below. Since the people become increasingly impoverished, isn't Lao-tzu's lament appropriate! Moreover, if forcing All under Heaven to display tactical plans and take up sharp implements isn't muddled, what is? "Muddled" is like chaotic.

"As human skill and artifice multiply, rarities are increasingly brought forth" that will inevitably perturb the minds of superiors. "As laws and edicts are further publicized, robbers and brigands become increasingly numerous," meaning that the people do not fear death. For these reasons, the Sage says, "I am actionless, so the people are transformed of themselves." This means that if he doesn't undertake military affairs, the people will be settled and transformed. "I mount no affairs, so the people become rich by themselves" points out that in the absence of taxes and impositions, the people will be ordered and daily grow richer. "I love tranquillity, so the people become upright by themselves" asserts that by going back to the root and returning to one's fate, the people will become upright by themselves. "I am desireless, so the people become simplified by themselves" says that if they don't pursue the ruler's tastes and desires, the people will become simple by themselves.

SAWYER   With the exception of the first two lines, the chapter clearly reprises themes previously raised, again advancing the specter of devolutionary consequences and the pernicious effects of "goods difficult to obtain." The concluding verses then portray the Sage ruler's actionless stance directly affecting the people so that they are transformed by themselves rather than through the efforts and interference of government. Wang Chen appropriately expands this crucial insight and concretely translates the indefinite nature of "prohibitions and interdictions" into those related to natural resources, thereby depriving the people of their means to livelihood, as much as actual criminal law.

More significant and unusual is Wang's reading of the first two lines, probably based upon a different character for "government." Most editions, and therefore most English translations, run: "With the orthodox, govern the state; with the unorthodox, employ the military." Wang then goes on to essentially gloss "government," a slightly different character from "orthodox," as "uprightness," which is another meaning of the character for "orthodox." Therefore, in theory, we might also understand his statement as "Here government means the orthodox. When the government leads with the orthodox, who will dare not be orthodox?" However, such a reading is unlikely, particularly as Confucius stressed uprightness in both rulers and individuals, believing that it would encourage a similar response, and Wang Chen previously cited his concept.

Wang's choice of this textual variant is also rather astonishing because historically these famous lines have essentially defined the contrast between civil government, being orthodox (synonymous with employing straightforward, upright measures), and the military itself ("the Tao of deceit," in Sun-tzu's words), manipulating and exploiting, using the crafty and devious. Moreover, they were repeatedly cited for more than two millennia thereafter whenever a bureaucrat wished to disparage and deprecate the military.

However, Taoist and military thought were closely intertwined and obviously influenced each other during the formative Warring States period in China, even though their exact relationship remains unclear. Furthermore, the "unorthodox"—which may be defined as acting and implementing tactics in an unexpected way, particularly through deception, indirection, and maneuver—furnishes one of the fundamental principles underlying every Chinese conception of warfare. First briefly enunciated by Sun-tzu (no doubt on the basis of common conceptualizations and battle practice during the

Spring and Autumn period) in his chapter entitled "Strategic Military Power," the concept is integrated by most subsequent military writings to constitute one of the basic approaches to war fighting. Wang Chen assumes it means creating a tactical imbalance of strategic power that can then be successfully exploited, but Sun-tzu's primary definition, which waxes almost mystical, delimits the methodology:

> What enables the masses of the Three Armies invariably to withstand the enemy without being defeated are the unorthodox and orthodox. In general, in battle one engages with the orthodox and gains victory through the unorthodox. Thus, one who excels at sending forth the unorthodox is as inexhaustible as Heaven, as unlimited as the Yangtze and Yellow Rivers. What reach an end and begin again are the sun and moon. What die and are reborn are the four seasons. The notes do not exceed five, but the changes of the five notes can never fully be heard. The colors do not exceed five, but the changes of the five colors can never be completely seen. The flavors do not exceed five, but the changes of the five flavors can never be completely tasted. In warfare, the strategic configurations of power do not exceed the unorthodox and the orthodox, but the changes of the unorthodox and orthodox can never be completely exhausted. The unorthodox and orthodox mutually produce each other, just like an endless cycle. Who can exhaust them?

Clearly the *Tao Te Ching*'s approach to warfare emphasizes the unorthodox, which is much like the pliant and weak's dominating the firm and strong or water's configuring to destroy its obstacles.

58

The Government
is Morosely Quiet

When the government is morosely quiet,
The people will be heartily substantial.
When the government is caustically intrusive,
The people will be morally deficient.
Misfortune is relied upon by good fortune;
Good fortune is subverted by misfortune.
Who understands the extremity?
Is there no uprightness?
Uprightness reverts to perversity;
Goodness reverts to weirdness.
People have indeed long been deluded.
For this reason, the Sage is square without cutting,
Pure without nicking,
Direct without being dissolute,
Radiant without scintillating.

WANG   Those who would practice the Tao of rulership must conceal their wisdom and intelligence, be liberal in their instructions and commands, and constantly be morose, for then the people will naturally be simple and unadorned. When superiors have caustic, pedantic minds, the people below will invariably be deceptive and contrary, sneaky and irresponsible, neither sincere nor trustworthy. Moreover, good fortune relies upon misfortune, whereas misfortune is concealed in good fortune. They are solely summoned by men, born through their endeavors. In the case of going and coming, victory and defeat, or in the distinction between pursuing and following, favor and disgrace, what is encountered will perhaps differ. Joy and sorrow must accompany them. From the individual to the family, the family to the state, and on throughout the realm, what everyone, whether great or small, ought to fear is just this "reliance" and "subversion."

Moreover, it is simply human nature to be elated about imminent good fortune; few trouble themselves over incipient misfortune. In the midst of calamity, people constantly think about good fortune, but when enjoying good fortune, no one takes precautions against misfortune. Thus, the *Tao Te Ching* asks, "Who knows the extremity?" Even worse, some take uprightness as perversity, goodness as weirdness. Thus, the *Tao Te Ching* states, "People have indeed long been deluded." For this reason, the Sage dwells by himself in his squareness without cutting others and preserves his purity uncontaminated. He rusticates his customs, demeans himself, and extends others, so is said to be "direct without being dissolute." He conceals his brightness and employs darkness, so is said to be "radiant but not scintillating."

SAWYER "The Government Is Morosely Quiet" is one of several grouped chapters that elaborate the fundamental theme that unintrusive but benevolent government both directly and indirectly benefits the people. Moreover, because extremes naturally revert, even uprightness and goodness eventually transform to their negative counterparts, implying that only government without attributes can successfully govern.

Consonant with this reversion of extremes, although not specifically attributed to it, is the principle that "misfortune is relied upon by good fortune; good fortune is subverted by misfortune." These verses frame an image of good fortune's somehow lurking within the worst situation, calamity's suddenly ambushing happiness and frivolity. In his commentary, Wang Chen concisely characterizes the psychological states of people immersed in these two different conditions: the inevitable tendency, no doubt basically a defensive mechanism, to hope for a turn for the best when enduring misfortune and the blissful confidence that largely precludes future concerns while enjoying fortuitous benefits. (Similar comments were made by Han Fei-tzu.) Just as Wang Chen's commentary elaborates, the *Tao Te Ching* discourages such tendencies and seeks to preclude the experience of misfortune brought on by "excessive" good fortune through its advocacy of minimizing the desires and maintaining a low profile when gains have been realized. As the T'ai Kung said, "Existence does not lie in existence but in thinking about perishing. Pleasure does not lie in pleasure but in contemplating disaster."

59

Governing the People and Serving Heaven

For governing the people and serving Heaven, there is
nothing like frugality.
Now only through frugality will they early submit.
Early submission is termed doubly accumulated Virtue.
For one of doubly accumulated Virtue, there are none
unconquered.
Since there are none unconquered, no one knows their
pinnacle.
Since no one knows their pinnacle,
They can possess the state.

Those who possess the mother of the state
Can long endure.
This is referred to as deepening the roots and solidifying
*   the base,*
The Tao to longevity and enduring vision.

WANG   To be frugal is like loving. This says that in governing the people and serving Heaven, the king must take benevolence and righteousness as his progenitor. Thus, the *Tao Te Ching* advises, "Nothing is like frugality." When the Tao of benevolence and righteousness is implemented, All under Heaven will early submit. Since All under Heaven early submit, it is referred to as "doubly accumulated Virtue." One marked by "doubly accumulated Virtue" will be victorious in warfare and solid in defense. Thus, the *Tao Te Ching* states, "there are none unconquered. Since there are none unconquered, no one knows their pinnacle. Since no one knows their pinnacle, they can possess the state. Those who possess the mother of the state can long endure." "Mother" here refers to the Tao. This means that if the king realizes the Tao in preserving the state, his roots and foundation will naturally be deep and solid, and he will enjoy the blessings of longevity and enduring vision.

SAWYER   Another in the *Te Ching*'s series on government, "Governing the People and Serving Heaven" identifies frugality as the defining aspect of unintrusive government. Wang Chen immediately envisions this in terms of the remarkably Confucian virtues of benevolence and righteousness rather than the Virtue of a ruler immersed in the Tao. Such a ruler would be naturally benevolent rather than consciously implementing such debased virtues as righteousness, which was itself strongly deprecated in "The Great Tao Abandoned" and "Eliminate Sagacity, Abandon Wisdom." However, enjoiners to frugality were common in the Warring States period, when most governments routinely imposed onerous taxes in their quest to survive the era's internecine strife and rulers indulged their whims at the expense of the people. Mencius, who decried warfare in general, vociferously condemned the debauchery and extravagance of the period's monarchs and even personally harangued them to abjure such inimical practices.

In addition, as expressed in the "Canine Secret Teaching" of the *Six Secret Teachings,* the classic military writers grounded their state-building doctrines on the assumption that a benevolent government that neither oppressed nor interfered with the people would not only garner the allegiance of its own subjects but also attract the disaffected and dispossessed of other states. For example, in discussing how to love the people, which turns out to be synonymous with profiting them, the T'ai Kung noted:

> When the people do not lose their fundamental occupations, you have profited them. When the farmers do not lose the agricultural seasons, you have completed them. When you reduce punishments and fines, you give them life. When you impose light taxes, you give to them. When you keep your palaces, mansions, terraces, and pavilions few, you give them pleasure. When officials are pure and neither irritating nor troublesome, you make the people happy.

No doubt the belief that frugal governments nurture their wealth by widely distributing it among the people, thereby ensuring the populace's enthusiastic participation in the crucial matters of warfare and public works, underlies the *Tao Te Ching*'s assertion that frugality results in submission and "none unconquered." ("All under Heaven Term Me Vast," which reiterates frugality's importance and role in gaining the willing allegiance of the people, might well be read in conjunction with this chapter.)

60

Governing
A Great State

Governing a great state is like poaching small fish.
When the Tao is employed to oversee All under Heaven,
Ghosts will not be spiritually potent.
It's not that ghosts won't be spiritually potent,
But that their spiritual power will not harm people.
It's not that their spiritual power will not harm people,
The Sage similarly will not harm people.
Since these two do not harm each other,
Virtue will intersect and abide there.

WANG   Those who govern one of the realm's states should act as if poaching small fish and leave it peacefully undisturbed. By thus making undisturbed tranquillity their foundation, they will naturally never lose the Tao. The Tao not being lost, yin and yang will be greatly harmonious. When yin and yang are greatly harmonious, wind and rain will be seasonable. Wind and rain being seasonable, the hundred numinosities will attain tranquillity. The hundred numinosities attaining tranquillity, the disciples of unnatural essence will not be able to effect their weird transformations. Thus, the *Tao Te Ching* states that "ghosts will not be spiritually potent."

Moreover, when an enlightened king resides above, weapons and armor will not be flourished, the people will accord with his sincerity, and Heaven and Earth will provide blessings. Isn't it therefore appropriate that Sages and spirits will cooperatively respond, that abundant Virtue will intersect and abide there?

SAWYER   The first line, which reflects the *Tao Te Ching's* overall philosophy and approach to "governing," is clearly discontinuous with the remaining verses, which resolve a difficult question that beset traditional China: how to defuse the evil and deflect the harm inflicted by so-called hungry ghosts. (In theory, "ghosts" might be controlled, although not rendered benign, by integrating them into the administrative continuum governing both the manifest and ethereal, the mundane and spiritual realms. However, ancestral spirits who no longer, or even never, enjoyed the filial sacrifices of the ceremonies of mourning and remembrance and were therefore "unpropitiated" could become particularly disruptive forces. Moreover, in addition to those created through the activities of witches and sorcerers, other perturbations in the ch'i might form local discontinuities and thereby provide ethereal material for evil spirits and specters.) The *Tao Te Ching's* verses vividly reflect a mind-set troubled by such "potencies," so the Sage's activities in deflecting (but not emasculating) them, rendering them nominally impotent if not latently harmless, remain important. When Taoist governments restore tranquillity and substantiality to the world, harmony results in all realms, both immanent and otherworldly. (Many commentators understand the line "Since these two do not harm each other" as referring to ghosts affecting the people rather than the Sage and ghosts not harming each other.)

61

Great States
Defer to the Flow

Great states should defer to the flow
Where All under Heaven intersect,
The realm's feminine.
Through tranquility the feminine constantly overcomes
  the masculine,
Employing tranquilly to be deferential.
Thus when great states act deferentially to small states,
They seize the small state.
When small states defer to great states,
They seize the great state.
Thus one seizes by being deferential;
One seizes through its subordination.
Great states want no more than to unify and nurture
  people;
Small states want only to enter the service of others.
Since they both gain what they desire,
The great should act deferentially.

WANG   This chapter exhaustively speaks about how kings
should constantly employ humility and deference in order to
be Virtuous. Could they then employ weapons and armor,
strength and power, to seek victory and domination? Moreover, intercourse among great and small states means cultivating human affairs. If you investigate the pattern of their
emotions, doesn't everyone exert themselves for what they
desire? Since everyone seeks what they desire, it's obvious
that the great should act deferentially. Now the Tao of humility always entails diminishing the superior and increasing the

inferior, so it is employed above, not below. Thus the *I Ching* states "When the noble defer to the lowly, they will truly gain the people." Isn't this it?

SAWYER   "Great States Defer to the Flow" apparently reflects the harsh political reality of the Warring States period and memories of the earlier Spring and Autumn, which saw the violent emergence of megastates through the rapacious conquest of smaller, contiguous entities. Wang Chen's brief commentary apart, small states that wax belligerent in these circumstances might gain a modicum of respect but would soon be zealously trampled for their arrogance. Powerful states such as Ch'in, Ch'u, and Ch'i not only could easily annex the many clan states scattered throughout the realm but actually did so, subjugating hundreds of them through ongoing campaigns in the Spring and Autumn period.

However, although many realist thinkers advocated conquest as the surest means to wealth and power, in actuality mounting military campaigns always proved expensive and battles invariably took a significant toll. More subtle alternatives to forcible conquest and annexation, such as alliance building and being deferential to smaller states, were therefore envisioned as potentially yielding superior results, just as the *Tao Te Ching* here counsels. Conversely, smaller states that managed to survive at the sufferance of others had to similarly practice deference and yielding—or simply surrender without fighting—so as to preserve themselves intact. However, the rapacious motivation of the larger states visible even here implies that a realpolitik underlies at least some chapters of the *Te Ching* beyond that normally recognized.

At the same time, the main theme of cleaving to the feminine and lowly, disdained terrain to which all must return is clearly a fundamental *Tao Te Ching* principle and its means for control and conquest, as advanced in "Know the Masculine" and "How Rivers and Seas Can Be Kings of the Hundred Valley Streams." (It should be noted that considerable disagreement exists about the reading of the verse "Thus one seizes by being deferential; one seizes through its subordination.")

62

Tao of the
Myriad Things

Tao is the mysterious obscurity of the myriad things,
The good man's treasure,
How the not good are preserved.
Beautiful words can display respect;
Attractive behavior can augment men.
The not good among the people,
How can they be rejected?
Thus when emperors are established,
The Three Dukes emplaced,
Even respectfully presenting discs of jade preceding teams
  of horses
Would not be as good as submissively advancing the Tao.
Why is it that the ancients valued the Tao?
Is it not said:
What is sought is obtained;
Transgressions are remitted?
Thus it is valued by All under Heaven.

WANG   Sages treasure the Tao because it can preserve,
meaning nurture, all the people under Heaven. Now among
the people under Heaven, the good are few, the "not good"
many, so how can they all be rejected? Therefore the Sages
"established emperors, emplaced the Three Dukes," and con-
centrated upon setting aside their shields and halberds, upon
not employing punishments and fines. They embellished
their words and made their actions respectful, hoping to
thereby reform the people, to principle and transform them.
They thus became what All under Heaven valued. How

could this be compared with the presentation of jade discs and matched horses?

SAWYER   "Tao of the Myriad Things" refocuses on the Tao itself, which tends to be de-emphasized throughout the *Te Ching*. In it the Tao, far from rejecting miscreants and the perverse, provides the "not good" with refuge and hope, as should be expected, for if the Tao were not all-encompassing, how could it be transcendently ineffable and pervasive? Furthermore, as elucidated in "All under Heaven Know," "not good" is simply a relative concept (although the case of murderers would seem to be offensive to the Tao and particularly problematic). In view of the willingness to repress brigands found in "Tao Eternally Actionless," the line "transgressions are remitted" is rather startling. Nonetheless, it surpassingly justifies the spirit expressed in "Those Who Excel in Moving Have No Tracks," wherein the Sage, who may be said to embody the Tao, "always excels at rescuing people, so there are no rejected people." Almost identically, this chapter rhetorically asks, "The not good among the people, how can they be rejected?"

The major political-philosophical perspectives of antiquity advanced different solutions to the problem of asocial and antisocial people. The Confucians believed in personally leading by example and educating the people to Virtue, thereby inducing a sense of shame. Legalists such as Lord Shang and Han Fei-tzu, deliberately indifferent to attitude and motivation, focused instead upon coercing desirable behavior with draconian laws, severe punishments, and the incentives of rewards. The Taoists of the *Tao Te Ching*—there are serious distinctions among later proponents—apparently believed that all men are encompassed by the Tao and that minimal government will effect the circumstances for self-transformation, as numerous chapters have already outlined. Moreover, "The People Do Not Dread Death" rejects the imposition of capital punishment even for murderers (though Wang Chen concludes differently), and "The Government Is Morosely Quiet" observes that good reverts to evil, the perverse to goodness, with unspecified implications. Thus Wang Chen, while clearly embracing the *Tao Te Ching*'s spirit and programs, also envisioned them being concretely realized through distinctly Confucian measures, as seen in his commentary to this chapter and the necessary imposition of punishment in "The People Do Not Dread Death."

63

Act Actionlessly

Act actionlessly;
Undertake insubstantial affairs;
Taste the tasteless.
Increase the small;
Make the few numerous.
Repay rancor with Virtue.
Plan against the difficult while it remains easy;
Act upon the great while it is still minute.
The realm's difficult affairs invariably commence with
  the easy;
The realm's great affairs inevitably arise from the
  minute.
For this reason the Sage never acts against the great,
So can achieve greatness.
Since promises carelessly made inevitably have little
  credibility,
And many easy affairs invariably entail numerous
  hardships,
The Sage still takes them as difficult
And thus to the end suffers no hardship.

WANG   Rulers who realize the Tao of true kingship begin by standing upright, folding their hands, and letting their robes hang down. Thus, the *Tao Te Ching* states "act actionlessly." They de-emphasize the martial and do not contend, so it says they "undertake insubstantial affairs." They embrace the Tao and are spiritual, so it says, "taste the tasteless."

Now the minds of the myriad states, the nature of the manifold people, are such that winter cold and summer rain cause them to sigh. How can the true king's mind be limited to large or small or prefer to discuss the many or few? In all cases he ought to soothe them with Virtue, to ensure they will be free from rancorous murmuring. Thus, the *Tao Te Ching* states, "Repay rancor with Virtue."

"The realm's difficult affairs invariably commence with the easy" means that if the ruler slights affairs, misfortune and difficulty will certainly be spawned amid them. "The realm's great affairs inevitably arise from the minute" says that by not ignoring minor actions, in the end the ruler will accumulate great Virtue. Accordingly, the Sage takes precautions against the subtle before it becomes obvious and accumulates the small in order to complete the great. If he wants to act when something has already become obvious and great, he will not succeed. Thus, the *Tao Te Ching* states, "For this reason the Sage never acts against the great, so can achieve greatness." Accordingly, "promises carelessly made inevitably have little credibility, and many easy affairs invariably entail numerous hardships" expresses an incontrovertible principle. Moreover, the Tao of focusing upon the easy is easily followed, but the error of slighting the easy gives birth to difficulty. For this reason "The Sage still takes them as difficult." Only through such extreme attentiveness and caution can he always avoid difficulty among the myriad affairs and subtle moments. Thus, the *Tao Te Ching* concludes, "to the end, [he] suffers no hardship."

SAWYER   "Act Actionlessly" and the next chapter, "The Tranquil Is Easily Grasped," are essentially continuous in stressing the importance of exploiting the easy path by acting at the earliest possible opportunity, at the incipient moment of change (witnessed in the Sage's taking precautions against the subtle before it becomes obvious) to preclude disaster and misfortune. Conversely, great achievements require initiating affairs from the very minute and relentlessly proceeding according to Wang Chen's interpretation of the second half of the verse, translated (in accord with his view) as "The realm's difficult affairs invariably commence with the easy; the realm's great affairs inevitably arise from the minute." (The second half of the verse could also be seen in a more negative light, as cautioning that "great affairs"—namely, revolutions—equally arise from the minute.) Wang Chen further interprets the admonitions as applicable for enlightened rulers, presumably on the assumption that through appropriating them, they will escape calamity.

However, the initial line's admonition to "act actionlessly" somewhat contradicts the idea of taking action early. For example, a state encountering urgent military problems might be well advised to act quickly and early, a course apparently justified by the verses' intent. Yet military strikes may prove precipitous and disastrous, and could also contravene the *Tao Te Ching*'s emphasis upon noncontention and deference to attract and nonviolently subdue others. The apparent conflict becomes resolvable only through the transcendent nature of "actionless" actions not contravening the Tao. It must therefore be concluded that there are moments when brusque martial strikes may be justified as truly benevolent in being for the people's benefit and therefore *defined* as "actionless" in the *Tao Te Ching*'s and Wang Chen's transcendent sense.

64

The Tranquil is
Easily Grasped

The tranquil is easily grasped;
What yet lacks signs is easily plotted against.
The brittle is easily split;
The minute is easily scattered.
Act upon them before they attain being;
Control them before they become chaotic.
Trees that require both arms to embrace
Are born from insignificant saplings.
A nine-story tower commences with a little
   accumulated earth.
A journey of a thousand kilometers begins
   beneath one's feet.
One who acts on things defeats them;
One who holds things loses them.
Being actionless, the Sage suffers no defeats;
Never grasping, suffers no losses.
In undertaking affairs, people constantly thwart
   themselves on the verge of success.
Being as attentive at the end as the beginning,
   there will be no thwarted affairs.
Accordingly, the Sage desires what is not desired
And does not value products difficult to obtain.
He studies what is not studied
And reverts the people's transgressions.
He sustains the naturalness of the myriad things
But does not dare act.

WANG   This entire chapter states that success and failure lie with men, that there is a Tao for beginning and ending. Accordingly, the Sage does not dare wantonly act just to seek the swift completion of things. Therefore, when secure he thinks of danger, which is why the chapter says "easily grasped." Since he does not contravene what precedes Heaven, it states [that such affairs are] "easily plotted against." If evildoers suddenly appear to foment difficulty, you must take advantage of their brittle beginnings to destroy them. Since you will then easily grapple with slender, minute beginnings, you will certainly scatter them without difficulty. Thus, it says, "act on them before they attain being; control them before they become chaotic." This is foresight and prescience. Before events sprout or show any signs, you want to act on them for fear that it will be difficult to plan against them when they are flourishing and overflowing. Moreover, great trees are given birth from insignificant saplings, high towers arise from overturning a basket of earth, and a distant journey commences from where you are. These three make it clear that by accumulating the small, one attains the great, that from the near, one reaches the distant, just like patiently following the river's flow to a destination. If you seek things too fervently, you will be entangled by a desire for quickness.

For this reason, military affairs cannot be undertaken; anyone who undertakes them will inevitably defeat himself. Weapons such as staves and halberds cannot be taken up; anyone who brandishes them will lose by himself. Therefore the Sage has nothing he does, nothing he grasps, so it is clear that he has nothing by which to be defeated, nothing through which to lose. Moreover, in prosecuting their affairs, the people of our age are all filled with doubt and prefer shortcuts when approaching the road. In mobilizing the army and defending the state, many are those who thwart themselves on the verge of success. In every case they lose the foundation and tip, confuse beginning and end.

Thus, it is said, "Being as attentive at the end as the beginning, there will be no thwarted affairs." Since the Sage desires what people do not want, the chapter also advises "do not value products difficult to obtain." He studies what other people do not study, so it says he "reverts the people's transgressions." Lao-tzu probably wants [rulers] to supplement and assist the myriad things, ensure that they naturally mature and attain completion, but at the same time not dare act presumptuously or manifest themselves, which would be called "taking action." Thus he concludes the chapter by advising that the Sage ruler "sustains the naturalness of the myriad things but does not dare act."

SAWYER   This chapter essentially continues the preceding one, reemphasizing the need to act before affairs mature, and thus represents the comparatively activist strain of thought in the *Tao Te Ching*. Although cognizant of its boldness, after the first paragraph Wang Chen's commentary reorients the theme somewhat to stress the idea that armies should not be employed, no doubt envisioning them as a deterrent rather than an actual implement for use except in truly inescapable circumstances. Moreover, simply relying upon military action invariably rebounds, if only because such efforts are always initiated too late. The key to Wang's vision thus probably remains a line from the previous chapter, "the Sage never acts against the great, so can achieve greatness."

The military writings—including the *Six Secret Teachings,* composed during the Warring States period—equally stressed the need for timely action. In a passage virtually mirroring this chapter, when asked how to preserve the state's territory, the T'ai Kung replied:

> Do not dig valleys deeper to increase hills. Do not abandon the foundation to govern the branches. When the sun is at midday you should dry things. If you grasp a knife you must cut. If you hold an ax you must attack.
>
> If, at the height of day, you do not dry things in the sun this is termed losing the time. If you grasp a knife but do not cut anything, you will lose the moment for profits. If you hold an ax but do not attack, then bandits will come.

If trickling streams are not blocked, they will become great rivers. If you don't extinguish the smallest flames, what will you do about a great conflagration? If you do not eliminate the two-leaf sapling, how will you use your ax when the tree has grown?

Wang Chen also echoes the *Tao Te Ching*'s observation that most people thwart themselves just on the verge of success and reiterates the need to be cautious about both the beginning and end of affairs, without again explicitly raising the Taoist perception that conclusions and achievements are brittle and temporary, doomed to inevitable failure in the indefinite future.

There is, of course, a fundamental contradiction between the first few lines, concluding with three examples of tendentious accumulation, and the disjointed assertion that follows—"one who acts on things defeats them"—condemning action to failure and thereby justifying the final statement, the Sage "does not dare act." Perhaps it may be resolved by understanding it within the framework of acting against the incipient, a form of nonaction because it strikes the invisible and thus constitutes the most radical action of all. (How this might "sustain the naturalness of the myriad things" remains puzzling in itself.) Another approach, basically disdained here, remains: physically and psychically opting out, achieved by distancing oneself from the concerns and desires of men, estranging oneself from society's claims. However, the Sage manages to participate in a positive way and therefore be integral to the universe.

65

In Antiquity, Those Who Excelled in the Tao

In antiquity, those who excelled in the Tao
Did not intend to enlighten the people but
  to stupefy them.
People are hard to govern when their wisdom is manifold.
Thus, one who governs a state with wisdom is the state's
  brigand;
One who does not govern with wisdom is the state's
  benefactor.
Knowing these two is also a pattern for emulation.
Constantly knowing this emulatory pattern is termed
  Dankly Mysterious Virtue.
Dankly Mysterious Virtue, profound and extensive,
Conjoins with things in reverting.
Only thereafter is great concord attained.

WANG   This chapter states that those rulers in antiquity
who excelled in implementing the Tao did not instruct the
realm's populace but instead forced the wise to conceal their
deceptions. They did so to stupefy all the people under
Heaven and thereby ensure they would remain in their
places. Thus the *Tao Te Ching* notes that "people are hard to
govern when their wisdom is manifold." Moreover, it also

states that "one who governs a state with wisdom is the state's brigand." How is this so?

By nature, the common masses are shallow and debased. Before wisdom and thought emerged, sly deceptions were first practiced. Did the resulting rancor and murmuring discriminate between right and wrong, contrary and according? The common people preferred to know who soothed, who brutalized. Some of them gathered like ants to form parties in the provinces; others arose like hornets amid the rivers and mountains. Ten thousand men responded to every evil leader who laid plots. Campaigns of rectification were constantly mobilized against them, so isn't this indeed what is meant by "one who governs a state with wisdom is the state's brigand"?

This says that if you increase the knowledge of the common masses, they will all become thieves capable of harming the state. Therefore, anyone who ensures that the people preserve their stupidity, directness, simplicity, and purity can achieve good fortune and blessings for the state. If the ruler can always remember these two [aspects of governing with and without wisdom], he will personally become a model for emulation. This is what is referred to as sharing the Virtue of Heaven. Now by saying that "Dankly Mysterious Virtue is profound and extensive," Lao-tzu sought to have rulers model on it and imitate it, thereby naturally returning to simplicity and purity. Then all the people under Heaven would undoubtedly be able to realize great concord. Therefore the chapter concludes, "only thereafter is great concord attained."

SAWYER   Chapters such as this are cited by those who vociferously claim that the *Tao Te Ching*—especially the *Te Ching* section—is a blatantly dictatorial tract that espouses only the ruler's interests. Probably no one would deny that "knowledge," while engendering freedom and facilitating progress, equally underlies all successful attempts to deceive, defeat, and exploit the sociopolitical structure and its laws. (The current proliferation of computer crimes provides a vivid, contemporary example.) Wang Chen interprets the chapter in a straightforward manner from a decidedly late Confucian perspective in saying, "by nature, the common masses are shallow and debased," hardly the sentiments of a true *Tao Te Ching* Taoist.

However, for ancient rulers, the political context was decidedly simpler, the most pressing—often insurmountable—concerns being social order and feeding the populace, thereby ensuring the state's survival. As already elaborated, according to the *Tao Te Ching*, they might be achieved through simplification, stressing life's basics rather than pursuing the artificial or anything that detracts from the focal task. Thus understood, the policy of stupefying the people (who are basically inclined to stupefy themselves in pleasure and artifice anyway) seems somewhat less pernicious, perhaps even viable, if it could truly resolve the core problems of starvation and antisocial violence.

(It should be remembered that the Sage, to the extent he is not completely oblivious to human concerns, is perturbed by the harm that antisocial acts inflict, not the acts themselves nor any significance they might have in violating the laws. Furthermore, although "stupefying" can only be a dictatorial, inconceivable policy to the modern mind, its odiousness diminishes drastically in comparison with the heinous dictatorial programs implemented in the twentieth century in China and elsewhere that proved responsible for untold suffering and the deaths of millions.)

66

How Rivers and Seas Can be Kings of the Hundred Valley Streams

Rivers and seas can be kings of the hundred
  valley streams
Because they excel at being below them,
And thus can be kings over the hundred valley streams.
For this reason, when the Sage wants to be above people,
In speech, he certainly defers to them.
When he wants to precede people,
In body, he puts himself behind them.
Accordingly, the Sage occupies a position above,
But the people are not weighed down.
He occupies a position in front,
But the people are not harmed.
Therefore, All under Heaven take unmitigated pleasure
  in being directed.
Because he does not contend,
None under Heaven are able to contend with him.

WANG   This chapter dramatically employs the great rivers and seas as an analogy because Lao-tzu wants rulers to epitomize circumspection, pliancy, humility, and weakness.

Through epitomizing circumspection, pliancy, humility, and weakness, rulers can gain the willing allegiance of All under Heaven. Only after gaining the willing allegiance of All under Heaven can they then ensure that the people will "take unmitigated pleasure in being directed." When they attain their taking unmitigated pleasure in being directed, upper and lower ranks will naturally not struggle with each other. Now the righteousness of noncontention is identical with Heaven's Virtue, for they both beautify and benefit the myriad things and excel at responding without speaking. Fully circulating among the six vacuities of the celestial points, they excel at conquering without plotting. Moreover, among all the men under Heaven, can anyone contend with one who does not contend? Certainly not.

SAWYER   The unspoken premise of this chapter is that China's great rivers, the Yellow and Yangtze, and seas somehow "conquer" the numerous smaller rivers and streams that meander down China's many valleys into them, whether directly or indirectly. Although Wang Chen does not mention it, rivers and oceans obviously derive their own overwhelming power and majesty by absorbing the waters of these various feeders. This image is suggestive in that the streams continue to flow and therefore maintain their temporal identity, while the oceans are unceasingly increased through mergence of their waters. Even though this partially mirrors the Tao's relationship with the myriad things in that they all return to the origin, to the Tao, the chapter is undeniably directed toward nurturing power through deference. As previously discussed, the presumption of significant position or rulership is naturally required if what might be termed negative, self-abnegating methods are to prove effective amid the power structures that characterize the mundane world of desire and if the ruler is to avoid being cast aside or simply trampled by aggressive, self-seeking hordes. However, as interpreted by Wang Chen, the chapter's approach provides a corrective for headstrong rulers rushing toward their own self-destruction.

67

All Under Heaven
Term Me Vast

All under Heaven term my Tao vast and unreal.
Only because it is vast is it unreal!
If it were real, it would have long been insignificant!
I have three treasures I grasp and preserve.
The first is called solicitude;
The second is called frugality;
The third is called not daring to precede the world.
Because of solicitude, there can be courage;
Because of frugality, there can be expansiveness;
Because of not daring to precede the world, one can be the
    leader of implements.
Now abandoning solicitude yet being courageous,
Abandoning frugality yet being expansive,
Abandoning being last yet being first,
Would be fatal!
Solicitude yields victory in warfare and solidity in defense.
When Heaven is about to rescue someone,
It protects him with solicitude.

WANG   In order to illuminate the essence of these three
treasures, the chapter first presents us with a discussion about
vastness. Now vastness is the Tao's embodiment. Inferior
scholars do not understand this, so they term it unreal. In
pointing this out, Lao-tzu wants rulers to deeply examine the
significance of the three treasures, to preserve and cling to
them. Thus he begins with a section about employing and
abandoning them in order to illuminate the potency [Te] of
solicitude and frugality.

"Because of solicitude there can be courage" means that a single man's [the ruler's] solicitude can gain the death-defying strength of All under Heaven. If this cannot be deemed courage, what can? "Because of frugality, there can be expansiveness" means that a single man's frugality and parsimony can acquire all the riches under Heaven. If such possession isn't expansive, what is?

Accordingly, the Three August Ones employed solicitude and frugality to conquer the Nine Li; the Five Emperors employed them to expel the four evil chiefs. King T'ang of the Shang and King Wu of the Chou employed them and their armies conquered All under Heaven. Kings Ch'eng and K'ang of the Chou and Emperors Wen and Ching of the Han employed them and their punishments and fines were emplaced. But Chieh of the Hsia and Chou of the Shang abandoned them and their states were extinguished. Kings Yu and Li of the Western Chou abandoned them and perished. Ch'in Shih-huang neglected them, and his son was torn apart. Hsiang Yü abandoned them, and his limbs were scattered. Han Wu-ti abandoned them and lost half the realm. Ts'ao Ts'ao abandoned them, and the states of Wu and Shu divided the empire into thirds.

Thus, the *Tao Te Ching* speaks about "abandoning solicitude yet being courageous, abandoning frugality yet being expansive." "Abandoning solicitude" means eliminating loving solicitude for other men. Since people will no longer repay the ruler with death-defying strength, his singular ardent courage must withstand the empire's enmity. How can he then implement his own courage and daring?

"Abandoning frugality" refers to not knowing to be frugal and parsimonious but instead imposing heavy impositions, building extravagant palaces, and augmenting the army. When both the state's wealth and foodstocks are exhausted, how will the ruler be sufficient?

Moreover, the *Tao Te Ching* advises that "putting yourself behind, you will be first" and adds that "if you want to precede men, you must put yourself behind them." For this reason the Sage never dares to precede any under Heaven, yet in the end precedes All under Heaven. This is illustrated by the beneficial examples of all those from the Yellow Emperor down through Emperors Wen and Ching, and further attested by [the ill fate of] all those who abandoned [this principle], from Kings Chieh and Chou down through Ts'ao Ts'ao. Accordingly, the *Tao Te Ching* concludes, "Now solicitude yields victory in warfare and solidity in defense. When Heaven is about to rescue someone, it protects him with solicitude."

SAWYER   Although the chapter opens with a rumination upon the term *unreal* as inappropriately applied to the Tao, the "three treasures" of solicitude, frugality, and deference lie at its core. (The first verse turns upon a question of perspective, for what appears "unreal" must inevitably be so from the limited viewpoint of mere men who are struggling to conceptualize the ineffable Tao. It essentially reframes the ideas of "The Tao That Can Be Spoken Of," "Looked at but Unseen," "When Superior Officers Hear about the Tao," and the spirit of "Great Achievement Seems Deficient.")

Frugality—synonymous with benefiting the people—has previously appeared in a number of chapters, including "Governing the People and Serving Heaven," and been thoroughly explicated by Wang Chen for its ability to attract and nurture the support and allegiance of the people. Its correlate "solicitude" (sometimes translated as "compassion," although the scope is much wider, meaning being concerned about or exerting oneself over something) is normally understood as a superior's active, emotional concern for an inferior in a two-party relationship, whether it be political power (ruler/subjects), the family (parents/children), or the military (commander/troops). Wang Chen's expansion, conceived against a background of military thought, well explains the psychodynamics whereby "solicitude yields victory in warfare and solidity in defense."

The military writings were especially aware of this need to develop strong attachments among the populace for their ruler and the troops for their commander, such as by having the latter personally share all hardships with them. The *Three Strategies* preserves an ancient dictum:

> A state about to mobilize its army concentrates upon first making its beneficence ample. A state about to attack and seize another concentrates upon first nurturing the people. Conquering the many with only a few is a question of beneficence. Conquering the strong with the weak is a question of people. Thus the good general, in nurturing his officers, treats them no differently than himself. Therefore he is able to direct the Three Armies as if they were of one mind, and then his victory can be complete.

Sun-tzu even likened the relationship to that between parents and their children, noting that the proper emotional basis must be established before the troops will truly follow commands and unhesitatingly submit to danger:

> When the general regards his troops as young children, they will advance into the deepest valleys with him. When he regards the troops as his beloved children, they will be willing to die with him. If they are well treated but cannot be employed, if they are loved but cannot be commanded, or when in chaos they cannot be governed, they may be compared to arrogant children and cannot be used.
>
> If you impose punishment on the troops before they have become attached, they will not be submissive. If they are not submissive, they will be difficult to employ. If you do not impose punishments after the troops have become attached, they cannot be used.

Part of Han Fei-tzu's explication of this chapter similarly raises the parent-child analogy, even expanding it to elucidate the Sage's performance as well:

> Anyone who loves children will be solicitous about them. Anyone who values life will be solicitous about his body. One who esteems accomplishments will be solicitous [exert

himself] in affairs. The solicitous mother exerts herself to obtain good fortune for her weak child. Because she exerts herself to obtain good fortune, she will direct her efforts toward eliminating misfortune. Because she directs her efforts to eliminating misfortune, she will think and ponder deeply. When she thinks and ponders deeply, she will realize the patterns of affairs. When she realizes the patterns of affairs, she will certainly be successful. Since she will certainly be successful, her actions will not be doubtful. Not being doubtful is termed "courage."

The Sage ponders the myriad affairs just as the mother does on behalf of her weak child. Therefore, he will discern the path he must follow. Discerning the path he must follow, the affairs he undertakes will similarly not be doubtful. Not being doubtful is termed "courage." Not being doubtful stems from solicitude. Thus, the *Tao Te Ching* states, "Because of solicitude, there can be courage."

Anyone who is solicitous about children will not dare cut off their food or clothes. Anyone solicitous about his body will never dare depart from the laws and regulations. Anyone who is concerned about ["solicitous" of] squares and circles will not dare abandon rulers and compasses. Therefore, when a general assumes command, if he is solicitous of his officers and staff, in battle he will certainly conquer the enemy. If he is concerned about ["solicitous" of] the weapons and armaments, his fortifications will be firm and solid. Thus, the *Tao Te Ching* states, "Solicitude yields victory in warfare and solidity in defense."

68

Those Who
Excel as Warriors
are not Martial

Those who excel as warriors are not martial.
Those who excel in combat do not get angry.
Those who excel in conquering the enemy do not do battle.
Those who excel in employing men act deferentially to them.
This is what is termed the Virtue of nonconflict.
This is what is termed employing the strength of men.
This is what is termed matching Heaven,
The pinnacle of antiquity.

WANG   Now rulers who embody the Tao all dwell amid actionless affairs and implement unspoken teachings, so how would they have any martial inclinations? Moreover, those who excel at combat are not defeatable because they esteem being placid and tranquil. Thus, on the day they are victorious, they still do not glorify their actions but in grief and sorrow constrain them with the rites of mourning, so what anger do they have? Furthermore, since the sagacious ruler's Virtue conjoins with Heaven and Earth, he naturally does not contend. Thus the *Tao Te Ching* says, "Those who excel in conquering the enemy do not do battle."

Now true kings are frugal, love the people, and employ them according to the seasons. Thus, the assistants they utilize for civil affairs may be compared with their limbs and heart. When they employ generals, they have them kneel and receive the symbolic ax of command, sending them off with a hand on their chariots. In this way they first gain their hearts, then employ their strength. Thus, the *Tao Te Ching* states, "Those who excel in employing men act deferentially to them," what is termed the "Virtue of noncontention." The Virtue of noncontention can be employed to match Heaven in establishing the extremities. Thus, it is called "the pinnacle of antiquity."

SAWYER "Those Who Excel as Warriors Are Not Martial" presents a startling image, one completely contrary to every conceivable combat scenario, whether individual or massive. Moreover, although the second line's assertion that "those who excel in combat do not get angry" connotes on some intuitive level such surpassing skill and superiority that anger would only prove inimical, it runs contrary to the general martial notion that anger provides the vital motivation for combat. For example, Sun-tzu said, "What motivates men to slay the enemy is anger."

These dramatically contradictory views on anger's role in battle may perhaps be reconciled by simply considering anger synonymous with intensely motivating emotions. Until some strong emotion compels the ordinary soldier or common person to act, he will remain reluctant to expose himself to danger and to kill other men. Thus, the *Ssu-ma Fa* observes, "In general, men will die for love, out of anger, out of fear of awesomeness, for righteousness, and for profit." Conversely, excessive anger rapidly leads to a loss of judgment and control and, except in the case of the unopposably berserk, almost certain defeat or death. (All the military writers therefore condemned commanders who were prone to anger because they would invariably commit errors and be easily manipulated.)

For those who attain surpassing skill and wisdom—namely the Sages—victory without combat, through overawing the enemy without becoming martial or manifesting their power, constitutes a definitive achievement. (The Sages are, of course, identifiable as such because they have escaped or transcended such powerful emotions as anger—according to the

Tao Te Ching's perspective, but not Chuang-tzu's or Neo-Taoism's.) Thus, in virtually mirroring the third line—"those who excel in conquering the enemy do not do battle"—Sun-tzu said:

> Attaining one hundred victories in one hundred battles is not the pinnacle of excellence. Subjugating the enemy's army without fighting is the true pinnacle of excellence. Thus, one who excels at employing the military subjugates other people's armies without engaging in battle, captures other people's fortified cities without attacking them, and destroys other people's states without prolonged fighting. He must fight under Heaven with the paramount aim of "preservation." Thus, his weapons will not become dull, and the gains can be preserved.

Wang Chen's commentary reintroduces the theme of post-combat sorrow instead of focusing on the warrior's crucial characteristics. However, he tangentially notes one of the procedures during the ceremony for commissioning commanding generals prior to their embarking on campaigns to signify the formal establishment of power and transfer of authority. (Essential aspects of such ceremonies are preserved in a chapter appropriately entitled "Appointing the General" in the *Six Secret Teachings*.) Unstated, but ever in the background, is the not always uncontested belief that generals should exercise completely independent authority once commissioned and in the field. As Sun-tzu taught and visibly exemplified (at his famous historical encounter with King Ho-lü when he beheaded two of the king's beloved concubines for failing to swiftly execute his commands while they were acting as captains for an ad hoc army training company), it was essential for field generals to reject orders they deemed unacceptable whenever dictated by actual battlefield circumstances even though such disobedience would probably result in their execution. (Correspondingly, the reward for defeat was likewise death.)

69

Those Who
Employ the Military
Have A Saying

Those who employ the military have a saying:
"I dare not act as the host but act as the guest;
I dare not advance an inch but withdraw a foot."
This is termed deploying without lines,
Displaying one's arms without laying them bare,
Being extant without enemies,
Grasping without weapons.
No disaster is greater than slighting the enemy,
For slighting the enemy borders on the loss of one's treasures.
Thus, when mutually opposing armies attack each other,
Those who feel grief will be victorious.

WANG   Lao-tzu, being humbly deferential, could not directly express himself, so he borrowed the phrase "Those who employ the military have a saying." Now armies invariably regard those who mobilize first as the "host," those who respond thereafter as the "guest." Moreover, Sages employ their armies only when there is no alternative, so they mobilize only in response to an enemy. Since they arise only in response to enemy forces, they always act as guests. Advancing little but withdrawing much is the concealed crux and mysterious employment of the military, evidence of its serious treatment of the enemy.

Thus, when an enemy draws up, even though the Sage excels in military affairs, he does not deploy. Since he excels in military affairs but does not deploy, he does not mount aggressive attacks. Thus, the *Tao Te Ching* states that he "deploys without lines." Since he does not employ aggressive formations while his infantry forces embrace righteousness and maintain a defensive posture, what "baring of arms" is there?

Now rulers who embody the Tao initially allow perverse, brutal invaders to wantonly advance, after which the army formally charges them with their offenses and performs martial dances with shields and arrows. The enemy will certainly respect such righteousness and withdraw, so naturally sagacious rulers will not have any enemies. Thus, the *Tao Te Ching* says, "extant without enemies." When the enemy has withdrawn, shields and halberds are put aside. Thus, it states, "grasping without weapons." Once weapons are stored away, Lao-tzu fears people will forget warfare, so he again admonishes, "No disaster is greater than slighting the enemy, for slighting the enemy borders on the loss of one's treasures." "Slighting the enemy" refers to being enthralled with conducting warfare outside the state while lacking preparations within it. However, rather than lacking preparations within the state, it is better to be enthralled with conducting warfare outside it because engaging in external battles will just result in victory or defeat, but lacking preparations within inevitably results in loss and extinction.

Although Sage rulers truly have no enemies under Heaven, if one speaks about ordinary rulers, about their order and disorder, their enemies are numerous. As the *Book of Documents* states, "Those who soothe us we regard as our ruler, those who oppress us we regard as our enemy." If this is so, then All under Heaven may be one's enemy. A single state may be the enemy, a village the enemy, a family the enemy, a person the enemy. Thus when kings do not neglect their most insignificant ministers, they gain the willing allegiance of the myriad states. When dukes and lords do not insult widows and widowers, they gain the willing allegiance of the hundred surnames. When chancellors and high officials do not neglect their ministers and wives, they gain the willing allegiance of both the small and great. When the common people do not neglect their self-cultivation, they gain true and substantial admiration. Only thus can I preserve what I treasure, my body and position.

"When mutually opposing armies attack each other, those who feel grief will be victorious." Whenever Lao-tzu speaks of grief, he means the solicitude and love that are sincerely manifest from within. If the ruler preserves a compassionate, loving mind and does not neglect the rites in employing his subordinates, they will exert themselves in the measures of loyalty and courage and fully realize the meaning of serving their ruler. Then, in what direction will the ruler not be victorious? Thus, the chapter concludes, "Those who feel grief will be victorious."

SAWYER   Throughout the book, and particularly in this chapter, the *Tao Te Ching* advances a vision of warfare as defensive and reactive rather than aggressive and initiative. Here Lao-tzu's exposition surprisingly commences by expropriating the concept of "guest" and "host," a fundamental tactical distinction also preserved in Sun Pin's *Military Methods* and the T'ang (or perhaps Sung) dynasty *Questions and Replies*. As Sun Pin defines them, in normal military usage "guest" generally refers to an invader and "host" to a defender fighting in his home state or on terrain he already occupies:

> Armies are distinguished as being a "guest" or a "host." The guest's forces are comparatively numerous, the host's forces comparatively few. Only if the guest is double and the host half can they contend as enemies.
> The host is the one who establishes his position first; the guest is the one who establishes his position afterward. The host ensconces himself on the terrain and relies on his strategic power to await the guest who contravenes mountain passes and traverses ravines to arrive.
> The *Tactics* states, "The host counters the guest at the border."

However, in the *Questions and Replies,* the great early T'ang general Li Ching theorized that the distinctions are not immutable, so conversion remains possible:

The T'ai-tsung said: "The army values being the host; it does not value being a guest. It values speed, not duration. Why?"

Li Ching said: "The army is employed only when there is no alternative, so what advantage is there in being a guest or fighting long? Sun-tzu says: 'When provisions are transported far off, the common people are impoverished.' This is the exhaustion of a guest. He also said: 'The people should not be conscripted twice; provisions should not be transported thrice.' This comes from the experience of not being able to long endure. When I compare and weigh the strategic power of host and guest, then there are tactics for changing the guest to host, changing the host to guest."

The T'ai-tsung said: "What do you mean?"

Li Ching said: "By foraging and capturing provisions from the enemy, you change a guest into a host. 'If you cause the sated to be famished and the rested to be tired,' it will change a host into a guest. Thus the army is not confined to being a host or guest, slow or fast, but only focuses upon its movements, invariably attaining the constraints and thereby being appropriate."

Therefore, according to such military theorists, the concept of "guest" should not be delimited solely to invaders moving into foreign territory. Rather it should be considered another tactical designation useful for comparative purposes because, in essence, it refers to a force in movement striking one already emplaced. Moreover, throughout history, defensive forces generally enjoyed almost insurmountable advantages through choosing the battlefield, exploiting the terrain, and establishing fortifications, thereby forcing their "guests" to possess overwhelming superiority to create even the possibility of victory.

However, the opening passage in the present chapter apparently inverts these key designations: "I dare not act as the host but act as the guest; I dare not advance an inch but withdraw a foot." Based upon commentators' explications over the millennia, it must be concluded that Lao-tzu is employing the terms *guest* and *host* in an idiosyncratic fashion because *host* here refers to the party that initiates the combat—the "master," which is the fundamental meaning of the character translated as "host" of the situation—and *guest* to the party that responds. (Wang Chen concurs because he designates those who move first as the "host.") In this light it becomes apparent that Lao-tzu here advocates adopting a temporizing strategy, one designed to force the enemy to commit and largely expend its energies before mounting a response. Lao-tzu's approach is not simply philosophical, reflecting the Taoist emphasis upon yielding and deference to overcome the brutal and powerful, but inherently accords with the quietest response to a perverse context.

It should be remembered, though, that the *Tao Te Ching* also characterizes the military as inherently unorthodox while the chapter itself continues on to discuss the deployment of the formless formation. (Wang Chen's discussion of the righteous simply shaming the enemy into withdrawing is, of course, undermined by his caveat that few rulers are Sages. Nevertheless, his reorientation on the comparative advisability of conducting warfare outside the state well merits noting.)

70

My Words Are Very Easy to Comprehend

My words are very easy to comprehend,
Exceedingly easy to implement.

None under Heaven are able to comprehend them,
None capable of implementing them.
My words have a progenitor;
My actions have a master.
Only because they lack knowledge
Do others not know me.
Those who know me are rare,
Who model on me are honored.
For this reason the Sage, though coarsely garbed,
Embraces pure jade.

WANG   In the realm of men, nothing exceeds the army's employment for severity, prompting Lao-tzu to earnestly and diligently address it. Although the previous chapter thoroughly discussed the importance of treating the enemy seriously whenever employing the army, Lao-tzu still feared later generations might be unable to penetrate his meaning. Therefore, he again particularly states, "My words are very easy to comprehend, exceedingly easy to implement." Moreover, he adds, "My words have a progenitor; my actions have a master," *progenitor* here referring to the root and foundation, *ruler* to control and preservation. This means that his words all have a foundation, his actions all have core assumptions, but people are simply incapable of comprehending them, incapable of implementing them. Dejected, he then says that "Those who know me are rare, who model on me are honored." "To model on" means to take as an example and follow, while "to honor" is similar to being rare. Lao-tzu thus asserts that since few are able to know and model on him, Tao and Te [Virtue] are not implemented. Since Tao and Te are not implemented, the Sage externally displays darkness while internally concealing his brightness and dwelling in isolation. Thus, the chapter concludes, "For this reason the Sage, though coarsely garbed, embraces pure jade."

SAWYER   In commencing his commentary, Wang Chen apparently assumes that this chapter continues the warfare theme of the previous two and envisions the ongoing presence of conflict being the result of failing to comprehend

Lao-tzu's teachings. However, despite the *Tao Te Ching*'s explicit advocacy of casting out wisdom and knowledge, the first two verses clearly turn upon achieving thorough knowledge of the transcendent, inexplicable Tao. While reflecting the essence of the book's opening lines—"The Tao that can be spoken of is not the ineffable Tao"—once penetrated, practice becomes easy. Accordingly, the Sage, who deliberately appears shadowy and insufficient, embodies this wisdom and thus the Tao.

71

Knowing, Not Knowing

Knowing, while acting as if one doesn't know, is superior;
Not knowing, while acting as if one knows, is an illness.
Now only by regarding illness as illness
Is one therefore not ill.
The Sage is not ill because he regards illness as illness
And is therefore not ill.

WANG   To know what one knows, but not speak about what one knows, is human superiority. To not know what one knows, yet forcefully speak about what one knows, is human illness. Realizing that this sort of wanton knowing constitutes an illness makes it not an illness. The subtle crux in employing military forces particularly lies in this. Only Sages and Worthies are capable of knowing it.

SAWYER   This famous but enigmatic *Tao Te Ching* chapter is open to many interpretations and translations. Although the first two lines are generally rendered "Knowing that one doesn't know is superior; to think one knows when he doesn't is an illness," our translation follows the manifest behavioral thrust of Wang Chen's commentary. (As Wang also points out in consonance with all the classic military writers, knowledge is the essence of the military. Without it, armies are doomed to errors and defeat, so its lack is truly a fatal illness!) However, our own inclination would be to translate it as "Knowing the unknown is superior; not knowing the known is an illness." Somewhat less appealing, but still possible and encompassing of the *Tao Te Ching*'s general viewpoint, would be "Knowing not to know is superior; not knowing to know is an illness." In this case, though, the second half of the verse would certainly have to be understood with reference to the Tao, not pragmatic knowledge in general.

72

People Do Not Dread Awesomeness

When people do not dread awesomeness,
Great awesomeness arrives.

Do not vex them in their dwellings;
Do not repress their means to life.
Only when there is no repression
Will they be unoppressed.
For this reason the Sage knows himself but does not
*   manifest himself,*
Loves himself but does not exalt himself.
Thus he rejects that and takes this.

WANG   "Great awesomeness" refers to armor and weapons. Now when the officers and common people have nothing they dread, punishments and fines result. When chancellors and high officials have nothing they dread, banishment and insult result. When lords and kings have nothing they dread, armor and weapons appear. Moreover, the *Book of Documents* contains a similar statement: "Not being fearful, one enters fearfulness."

Lao-tzu further admonishes rulers to maintain a generous, encompassing heart, never allowing the narrow and constrained to be their body, never deprecating their own patterns to life. When they do not deprecate their own patterns to life, they will certainly emphasize governing the people. When they emphasize governing the people, the populace will invariably take pleasure in being directed. When they already take pleasure in being directed, who will feel oppressed? Therefore, only after implementing affairs that cannot cause oppression will the people not be repressed. Thus, Lao-tzu says, "Only when there is no repression will they be unoppressed."

Now the Sage is enlightened and therefore surely knows himself, so how would he ever willingly flaunt himself and expose his talents in order to manifest himself? The Sage is benevolent and therefore assuredly loves himself, so how would he ever willingly be overbearing to men or arrogant to things in order to make himself respected and honored? Therefore he rejects this great delusion of self-manifestation and self-aggrandizement and seizes upon the vast augmentation of self-knowledge and self-love. Thus, the *Tao Te Ching* states, "He rejects that and takes this."

SAWYER   Although the chapter's two parts are internally coherent and continue earlier themes (and also closely prefigure "The People Do Not Dread Death"), they in fact have only a tenuous connection and were probably simply cobbled together with "for this reason" to loosely integrate them. Wang Chen's explications are clear and concise, capturing the main point that when government does not perturb the people, the people will not feel rancor or reach the point of disdaining punishments and ignoring regulations. Even though there is some wordplay on the concept of awesomeness, adherence to its lesser form through maintaining proper respect thus precludes the germination of the greater, more terrifying—and therefore more severe—extremes of warfare and capital punishment. (The idea of entrusting the empire only to those who love themselves, who are solicitous of their bodies, previously appeared in "Be Startled at Favor and Disgrace," which states "One who loves his body when acting on behalf of the realm apparently can be fully entrusted with All under Heaven.")

73

One Courageous in Daring Slays

One courageous in daring slays;
One courageous in not daring gives life.
Among these two,

One is beneficial, one harmful.
For what Heaven abhors,
Who knows the reason?
For this reason the Sage still regards it as difficult.
The Tao of Heaven is to not contend, yet excel at conquering,
Not to speak, yet excel at being responsive,
Not to summon, but come by itself,
To be lax, yet excel at strategy.
Heaven's net is spaciously wide,
Expansive without any losses.

WANG   This chapter asserts that decisively daring and courageously fierce rulers are always enthralled with forging the strongest armies possible under Heaven and killing men. However, if they were instead decisively daring without being courageously fierce, they would invariably concentrate upon implementing the Tao throughout their region and preserving the people's lives. Thus the chapter states that in knowing these two, there is benefit and harm.

"What Heaven abhors" are those who love to slay men. Since the Sage has long known this, to intensify his admonition, Lao-tzu reiterates that "he still regards it as difficult." Modeling on Heaven and implementing the Tao, the Sage undertakes actionless affairs and establishes unspoken instructions. How could there be any contention anywhere in the realm? Since there isn't any contention, how could there be anyone he wouldn't conquer? Thus, the chapter states, "Without contending, he excels at conquering."

Heaven follows human desire with the rapidity of a shadow or echo, so isn't this excelling at response? Summer comes after cold, winter arrives after heat, so don't they come by themselves? The myriad things are formed and shaped so that each realizes its proper nature and destiny, so isn't this excelling at planning? The ruler models upon Heaven's broadly expansive net. No unintentional transgression is too great for his leniency, so if this isn't being broad, what is? No intentional crime is too small for his punishment, so if this isn't not losing, what is? Moreover, the *Book of Documents* states,

"Retribution imposed by Heaven can still be contravened; retribution imposed on oneself is inescapable." Isn't the meaning identical?

SAWYER   The first two lines are normally rendered "One courageous in daring will be killed; one courageous in not daring lives." However, our grammatically more direct and correct translation actually follows Wang Chen's cogent views, which well cohere with the overall spirit of the Tao and the chapter's subsequent expansion of being courageous in not daring as beneficial. (To be courageous in not killing is often more difficult than simply slaying other men, as well as requiring greater emotional control in combat to avoid succumbing to hatred or anger.) The idea that Heaven excels in conquering is concisely recast by Wang Chen here into the actionless mode of noncontention. (It should be noted that this is the only direct statement of Heaven's power being so employed, even though the few remaining chapters often convey a darker image of it as potentially repressive.) Naturally, the image of Heaven's patterning and thereby structuring the myriad things in their passage from life to death, apparently without conscious intent to do so, remains pervasive. However, since Heaven is inescapably powerful, even without any intention to interfere or intrude, it inevitably dominates. Thus, its net "is spaciously wide, expansive without any losses."

Unexpectedly, Wang Chen interprets this as referring to punishment, perhaps prefiguring the next chapter which coincidentally points out that Heaven abhors the infliction of capital punishment. Wang's citation of the incisive saying from the *Book of Documents,* one of the Confucian classics, skillfully shifts the responsibility back onto the individual: people commit offenses and thereby condemn themselves because responses thereafter are natural and inescapable. (Han Fei-tzu particularly seized upon this insight to infuse his vision of a government that automatically reacts to the commission of offenses.)

In explicating the chapter, Wang Chen also notes that "Heaven follows human desire with the rapidity of a shadow or an echo," an odd encumbrance inflicted upon Heaven that perhaps derives from the Sage's behavior in "The Sage Has No Preset Mind," regarding which Wang states, "'The Sage takes the minds of the hundred surnames as his mind' basically means that he follows the desires of others."

A more succinct translation of the eighth through tenth lines would be:

The Tao of Heaven is to conquer without contending,
To excel at responding without speaking,
To come unsummoned.

74

The People Do Not Dread Death

The people do not dread death,
So how can you terrify them with death?
Once we cause the people to constantly dread death,
And I grasp and slay those who act perversely,
Who will dare?
Always have the executioner slay them,
For substituting for the executioner in slaying
Is termed substituting for the Great Carpenter in
    hewing.
One who substitutes for the Great Carpenter in hewing
Rarely avoids injuring his hands.

WANG   Now when the army is exhausted and the soldiers worn out, regulations dangerous and punishments severe, the people will invariably lack the means to live. When the people lack the means to live, clearly they will no longer fear death. When they no longer fear death, how can they be punished with punishments? That the people avoid punishment and have no shame lies in this. If the ruler were to transform them with Tao and Te [Virtue], they would certainly embrace life and fear death, naturally have a sense of shame and be correct. Once they have acquired a sense of shame and become correct, should hooligans and evildoers suddenly arise and again commit perverse acts, "I grasp and slay them."

This means that if the disciples of militarism employ artifice and deception to disorder the people and delude the masses, I will take hold of them and execute them. However, as this is what Heaven abhors, I still cannot assume sole responsibility. Thus, the *Tao Te Ching* asks, "Who would dare? Always have the executioner slay them." Here "the executioner" refers to Heaven's net. Moreover, since the king has certainly committed numerous offenses, he should berate himself and wait for the spirits of Heaven to carry out the extremity of execution. How can he vent his emotions, shift his anger, and recklessly punish the innocent? Thus, the chapter concludes, "One who substitutes for the Great Carpenter in hewing rarely avoids injuring his hands."

SAWYER   This chapter might well be read in conjunction with the next, "The People's Hunger," because inverting their order will explain why the people no longer fear death and therefore come to disdain both corporeal and capital punishment. As "People Do Not Dread Awesomeness" has already noted, when the people no longer fear anything, they cannot be coerced with threats of punishment and, lacking natural virtue, incline to disorder. Here the quest remains resolving this disorder and attaining social tranquillity, whereas the next chapter proffers a solution based upon rectifying the government (which is no doubt assumed here as well). This appropriately requires reestablishing a sense of dread among the people and then imposing corporeal punishment, but since Heaven is known to abhor punitive inflictions, problems of implementation still remain. Furthermore, Wang Chen is clearly troubled by the chapter's almost blatant advocacy of punishment—despite the caveat that Heaven condemns it—and therefore understands the lines as referring to conditions that have accrued through prolonged warfare and deprivation.

The previous chapter has already discussed the need to be courageous in not killing, in giving life; here Wang advocates intensifying nurturing programs through the implementation of Tao and Te. Apparently, the latter is synonymous with the Confucian virtues because they inculcate a sense of shame and achieve uprightness, the very bastions of Confucian psychodynamics. In a surprising bow to reality, Wang acknowledges that most rulers are themselves morally deficient and therefore counsels restraint, waiting "for the spirits of Heaven to carry out the extremity of execution." How this abstraction will be concretely realized remains puzzling but is perhaps understandable if the miscreants have all gravitated to some perverse state soon to be chastised.

75
The People's Hunger

The people are famished because their superiors consume
excessive taxes,
Making them hungry.
The people are difficult to administer because their supe-
riors are active,

Making them difficult to govern.
The people are untroubled by death because their superiors
seek life's abundance,
Making them oblivious to death.
Now it is only one who does not act for life
Who is more worthy than one who values life.

WANG   This chapter asserts that misery and famine stem from the ruler's establishing numerous labor services, heavy military impositions, and onerous taxes, thus taking in a great deal. This certainly is true! Moreover, in speaking about being active, it is referring to rulers who love to undertake military affairs. Now when one family has weapons, it affects its village. When a village has weapons, it affects its state. When a state has weapons, it affects All under Heaven. When All under Heaven have weapons, chaos is preordained. Farmers then abandon their hoes to take up staffs and halberds, and women abandon their weaving work. Among the common people and registered households, more than half thus engage in military activities. Fathers and sons, elder and younger brothers, neighbors and clans, villages and cliques all become armed knights and perpetrate villainy. Even among those tempted to goodness, who speaks about Confucius and the *I Ching*? Therefore they are said to be "difficult to govern."

People treat death lightly because the ruler's demands are so excessive that they have no means to live and so disregard death. Accordingly, Lao-tzu dejectedly comments, "Now it is only one who does not act for life who is more worthy than one who values life." Here "worthy" means something like "being good at." This refers to those who love to accumulate wealth in order to ennoble their lives, not to those who embrace the Tao in order to nurture their lives.

SAWYER   Lao-tzu's observations in this chapter might well be seen as a fervent condemnation of conditions and practices in his era, the Warring States period, as well as basically characterizing most developed countries today. The verses succinctly express the Taoist disinclination to activist government in general and convey abhorrence of oppressive, extravagant rulers in particular. Although the insight that poverty and destitution cause people to fear death was hardly unique—the Confucians all spoke of the difficulty of being virtuous in the face of want and deprivation and frequently condemned the extravagant practices of licentious, self-indulgent rulers—the chapter's envisioned resolution is. Wang Chen, in accord with his penchants and focal intent, again interprets the disorder portrayed as stemming solely from warfare rather than simply the government excesses portrayed in "If I Minutely." However, his depiction of even minimal military activities, unavoidably compelling other people, in an ever-widening circle, to pursue martial practices is instructive, especially as the *Tao Te Ching* counsels a different path altogether.

76

Life of the People

Human life is pliancy and weakness;
Death is stiffness and strength.
Alive, the myriad things, grasses, and trees are pliable
  and fragile;
Dead, they are dry and withered.
Thus the firm and strong are disciples of death;
The pliant and weak are disciples of life.
For this reason strong armies will not be victorious;
Strong trees will break.
The strong and great dwell below;
The pliant and weak dwell above.

WANG This chapter once again speaks about employing pliancy and weakness and elucidates the partisans of life and death. In my ignorance, I think its profound essence lies in the idea that strong armies will not be victorious. Moreover, the chapter subsequently states, "Strong trees will break. The strong and great dwell below; the pliant and weak dwell above." This is another severe warning against misfortune arising from armies being too strong. Why? Armies are termed baleful, dangerous implements, tools for fighting and conflict, the scope of their impact being the enemy opposite. Accordingly, when their armies are strong, rulers are unworried. When rulers are unworried, their generals are arrogant. When generals are arrogant, their troops are brutal. When a complacent ruler controls arrogant generals who in turn command brutal troops, before long they will be defeated and overturned, so how will they conquer the enemy?

The decline of the Hsia and Shang resulted from raising massive armies and overturning all within the four seas. In the end, Ch'in Shih-huang unified the realm but lost the Nine Regions. Hsiang Yü suddenly became hegemon and then raced toward extinction. Wang Mang of the Hsin usurped imperial power and was obliterated. Fu Chien was indecisive at Huai-shang [and was destroyed] while Sui Yang-ti was torn asunder in Ch'u Palace. The largest of their forces surpassed a million; the least attained it. Since every single one of them seized defeat through relying on achievements, they furnish explicit evidence of the strong not being victorious. Moreover, wresting military victory is not hard, but preserving it is! Only a ruler who has realized the Tao can hold onto victory. These rulers were all defeated because they failed to hold onto victory. Isn't this truly the case!

SAWYER This *Tao Te Ching* chapter provides key imagery summarily expressed in terms that have become watchwords throughout Chinese civilization, often shedding their origins to become misconstrued and misapplied in many realms. Wang Chen emphasizes the problems occasioned by the army's being too strong, thereby fating it to defeat, a theme that will reappear in his commentary to "The Pliant and Weak under Heaven." Since Warring States forces frequently exceeded 200,000, in the absence of modern communications, their sole recourse would have been rigid battle plans, strictly hierarchical control, and preassigned responsibilities that precluded the flexibility necessary to successfully cope with ever-evolving events.

However, even though the soft and pliant may well prevail over the strong and hard in individual life, particularly as the strong tend to become increasingly brittle and easily snapped, only the naive assume that the weak can invariably defeat the strong, as Wang Chen previously warned. (Chinese military theorists accordingly devised ways for the weak to overcome the strong—the very essence of maneuver warfare—but also realistically noted that only through flexibility might a weaker force contend with a significantly superior foe.) Temporary strength may also result from overstressed and overtrained forces whose spirits have been raised to such a pitch that they easily shatter with the least exhaustion and collapse at the first reversal, as history well attests. (These references to armies' being strong also have an underlying connotation of "weapons" being strong, in consonance with the term's derivation.)

The ancient military theorists repeatedly admonished commanders about the difficulty of sustaining the fruits of victory as well as the fatal exhaustion that numerous victories would entail. Moreover, following Sun-tzu's dictums, they cautioned against undertaking prolonged warfare of any kind because it could only enervate and impoverish the state. Many of the initially successful campaigns and great victories of the twentieth century may thus be seen as poignant evidence of their wisdom and the *Tao Te Ching*'s fundamental viewpoint that reversal is the essence of the Tao.

(An alternate translation for the first verse would be:

Alive, man is pliable and weak;
Dead, he is firm and strong.)

77

The Tao of Heaven

The Tao of Heaven is like tensioning a bow:
Repress the high and raise up the low;
Reduce the excessive and augment the insufficient.
The Tao of Heaven reduces the excessive and augments
   the insufficient,
But the Tao of man is not thus,
For men reduce the insufficient to support the excessive.
Who can have a surplus and thereby support All under
   Heaven?
Only one who has attained the Tao.
For this reason the Sage acts but doesn't rely,
Completes his achievements but does not dwell in them,
Not wanting to manifest his Worthiness.

WANG   The reason this chapter brings in the analogy of tensioning a bow lies precisely in the Tao of diminishing and augmenting. It asserts that if dukes and kings are able to know the essentials of diminishing and augmenting, of benefiting and harming, then All under Heaven will, by themselves, become equalized and tranquil. The *I Ching* asks, "With what does one gather men? It is called wealth. Imposing principles on wealth, making language correct, and prohibiting the people from acting incorrectly are termed righteousness." Moreover, farmers and weavers create wealth, but the army's soldiers destroy it. When few men create wealth while hordes destroy it, the already insufficient is reduced and the excessive supported. However, if you transform the soldiers into farmers, reducing those above and augmenting those below, naturally there will not be any cliques or parties, and the distribution of wealth would essentially equalize. Thus, the chapter observes, "Who can have a surplus and thereby support All under Heaven? Only one who has attained the Tao." This elucidates the *I Ching*'s idea about the righteousness of patterning wealth and correcting language in order to assist the people. Furthermore, although the Sage is able to change and transform yin and yang without relying upon his strength, and engender the myriad things without dwelling in the achievements, because he wants to obscure his Virtue and act clandestinely, he does not speak about those he benefits. Thus, the *Tao Te Ching* notes that he does "not want to manifest his Worthiness." "Manifesting one's worthiness" refers to exalting oneself and boasting of one's goodness.

SAWYER   Although the image of tensioning a bow is strikingly clear and easily understood, the actual process—namely, what is being reduced, what augmented—is not, despite speculation that it refers to the thickness of the staves, the balance of the string resulting from its tie points at the ends, or the curvature of the arms on a reflex bow itself. However, the principle is clearly applied in the next two lines, and the chapter develops in a coherent fashion that allows Wang Chen to envision it as a meditation on the creation and distribution of wealth, a crucial though hardly Taoist or Confucian theme. (Wang cites an unusual *I Ching* passage that encompasses critical methods for achieving the Confucian goal of righteousness—controlling wealth and what came to be known as the doctrine of the rectification of names. However, this probably reflects less his own orientation than a felt need to justify his views for his intended audience, the emperor and the latter's bureaucratic advisers.)

In turning his focus to warfare, Wang expands the incontrovertible point made earlier in "Assisting the Ruler with the Tao" that war destroys resources to subsume both direct casualties and the indirect removal of men from the productive labor and vital agricultural work that sustains the people and increases the state's wealth. Within this context, Sages are thus needed to rectify the tendencies to self-inflicted calamity and bring rationality to the world, changing and transforming it without becoming focal points themselves.

78

The Pliant and Weak Under Heaven

Under Heaven, there is nothing more pliant and weak
than water,
But for attacking the firm and strong nothing surpasses it,
Nothing can be exchanged for it.
The weak being victorious over the strong,
The pliant being victorious over the firm,
No one under Heaven is capable of knowing this,
No one capable of implementing it.
For this reason the Sage says,
"One who accepts the state's contamination is termed
Master of the altars of grain;
One who accepts the state's calamities is termed King of
All under Heaven."
Correct words seem contrary.

WANG   This chapter once again specially invokes the potential of water's pliancy and weakness to attack the firm and strong. I once tried to explain this by saying that according to the interrelationship of the five elements, earth is able to control water at its source, but in the extreme case, earth is found in water. Since water can bore through rock and float metal, there is nothing it does not conquer. The myriad streams pay court to the seas, the four seas pay court to the progenitor, so who would say the firm and strong can conquer water? Thus, the *Tao Te Ching* states, "Nothing can be exchanged for it." For this reason, Lao-tzu deeply regretted that all the people under Heaven were incapable of understanding its marvelous employment, of exerting themselves to exploit it. Thus, he says, "No one under Heaven is capable of knowing this, no one capable of implementing it." Thereafter, the chapter again cites what the Sage said about accepting the state's contamination and calamities, what is meant by any transgression of the hundred surnames lying with the ruler, the one man. Similarly, offenses anywhere accrue to him, the one man. If the king's mind can sincerely embrace this idea, what he actually says will seem upside down. Thus, the chapter concludes by saying that "correct words seem contrary."

SAWYER This pivotal chapter, well known for its first two lines, derives its power not just from the principle being expressed but also from the latter's juxtaposition with normal expectation. Who is not familiar with the "pliancy" and "flexibility" of liquids, especially water, in contrast to solids, as well as their ability to conform to any hard surface they encounter while flowing downward? From stories and reports, if not personal experience, virtually everyone in China would know well the devastating effects of flood and inundation, especially if they happened to dwell near the unpredictable Yellow River, and therefore water's potential power when massed in quantity. The clash between the two startles the reader because the softness and pliancy of water is not just able to circumvent the hard and inflexible but actually destroy it.

As a naked, unqualified principle, inherent problems remain, mainly derived from the requirement for quantity but also stemming from position, since water will not "run uphill." However, its tactical application was not confined to assaults on enemy camps or breaking dikes to inundate advancing forces, for it also grounds many techniques and theories in the individual martial arts. In the latter, the small and weak can sometimes (but not invariably) defeat the strong and belligerent by exploiting the latter's strength and tendency to imbalance and overextension, the inability to reverse and revert once committed. Similar risks mark massive, overly strong armies (as discussed in "Life of the People" and its commentary), while the principle even pertains to personality, character, and commanders.

In pondering the effects that quantity and movement impart to water, Wang Chen's commentary displays a reasoned approach to unspoken innate limitations on the weak and pliant overcoming the firm and strong. Moreover, he revisits the theme of the seas conquering the rivers earlier raised in "How Rivers and Seas Can Be Kings of the Hundred Valley Streams" in support, integrating it with the concept of deference, that voluntarily occupying the lowest terrain will lead to ultimate power as seen in "Great States Defer to the Flow" and other chapters as well.

79

Harmonizing
Great Rancor

When harmonizing great rancor,
There will certainly be remnant annoyance,
So how can one do good?
For this reason the Sage grasps the left tally
But does not upbraid others.
The virtuous control tallies;
The nonvirtuous control tracks.
The Tao of Heaven has no intimates;
It always associates with good men.

WANG   Now when Heaven gave birth to festering humanity, all the great desires were lodged in their minds. They fought for conquest, pursued profits, turned away from uprightness, and acted perversely. The greatest were mutual enemies; the least, mutually rancorous. Heaven, having compassion for them, established rulers to bring order. However, in rectifying their distress, remnant distress was still engendered, so how could they do good? Thus, the chapter asks, "How can one do good?" For this reason, the Sage maintains a heart of Virtue and trust, implements unspoken instructions, bespreads his beneficence over the Nine Regions, and pardons offenses throughout the myriad realms.

Now "tallies" emblemize virtue and trust, whereas auspicious affairs esteem the left. Irrespective of one's wisdom or stupidity, all are like infants in this. Thus, the chapter states, "He grasps the left tally but does not upbraid others." Now if the ruler does not transform All under Heaven with the Tao but instead orders them with punishments and leads them with government, he will be unable to fully realize the Tao of goodness. Thus, the chapter states, "The nonvirtuous control the tracks," whereby "tracks" refer to traces, meaning that the ruler clings to the traces of the rites and laws. Moreover, the *Tao Te Ching* also notes that if someone can long embody the Tao and rectify the state, the spirits of Heaven and Earth will certainly magnify his blessings and happiness. Thus, the chapter concludes, "The Tao of Heaven has no intimates; it always associates with good men."

SAWYER   Wang Chen's commentary provides a clear sense of the chapter's thrust, an admonition not to attempt to reconcile combatants or the disaffected but to focus upon mimicking the Tao of Heaven. In so doing, the ruler will eschew punishments in favor of Virtue, allowing the laws and rites—which impose obligations and set standards that, when violated, cry out for punishment—to fall into disuse. Thus the chapter employs the image of accepting the left tally, generally understood as the debtor's rather than creditor's, although Wang Chen, perhaps appropriately, expands the significance to a certain extent.

Somewhat more astonishing, Wang initiates his comments with the stark assertion that desire plagued humanity at its very birth, dramatically in contrast to the Taoist theory of devolvement previously elaborated in "The Great Tao Abandoned" and "Superior Virtue Is Not Virtuous." Moreover, Confucians generally attribute the creation of civilizing influences to the great Sages of antiquity, to such cultural progenitors as the Yellow Emperor and the Five Sage Emperors, including Yao and Shun. Here, in contrast, Heaven suddenly becomes active, even though it has expressly been characterized as not benevolent (in any constrained sense) in "Heaven and Earth Are Not Benevolent." The only resolution is Sagely rule, patterned on the Tao, actionless and quiescent, yet leaving nothing unaccomplished.

80

A Small State with Few People

Given a small state with few people—
Cause them to have military organizations of ten and a
*   hundred*
But not employ them,
And ensure the people value their deaths and do not
*   travel far off.*
Even though they have boats and wagons, they will then
*   have no place to ride them;*

Even though they have armor and weapons, they will then
have no place to deploy them.
Bring it about that the people revert to knotting ropes
and using them,
Make their food sweet,
Beautify their clothes,
Provide stability to their dwellings,
And make their customs pleasurable.
Then, although neighboring states look across at each other,
And the sounds of roosters and dogs be mutually heard,
Unto old age and death, the people will not travel back
and forth.

WANG   This chapter speaks about the Tao of rulership. Even with the strength of a large state, it is necessary to always make oneself humbly insignificant. Even with the strength of innumerable commoners, it is similarly necessary to always display solitary weakness.

Now one who makes himself humbly insignificant and avoids the error of boasting about his greatness will never neglect the Tao of humility and pliancy. One who manifests solitariness and weakness and lacks the worry of relying upon others will not neglect defensive preparations. Even if the state has leaders for every ten men, or captains for a hundred, they will similarly not be employed except when given birth by necessity. This being the case, every man will embrace and cherish his life, respect and value his death. When they are already settled amid their village lands, why would they want to travel or move far off? Moreover, when it's unnecessary to transport military rations, boats and wagons will be useless. When warfare has ceased, armor and weapons will not be deployed. People will then naturally attain great tranquillity, reverting to a simple form of government that employs knotted ropes rather than written documents. Thereafter, "make their food sweet and beautify their clothes" so that they will naturally rest in their allotments. "Provide stability to their dwellings and make their customs pleasurable" so that the winds of transformation will be implemented in timely fashion. Since abutting states will naturally not desire each other's possessions, deception and artifice will not be practiced. Moreover, as loyalty and good faith become treasures, their people will not be mutually solicitous, issue personal invitations, or undertake visits. Because they will not harbor any concealed deceptions, they will reject the ceremonies of mutual intercourse by themselves. Thus, the chapter concludes, "Even unto old age and death, the people will not travel back and forth."

SAWYER   Another of the *Tao Te Ching*'s core chapters, "A Small State with Few People" depicts an idyllic form of self-contained community life that must have been even highly appealing to those trapped in a world beset with the miseries of constant warfare and interminable suffering. (It continues to be, if not scrutinized too closely.) Although critics through the ages vociferously condemned one aspect or another—such as the inconvenience of abandoning transport equipment or the inhumaneness of rejecting human contact—reaction in this century has even extended to labeling it fascist and dictatorial, not to mention stifling and boring. Such criticism, of course, obscures the spirit of the central, pastoral vision expressed by many of the previous seventy-nine chapters, including "Do Not Esteem Worthies," emphasizing simplification, the essentials of life, and harmonizing with the Tao.

Although the chapter numbers among the *Tao Te Ching*'s most transparent, Wang Chen's commentary still provides a usefully integrated overview. Particularly noteworthy in both is the extant nature of military forces and organizations: they have not been discarded any more than boats and wagons; only their employment has been obviated. Thus even in this romanticized tranquillity, the people still require a deterrent force to be truly untroubled and preclude warfare's rearing its ugly head.

81

Credible Words
Are Not Beautiful

Credible words are not beautiful;
Beautiful words are not credible.
The good do not dispute;
Disputers are not good.
Wisdom is not eclectic;
Eclecticism is not wisdom.
Sages do not accumulate,
So they think they have an abundance
When what they have given to men is much greater.
The Tao of Heaven is to benefit, not harm;
The Tao of the Sage is to act, not contend.

WANG   This chapter, which summarizes the five thousand words that Lao-tzu personally wrote for transmission down through interminable ages and generations, clearly illuminates the sun and moon, the harmonizing Virtue of Heaven and Earth, and how the Vast Tao, preceding Heaven, gave birth to yin and yang. The Sage takes Earth as his model to determine the relative good points of Virtue and benevolence and discuss the weightiness and lightness of the rites and righteousness and thus rejects thin floweriness to dwell in thick substantiality. Accordingly, Lao-tzu breaks the discussion into three sections, wanting to illuminate it with paired principles. They come out from the same source but by different paths, so great circumspection is enjoined for both words and actions. The truly credible do not exert themselves in flattery and obsequiousness; do not boast of their skill in verbal jousting; lack unctuous and artful speech; and abjure crafty and decorous words. How, then, could their language be referred to as beautiful? Excelling at Virtue and speech is the Tao of Heaven. The Sage raises and implements them, so how could he allow sophistry and artifice to be spawned amid them?

Moreover, the chapter states that "Sages do not accumulate." This doesn't mean that the Sage doesn't accumulate anything but that when his wealth has accumulated, he can disperse it, when his Virtue has accumulated he can implement it. Thus the chapter subsequently says, "The Tao of Heaven is to benefit, not harm." So in the end, Lao-tzu wants to emphasize that the Sage imitates the Great Virtue of Heaven and Earth in assisting the patterns of unfolding life. Thus, the chapter reiterates, "The Tao of the Sage is to act, not contend."

Now the Sage values actionlessness, so why is it said here that he acts but does not contend? I believe that this chapter constitutes the ultimate one among the other eighty and that this single sentence is similarly the ultimate one among his five thousand words. Therefore we know that Lao-tzu's quintessential meaning lies here. The reason he doesn't discuss action and actionlessness but directly speaks about acting is that he wants rulers to act actionlessly. Moreover, he wants them to have nothing undone. His meaning is clear. When a family is not contentious, fighting and quarreling cease. When a state is not contentious, deployment for warfare ceases. When All under Heaven are not contentious, punitive campaigns cease. When fighting and quarreling cease in the family, military deployments cease in the states, and punitive expeditions cease throughout the realm, the Sage's principles will be realized. Thus, the *Tao Te Ching* states, "The Tao of the Sage is to act, not contend." This is what he means.

SAWYER The last chapter, in adopting the verbal tack of reversed but correlated pairs to startle the reader, echoes the book's initial verse, "The Tao that can be spoken of is not the ineffable Tao." Moreover, its final lines return to the concept of Heaven as beneficial (though according to previous chapters not necessarily benevolent, except in the most expanded sense) and conclude with the surprising assertion that

Index

Ability 89
Above 148, 234, 260, 261
Abstruse 58, 72, 73, 179
Abundant 192, 199, 272
Abysmal 81, 106
Abyss 109
Acceptance 56
Accord with 20, 232
Accumulate 93–95, 227, 228, 230, 272, 273
Achievement 12, 14, 42, 45, 54, 56, 57, 59, 61, 71, 74, 75, 77, 87, 88, 95, 104, 113, 117, 120, 125, 129, 137, 142, 147, 167, 171, 175, 178, 182, 183, 186, 196, 226, 238, 239, 242, 263, 264, 269
Act 64, 71, 74, 78, 79, 195, 227, 228, 261, 263, 272–274
Action 8, 22, 23, 28, 29, 41, 45, 55, 59–61, 67, 68, 70, 72, 81, 92, 96, 97, 129, 139, 160, 178, 179, 222, 249, 251, 259, 272
actionless (wu-wei) 8, 22, 23, 29, 32, 54, 55, 57, 59–61, 64–66, 72, 75, 76–78, 80, 81, 84, 90, 92, 96, 97, 107, 110, 119, 128, 148, 158–160, 164, 170, 174, 178, 183, 186, 188, 189, 198, 209, 210, 223–227, 254, 255, 269, 273, 274
inactive 2, 36, 54, 64, 81, 90, 91, 171, 186
Active 11, 17, 40, 51, 54, 83, 84, 112, 130, 131, 171, 178, 182–184, 258, 269
Activism 60, 65, 229
Activist 3
Administration 3, 89, 137, 174, 179
Admonition 5, 142
Advance 48, 109, 172, 173, 222, 239, 244, 245, 247
Advantages 72, 100, 138, 178
Affairs 14, 15, 25, 29, 53, 54, 57, 65–67, 89, 90, 113, 128, 133, 140, 145,156, 158, 170, 188, 189, 197, 202, 209, 224-228, 230, 240, 268

actionless 7, 50, 56, 74, 121, 170, 178, 241
Age 12, 202, 270–272
Aggressive 47, 194, 244–246
Agriculture 102, 200, 217, 264
All under Heaven 6, 9–12, 14, 18, 23, 25, 28–30, 33, 38–40, 46, 52, 54, 56, 61–65, 71, 73–75, 79, 83, 84, 86, 87, 98, 99, 103, 104, 106, 121, 125, 130, 131, 136–139, 150, 153, 154, 159, 167, 179, 183, 185–191, 196–198, 201, 202, 208–210, 216–218, 220, 222, 223, 234–238, 245, 253, 259, 263–265, 268
Allegiance 6, 14, 40, 45, 62, 87, 98, 113, 140, 151, 154, 175, 191, 217, 235, 238, 245
Alliances 10, 93, 150, 221
Alone 168
Altar 265
Ambition 26, 34, 35, 145, 146
Amorphous 14, 40, 47, 58, 107, 124, 155, 161, 175
An Lu-shan 3, 4
Analects 23, 79, 91, 92, 159, 202
Ancestor 11, 81, 82, 131, 148
Ancient 36, 125, 222, 233, 239
Anger 1, 5, 6, 10, 20, 26, 31, 51, 64, 75, 91, 105, 136, 194, 241, 242, 255, 257
Animals 5, 19, 74, 101, 203, 204
Annoyance 15, 16, 20, 51, 127, 252, 267
Anticipation 110
Antiquity 4, 11, 14, 15, 20, 35, 46, 51, 108, 110–114, 119, 123, 131, 138, 145, 165, 167, 202, 203, 223, 231, 241, 242, 269
Ants 232
Anxiety 37
Appearance 106
Apprehensive 108, 109
Armor 7, 15, 19, 22, 23, 32, 64, 75, 79, 83, 91, 92, 113, 121, 174, 191, 192, 193, 209, 218, 220, 225, 270
Arms 166, 247

Army 1, 4–7, 10, 20, 26, 27, 29, 30, 31, 33, 34, 41, 42, 44–47, 50, 51, 53, 63, 88, 90–92, 99–102, 108, 125, 128, 136, 139, 140, 142, 146, 150, 154–59, 168, 176, 179, 192, 193, 198, 204, 206–208, 212, 219, 228, 229, 237, 239, 244–247, 250, 251, 254, 257, 260, 261, 263, 266, 271
Arrogance 5, 42, 44, 46, 54, 93, 94, 103, 105, 109, 121, 129, 141, 142, 157, 177, 183, 221, 239, 252, 261
Arrows 33, 48, 99, 245
Art of War 72, 110, 135, 155, 177, 205
Artifice 15, 22, 24, 25, 60, 112, 114, 116, 118, 119, 166, 182, 209, 210, 233, 257, 271, 272
Associates 267, 268
Astonishment 104
Attack 6, 31, 48, 52, 100, 155, 226, 229, 239, 243, 244–247, 265, 266
Attentiveness 68, 227
Attraction 14
Augmentation 30, 53, 176, 204, 220, 222, 224, 263, 264
August Ones 63, 117, 164, 202, 237
Auspicious 34, 35, 43, 145, 204, 268
Authority 100, 117,158, 243
Awesome(ness) 10, 16, 31, 33, 82, 95, 99, 104, 126, 132, 136, 235, 242, 251–253, 257
Ax 74, 229, 241

Bad 18
Baleful 34, 35, 90, 140, 143–145, 146, 261
Bamboo 86
Bandits 229
Barbarians 87, 88, 150
Basis 216, 239
Battle 34, 51, 88, 99, 126, 134, 150, 179, 182, 205, 208, 211, 221, 240, 241, 243
Battleground 6, 206, 243
Beak 74
Bears 101

Beauty 18, 60, 73, 76, 116, 117, 270, 272
Beginning 45, 46, 66–68, 70, 73, 107, 123, 134, 137, 147, 148, 151, 157, 159, 164, 197, 198, 208, 212, 227, 228, 230
Behavior 5, 127, 222
Behind 234, 237
Being 18, 32, 33, 66, 71, 87, 99, 107, 170, 171, 227, 228
Belligerent 266
Bellows 83, 84
Belly 19, 22, 23, 64, 79, 102
Below 148, 234, 260, 261
Benefactor 231
Beneficence 14, 56, 83, 113, 147, 153, 205, 239, 268
Beneficial 49, 89, 92, 152, 159, 160, 254
Benefit(s) 15, 21, 25, 32, 50, 57, 60, 72, 75, 77, 99, 113, 118, 119, 159, 183, 189, 193, 196, 198, 214, 215, 235, 238, 263, 264, 272–274
Benevolence 6, 14, 21, 22, 25, 38–40, 60, 83, 84, 87–90, 92, 113, 115, 116, 118, 132, 134, 148, 149, 157, 158, 164–166, 174, 191, 202, 203, 214, 216, 217, 226, 252, 269, 272
Bespreading 172, 175, 175
Beyond 11
Birds 19, 74, 111, 141, 203, 204
Birth 4, 55, 96, 98, 153,170, 175, 177, 195, 196, 264, 267, 269, 270, 273
Bite 203
Black 9, 73, 136
Blade 82, 192, 193, 204
Blessings 21, 53, 119, 156, 157, 218, 232, 268
Blindness 19, 101
Block 197, 207
Blow 119
Boast 3, 17, 18, 26, 32, 42, 78, 87, 91, 95, 109, 121, 125, 129, 140–143, 152, 183, 199, 200, 252, 264, 270, 272
Body 10, 20, 36, 37, 43, 76, 87, 101–104, 111, 122, 136, 180, 181, 185, 197, 201, 204, 234, 239, 245, 253,
Bones 22, 23, 64, 78, 79, 203
Border 1, 3, 4, 246
Bottom 138
Bowl 99
Bows 33, 99, 263, 264

Brambles 140, 185
Branch 5, 229
Break 144, 260
Breath 97, 189
Bridge 143
Brigade 58, 71
Brigand 18, 20–22, 24–26, 79, 91, 102, 118, 200, 209, 210, 223, 231, 232
Bright 120, 125, 193, 197, 198, 214, 249
Brittle 54, 66, 67, 227, 228, 230, 262
Brothers 30, 202, 259
Brutal 26, 28, 44, 91, 141, 170, 245, 247, 261,
Buddhism 2
Bureaucracy 24
Bureaucrats 3, 117, 187, 211

Calamity 29, 34, 38, 54, 93, 94, 112, 137, 139, 142, 165, 176, 184, 185, 196, 214, 226, 264–266
Calculation 45, 109, 134, 151
Camp 93, 185, 266
Campaign (military) 7, 21, 61, 100, 185, 221, 232, 243, 262, 273
Captain 32, 243, 270
Capture 243
Carpenter 256
Casualties 1, 3, 34, 35, 143
Cautious 53, 109, 110, 139, 157, 177, 208, 225, 230
Cavalry 101
Cessation 99, 148
Change 66, 71, 84, 117, 212, 226, 264
Chao 28, 141
Chao Kao 28, 141, 142
Chaos 3, 5, 7, 16, 23, 26, 30, 40, 66, 79, 90, 164–166, 239, 259
Chaotic 26, 91, 165, 210, 227, 228
Characters (Chinese) 4, 99, 100
Chariot 32, 33, 98, 99, 121, 132, 242
Ch'eng, King 237
Chieh, Emperor 63, 227, 228
Child 9, 81, 120, 136, 137, 190, 191, 238–240
Ching, Emperor 237, 238
Ch'i 43, 58, 70, 82, 85, 86, 96, 97, 123, 124, 136, 137, 159, 160, 176–178, 89, 193, 194, 204–206, 219

Ch'in 28, 141, 150, 221
Ch'in Shih-huang 44, 142, 237, 261
Chou 4, 150, 165, 202, 237, 238
Ch'u 150, 221
Chuang-tzu 175, 181, 243
Circle 240
Circumspection 234, 235
City 24, 29, 30, 91, 176, 197, 243
Civil, the 5, 75, 146, 188, 189, 241
Civilization 3, 24
Clans 30, 259
Clarity 168
Close 134, 192, 207
Clumsy 182, 183
Claws 19, 74, 192
Clay 32, 98
Clear 90, 108, 109, 167, 174, 183
Cleaving 10, 108–110, 136, 137, 159, 197
Clothes 17, 199, 240, 270
Clunk 168
Coercion 10, 94, 140, 164, 182, 223, 257
Cold 54, 182–184, 225, 254
Colors 19, 36, 101, 122, 198, 199, 212
Combat 2, 5–7, 26, 27, 46, 51, 61, 74, 91, 100, 125, 144, 151, 169, 194, 205, 206, 212, 241–243, 247, 255, 261, 268
Come 254, 255
Command 3, 4, 155, 179, 206, 213, 240, 241
Commanders 3, 42, 51, 72, 94, 138, 143, 145, 147, 155, 238, 266
Compassion 43, 49, 204, 238, 268
Completion 11, 18, 50, 74, 108, 109, 130, 168, 172, 174, 175, 196, 227–229, 239
Compliant 23, 128
Comprehend 186, 248, 249
Concealed 72, 249
Concept 18, 20, 23, 72, 76, 124, 155
Conflict 2, 4, 26, 44, 45, 60, 76, 80, 122, 134, 171, 194, 196, 249, 261, 273
cessation of 8, 12, 84, 90, 122, 273, 274
origins of 7, 18, 22, 26, 27, 30, 74, 79, 80, 83, 84, 91
Conflagration 230

276   INDEX

Confucian 1–4, 36, 38, 40, 54, 73, 77, 80, 88, 89, 92, 97, 114-116, 121, 126, 140, 141, 149, 151, 158, 160, 166, 174, 187, 202, 216, 223, 224, 233, 255, 258, 260, 264, 269

Confucius 1–4, 12–14, 21, 22, 25, 28, 31, 84, 92, 158, 166, 173, 187, 211

Confusion 37, 81, 82, 116, 180, 207

Conquest 32, 49, 50, 51, 71, 100, 149, 150, 151, 158, 178, 185, 221, 235, 240, 241, 243, 254, 255, 268

Constant 111, 197, 204

Constraint 26, 27, 53, 119, 157, 192, 247, 252

Contamination 10, 97, 136, 173, 265, 266

Contemplation 9

Contention 7, 23, 27, 60, 78, 92, 168, 169, 175, 196, 254
cessation 174, 254

Contentment 37, 38, 184, 185

Continuous 106

Contrary 20, 26, 42, 43, 67, 91, 204, 205, 232, 265, 266

Contrast 74

Control 62, 66, 96, 97, 155, 221, 227, 228, 249, 262

Corner 172, 173

Correction 10, 265, 266

Cosmogony 4, 11, 30, 72, 123, 130, 168, 171, 176, 177, 272

Cosmology 2, 7, 68, 72

Cosmos 11, 12, 128, 130,

Courage 26, 49, 50, 62, 91, 101, 189, 236, 237, 240, 246, 253-255, 258

Court 17, 102, 117, 199,

Crack 167, 168

Credibility 224, 225, 272

Crime 16, 20

Crooked 43, 124, 137, 204

Crux 250

Cultivate 201, 202

Culture 3, 4, 24, 116, 146, 269

Curved 42, 50, 124, 125, 142, 169, 182, 183

Customs 214, 270

Cutting 213, 214

Daggers 10, 17, 94

Dances 48, 245

Danger 5, 29, 37, 67, 111, 148, 180, 182, 194, 197–199, 205, 228, 239, 242

Dank 5, 15, 55, 207, 208

Dankly Mysterious 70, 71, 73, 85, 86, 96, 97, 108, 110, 195, 196, 231

Daring 49, 50, 62, 189, 236, 237, 244, 253–257

Dark 10, 71, 72, 81, 123, 137, 172, 173, 214, 249

Day 101, 206

Deaf 19, 101

Death 15, 17, 25, 30, 32, 37, 43, 44, 51, 85, 98, 114, 126, 150, 176, 180, 182, 192–194, 206, 210, 212, 215, 223, 224, 242, 243, 255–257, 259, 260, 262, 269–271

Debilitating 160, 180

Decay 18,

Deception 15, 16, 20, 114, 175, 211, 213, 231, 232, 257, 271

Declination 74

Deep 156, 157, 216

Defeat 26, 28, 30, 33, 43, 45, 49, 66, 72, 91, 104, 105, 135, 139, 152, 157, 176, 183, 212, 213, 227, 228, 230, 232, 241-245, 251, 260, 262

Defects 45, 133

Defense 39, 45, 47, 62, 64, 134, 155, 208, 216, 236, 238, 240, 244–247, 270

Deference 2, 31, 46–48, 52, 75, 92, 149, 220, 221, 226, 234, 235, 241–244, 247, 267

Deficient 167, 182, 183, 213, 238

Delusion 112, 125, 113, 135, 213, 214, 252

Demon 86

Deployment 6, 31, 45, 48, 244, 245, 247, 270

Depressed 124

Description 11,

Designation 11

Desire 1, 2, 5, 6, 9, 18–20, 22, 23, 29, 36, 37, 56, 57, 64, 67, 77–80, 102, 112, 119, 121, 122, 152, 153, 158–161, 171, 181, 183, 185, 190, 200, 215, 227, 228, 235, 254, 256, 267, 269, 271
effects 19, 20, 25, 38
reduction 19, 21, 80, 118, 119, 188, 192, 220

Desireless 57, 209, 210

Desist 93

Destruction 1, 141, 148, 177, 198, 243, 263

Deterrent 271

Detest 14, 113,

Devolution 14, 15, 24, 25, 113, 114, 116, 119, 164–166, 210, 269

Difficult 18, 65, 66, 74, 105, 138, 224–226, 254, 258

Dike 143

Dim 120

Diminish 5, 21, 30, 43, 64, 118, 119, 176, 188, 220, 263

Direction 11, 131

Directness 21, 213

Disaster 1, 7, 10, 28, 29, 38, 48, 49, 66, 90, 104, 105, 111, 112, 142, 168, 176, 185, 215, 226, 244, 245

Disciples 257, 260

Discipline 6, 31

Disgrace 10, 36, 87, 103, 104, 136, 137, 173, 180, 181, 213, 253

Disharmony 82, 116

Disorder 18, 21, 36, 40, 64, 80, 95, 101, 245, 257,
causes 20, 21, 23–25, 95

Dispersion 11, 109, 131, 273

Dispute 272

Distant 11, 67, 130, 207, 208, 228

Distress 5, 268

Documents, Book of 28, 35, 141, 245, 252, 254, 255

Doctrine of the Mean 140, 202

Dog 83, 270

Dominate 220

Door 32, 71, 99, 186, 192

Doubt 67, 112, 190, 228, 240

Dragon 4, 101

Drink 154, 199

Drought 28, 142

Dry 44, 168, 229

Dull 81, 207

Dusky 120, 121

Dust 81, 82, 173, 193, 207

Dwell 252, 260, 263, 264, 270

Dynasty 6, 202

Ear 19, 101, 110, 190, 191

Earth 4, 10–12, 23, 40, 53, 58–60, 66, 67, 70, 71, 73, 78, 83, 85–87, 92, 96, 97, 106, 117, 123, 127, 130, 131, 141, 147, 148, 156, 159, 167, 168, 170, 173, 176, 186, 189, 196, 218, 227, 228, 265, 268, 269, 272, 273

Earthquake 196
Ease 168
Easy 18, 65, 66, 71, 72, 74, 75, 105, 106, 199, 224–226
Echo 18, 254, 256
Eclectic 272
Edicts 24, 209, 210
Effort 14, 84
Elixir 194
Emptiness 10, 86, 88, 99
Emotion 19, 74, 77, 88, 95, 116, 155, 194, 220, 242, 257
Emotionless 102
Empire 237
Emulation *See* Modeling
Endure 36, 37, 39, 40, 87, 111, 112, 150, 151, 158, 180, 204, 216, 247
Enemies 30, 35, 44, 48, 49, 52, 90, 93, 99, 100, 105, 126, 145, 152, 176, 179, 205, 208, 212, 240, 241, 243–249, 266, 268
Enervate 205
Elimination 22
Emaciated 139
Embody 198, 203, 205, 223, 241, 245, 250, 268
Emblem 47, 154, 172, 174
Embrace 201, 202
Emperor 3, 63, 82, 105, 114, 117, 141, 150, 187, 202, 222, 264, 269
Employment 169, 170, 182, 239, 241, 242, 269
Empty 136, 199
Encompassing 111
End 45, 66–68, 107, 109, 134, 151, 157, 212, 227, 228, 230
Endangered 29, 112, 180, 189
Energy 248
Enigma 251
Enlightened 53, 111, 129, 134, 149, 150, 151, 156, 170, 172, 173, 204, 218, 231, 252
Entangled 228
Envision 43
Ephemeral 124
Equanimity 34, 35, 47, 145, 147, 154, 172, 173
Error 10, 19, 101, 137, 147, 242, 251
Essence 7, 43, 123, 174, 189, 204, 218
Essential 135, 142
Estrangement 96, 136, 189
Ethereal(ity) 9, 15, 47, 70, 85, 106, 108, 110, 125, 134, 135, 148, 154, 193, 219

Eternal 59, 119, 153, 158, 160, 181, 223
Evil 2, 5, 6, 10, 21, 31, 36, 46, 67, 76, 88, 100, 104, 120, 121, 136, 147, 165, 191, 204, 219, 223, 232, 237, 257,
Excel 42, 201, 231, 234, 241–243. 254, 255
Excess 18, 101, 102, 109, 139, 188, 194, 199, 200, 263, 266
Execution 256, 257, 258
Exemplification 23, 75, 79, 84, 167, 178, 179, 183, 185
Exhaustion 5, 43, 105, 108, 109, 124, 144, 167, 168, 179, 183, 204, 212, 257, 262
Existence 14, 57, 123, 177, 181, 244, 245
Expansive 50, 62, 63, 83, 108, 111, 131, 172, 173, 236, 237, 254, 255
Expenditure 28, 141
Extensive 201, 231, 232
Extinction 2, 9, 15, 44, 167, 189, 198, 245, 261,
Extravagant 9, 10, 54, 102, 139, 185, 217
Extremity 41, 95, 128, 139, 140, 152, 171, 213, 214, 241
Evanescent 108
Eye 19, 101, 102, 110, 190, 191

Failure 67, 151, 228, 230
Fame 36, 37, 94, 180, 181, 185
Family 2, 24, 26, 30, 35, 61, 91, 201, 202, 214, 238, 245, 259, 73
Famine 27, 144, 258, 259
Farmers 30, 259
Fast 247
Fatal 236
Fate (destiny) 47, 71, 111, 155, 159, 210, 254, 261
Fathers 30, 191, 259
Favor 36, 87, 103, 104, 181, 213, 253
Favorites 26, 91
Fear 14–16, 46, 108, 109, 113, 120, 194, 199, 210, 223, 224, 242, 251–253, 256, 257,
Feast 120, 121, 154
Feminine 9, 10, 52, 85, 86, 96, 123, 136, 204, 220, 221
Feudal Lords 10, 11, 19, 26, 53, 59, 71, 90, 91, 93, 94, 103, 104, 112, 117, 131, 132,

142, 150, 155, 157, 159, 167, 168, 176, 196, 199, 222, 245, 252, 263
Few 65, 102, 125, 225, 239, 269
Fields 17, 37, 38, 184, 185, 199,
Filiality 21, 22, 116, 118, 148
Fill 93
Fines 15, 63, 83, 191, 217, 222, 237, 252
Firm 44, 144, 178, 179, 212, 240, 260, 265–267
First 236, 237
Fishing 25, 53, 61, 156, 157, 210, 218
Fissure 167, 168
Five Elements 166, 265
Five Emperors 23, 78, 165, 237
Flame 230
Flavors 19, 101, 212
Flood 34
Flourishing 67, 156, 201, 228
Flow 138, 220, 267
Flower 164
Flux 128
Food 17, 129, 154, 196, 199, 240, 247, 265, 270
Foot 48, 66, 74, 109, 227, 247
Follow 74, 139
Forces 9, 48, 52, 58, 140, 146, 177, 203, 208, 246, 262, 266, 271
Form 106, 107, 171, 251
Formless 45, 155, 174, 208, 248
Fortifications 93, 184, 185, 240
Fortune, Good 21, 137–139, 213–215, 232, 240
Foundation 39, 60, 90, 168, 216, 218, 228, 229, 249
Four Quarters 96, 111
Four Seas 26, 44, 91, 117, 261
Fragile 44, 260
Fragmentation 3
Freedom 40, 122, 232
Friend 148
Front 18, 74, 234
Frugality 39, 62, 63, 189, 215, 216, 236, 237, 241
Fu Chien 44, 261
Full 53, 108, 109, 124, 156, 167, 168, 182, 183
Funeral 89

Gain 36, 37, 103, 125, 138, 180, 196, 215, 243
Gap 178, 179
Gate 70, 84, 96, 97, 192, 197, 207
Generals 17, 28, 34, 44, 90, 105, 110, 141, 142, 145, 146, 155, 199, 206, 239–241, 243, 261
Ghost 53, 156, 218, 219
Giving 37, 156, 180
Glory 10, 34, 35, 109, 136, 137, 145, 185, 241
Gluttony 17
Gold 93, 94, 181, 182
Good, the 18, 21, 25, 31, 65, 74, 76, 89, 92, 120, 121, 165, 190, 191, 202, 267, 268
Goodness 96, 213, 214, 223, 259, 264, 268
Goods 17, 19, 20, 23, 36, 37, 151, 180, 181, 199, 227
Governing 12–14, 16, 20, 21, 23, 25, 32, 36, 38, 39, 46, 51, 53, 57, 58, 61, 62, 64, 68, 71, 75, 78, 89, 96, 97, 104, 106, 107, 113, 114, 117, 128, 156, 157, 165, 174, 187, 189, 191, 198, 211, 215, 216, 218, 219, 223, 229, 231, 234, 245, 238, 241, 252, 253, 258–260, 270, 271
Government 3, 4, 6, 7, 9, 11, 14–18, 20, 22, 24, 36, 47, 57, 64, 73, 80, 102, 112, 115, 159–161, 174, 183, 188, 191, 196, 198, 203, 209–219, 223, 253, 257, 255, 259, 268
Grace 37
Grain 265
Granaries 17, 199
Grasp 48, 49, 53, 62, 65, 66, 93, 156, 174, 201, 203, 225, 227, 228, 244, 245, 249, 256, 257, 267, 268
Grasses 44, 260
Great 1, 56, 65–67, 130, 131, 152, 153, 168, 170, 173, 175, 198, 220, 224, 225, 228, 229, 245, 260, 261, 267
Great Learning 202
Great Wall 141
Greed 1, 5, 6, 9, 18, 31, 37, 182, 184
Grief 35, 48, 49, 145, 241,

244, 246
Guest 48, 108, 109, 154, 244, 246–248

Halberd 19, 29, 30, 35, 40, 48, 67, 74, 88, 100, 112, 139, 145, 148, 189, 191, 200, 222, 228, 245,259
Hall 93
Han Dynasty 8
Han Fei-tzu 76, 77, 182, 187, 193, 215, 223, 239, 255
Han Wu-ti 63, 237
Hand 74, 256, 257
Handles 5, 158
Happiness 20, 64, 75, 217, 268
Hard 52, 53, 144, 156, 177, 178, 262
Hardship 66, 124, 139
Harm 15, 26, 37, 49, 50, 53, 55, 60, 61, 75, 81, 90, 92, 97, 98, 102, 104, 111, 117, 141, 156, 159, 180, 189, 192, 193, 198, 202, 204, 205, 207–9, 218, 219, 232–234, 254, 256, 257, 263, 272–274
Harmony 20, 22, 31, 40, 43, 54, 59, 72, 74, 81, 100, 116, 119, 148, 160, 176, 191, 194, 202, 204, 205, 207, 218, 219, 231, 232, 267, 271, 274
Hatred 19, 26, 35, 64, 74, 75, 89, 91, 176, 187, 254, 255, 257
Head 106, 107
Hear 47, 97, 101, 105, 106, 172, 173, 183, 212, 270
Heart 46, 114, 151, 241
Heat 182–184, 254
Heaven 4, 10–12, 23, 28, 34, 35, 38–41, 49–51, 53, 58–64, 67, 70–73, 78, 83, 85–87, 92, 93, 96, 97, 103, 105, 106, 111, 112, 117, 123, 127, 130, 131, 137, 145–149, 151, 154, 156, 159, 160, 167, 168, 170, 173, 174, 176, 178, 179, 189, 190, 196, 207, 208, 212, 215, 216, 218, 228, 231, 232, 235, 236–238, 241, 243, 245, 249, 252, 254–258, 265–269, 272–274
Heavy 132
Hegemon 23, 44, 46, 78, 105, 117, 150, 151, 261,
Hero 10

Hesitate 108, 109
Hew 256, 257
Hexagram 4, 177
High 18, 74, 167, 168, 262
Hill 229
Ho-lü, King 243
Hoarding 36, 93, 94, 95, 180, 199
Honor 10, 103, 207, 208
Hope 139
Horns 192
Horses 19, 37, 38, 101, 132, 184, 185, 222, 223
Host 48, 109, 244, 246–248
Hsia 44, 63, 165, 202, 237, 261
Hsiang Yü 44, 63, 150, 237, 261
Hsin 44
Hsüan 73
Hsün-tzu 80
Hu Hai 141
Huai-nan Tzu 76
Huang-shih Kung 116
Hub 98
Human 18, 84, 89
Human Nature 10, 13, 19, 26, 29, 91–93, 119, 137, 171, 214, 269
Humble 7, 46, 51, 53, 79, 94, 104, 121, 127, 178, 183, 193, 244, 270
Humility 2, 9, 31, 32, 52, 53, 121, 133, 156, 169, 177, 220, 234, 235, 270
Hundred 269, 270
Hundred Surnames 14, 64, 75, 83, 113, 134, 189–191, 245, 256, 266
Hunger 17, 30, 85, 219, 257, 258
Hunting 19, 25, 31, 101, 102, 193, 210
Husband 148

I Ching 4, 31, 171, 177, 221, 259, 263
Ice 108, 109, 173
Ignorance 20, 41, 112, 174, 184, 250
Illness 10, 41, 91, 136, 250, 251
Illustrious 125, 129
Image 4, 106, 107, 123, 131, 261
Imageless 131
Impediment 112
Imminence 148
Immoral 16, 213

Immortality 85
Impartial 111
Imperceptible 14, 47, 105, 106, 107
Imperfections 96
Implements 27, 33, 35, 44, 53, 62, 144–146, 156–158, 209, 210, 236, 248, 249, 261
Implementing 265, 266
Imponderable 107
Impositions 63, 75, 148, 239
Impoverished 209
Inactive 3, 22, 23, 54, 58, 76, 79, 81
Inch 109, 244
Incipient 66, 171, 198, 226, 230
Increase 29, 188, 202
Incursion 3, 99
Indistinct 105, 106, 123, 124
Ineffable 3, 15, 40, 70, 107, 171, 175, 208, 223, 238, 250, 273
Inexhaustible 11, 47, 81, 83, 120, 131, 154, 155, 182, 212
Infant 42, 43, 96, 120–122, 144, 194, 203, 206, 268
Infantry 48
Inferior 75, 168, 221, 238
Inhumanity 22
Insects 19, 174, 175, 203, 204
Inescapable 255
Insight 96, 97
Insignificant 236
Instability 95
Instruction 5, 7, 30, 74, 176, 213, 231
   unspoken 50, 74–76, 178, 179, 235, 241, 254, 268
Insubstantial 224, 225
Insufficiency 46, 47, 120, 154, 172, 174, 175, 188, 200, 250, 263
Insult 252
Intelligence 16, 213
   military 100, 187, 203
Intentions 22, 23, 64, 78, 79, 96, 194, 255,
Interdictions 24, 209, 210
Intervention 3
Intimates 267, 268
Intrusive 213
Intuitive 116
Invasion 27, 31, 32, 245–247
Isolation 249

Jade 93, 94, 168, 222, 223, 249
Joy 214
Journey 66, 67, 227, 228

Jumble 106, 107, 123, 124
K'ang, King 237
Kill 34, 35, 42, 49, 50, 100, 101, 142, 145, 193, 242, 253–257 King 6, 11, 12, 15, 19, 23, 26, 33, 39, 46, 53, 58, 59, 71, 72, 74, 78, 83, 90, 91, 94, 101, 103–105, 111–113, 117, 130, 131, 145, 159, 154, 157, 159, 165–168, 176, 188, 196, 197, 199, 202, 216, 218, 220, 225, 234, 241, 245, 252, 257, 263, 266, 267
Knights 30, 259
Knot 45, 134, 270
Know 14, 18, 136, 149, 179, 186, 223, 252,
Knowing 41, 113, 148, 152, 231, 250, 251, 265, 266
Knowledge 21, 23, 40, 41, 56, 72, 78–80, 96, 97, 112, 116, 119-122, 152, 174, 175, 185, 187, 189, 198, 199, 207, 232, 249, 250
   eliminating 22, 120, 121
   self 104
Kuei Ku-tzu 86

Land 143, 192, 270
Language 5, 15, 114, 263
Languid 120
Lao-tzu 5–8, 10, 18, 19, 25, 29, 30, 33, 35, 41, 48–50, 58–60,68, 71, 82, 84, 90, 96, 99, 102, 107, 109, 118, 119, 121, 123, 125, 128, 129, 131, 133, 134, 136, 137, 139, 145, 148, 157, 159, 165, 168, 173, 176, 178, 179, 183, 193, 200, 204, 209, 229, 232, 234, 236, 244, 246–250, 252, 254, 259, 265, 272
Large 225
Last 236
Late 172, 173, 229
Laughter 172–174
Laws 16, 24, 26, 91, 92, 188, 209–211, 223, 233, 240, 268
Lax 254
Leader 236
Leaves 5
Left 5, 34, 35, 55, 144, 145, 152, 153, 267, 268,
Legalist 3, 114, 182, 223
Li, King 237
Li Chi 88
Li Ching 246
Li Ssu 28, 42, 141, 142,

Licentious 26, 54, 91, 260
Life 15, 16, 32, 37, 43, 44, 87, 98, 104, 108. 109, 114, 128, 181, 192–194, 204, 206, 217, 239, 252, 255–260, 270–273
Light 132
Limb 192, 241
Lock 45, 134
Long 18, 74
Longevity 39, 54, 150, 151, 157, 160, 181, 192, 216
Loss 36, 37, 59, 60, 66, 103, 127, 128, 138, 180, 227, 228, 245, 254, 255
Love 6, 19, 21, 22, 26, 31, 36, 49, 56, 64, 74–76, 91, 96, 97, 100, 113, 116, 118, 126, 150, 153, 165, 180, 187, 204, 216, 217, 241, 242, 246, 252
Low 18, 74, 168, 235, 262
Lowest 14
Lowly 10, 53, 221
Loyalty 23, 49, 79, 116, 148, 164, 165, 246, 271
Lucid 120
Luo River 4

Madness 19, 101,
Man 58, 70, 127, 131, 151, 245
   common 6, 26, 30, 71, 91, 120, 122, 127, 173, 208
   perfected (chün-tzu) 35, 91, 126, 132, 144–146
Maneuver 47, 211
Manifest 70, 125, 126, 129, 152, 163
   non-manifestation 104, 112
Manipulate 126, 156
Mantra 194
Many 65, 125, 180, 224, 225, 239
Mao Tze-dong 142, 143
Market 194
Marsh 25, 210
Martial 4, 5, 34, 48, 51, 65, 75, 99, 100, 135, 141, 142, 146, 152, 188, 189, 194, 225, 241, 242, 245, 260, 274
Masculine 9, 52, 86, 119, 123, 136, 204, 220, 221
Masses 7, 12, 20, 21, 34, 101, 112, 120, 121, 134, 145, 232, 257, 270
Massacre 28
Master 41, 56, 87, 153, 155, 196, 247, 249, 265
Meanness 167, 168, 207, 208

Measure 16, 186, 188, 189, 224
Melancholy 120
Men 11–13, 23, 26, 34, 45, 46, 50, 51, 67, 72, 78, 120, 134, 142, 149, 151, 176, 187, 200, 202, 213, 228, 241, 264, 267, 268, 270, 272
employing 51, 137
knowing 151
Mencius 13, 76, 88, 100, 185, 202, 217
Meng T'ien 28, 141
Metal 93
Metaphysics 7, 9, 51, 72
Middle 45
Militarism 9, 199, 257, 274
Military 6, 14, 31, 42, 55, 92, 117, 135, 138, 151, 186, 189, 209, 211, 238, 244, 269
affairs 48, 57, 61, 67, 79, 97, 107, 109, 177, 183, 210, 228, 259, 260
employment 7, 41, 48, 104, 109, 142–144, 206
objectives 42, 142, 164, 174
writings 3, 4, 13, 47, 98, 100, 104, 105, 109, 116, 126, 138, 143, 151, 157, 182, 194, 205, 212, 217, 229, 238, 242, 247, 251, 262
Military Methods 306, 246
Mind 19, 20, 22, 23, 25, 29, 43, 49, 64, 78, 79, 82, 89, 90, 96, 102, 120, 122, 137, 151, 160, 189, 190, 191, 204–206, 213, 225, 239, 246, 256, 266, 267
Ministers 17, 28, 71, 78, 88, 116, 117, 132, 133, 141, 199, 245
Minute 65, 66, 110, 148, 193, 198, 224–228
Misery 17, 20, 36, 37, 55, 81, 87, 103, 181, 185, 259
Misfortune 37, 38, 44, 47, 65, 87, 98, 103, 104, 137, 138, 157, 184, 185, 196, 197, 213–215, 225, 226, 240, 261
Mo-tzu 76
Model 10, 12, 125, 130, 136, 137, 154, 196, 202, 232, 254, 272
Modeling 11, 130, 173, 231, 249, 254
Moment 5, 45, 65, 66, 171, 180, 225, 226, 230
Month 101
Moon 5, 60, 71, 212, 272
Morality 213

Morning 127, 173
Morose 16, 23, 214, 223
Mother 11, 39, 70, 73, 120–122, 130, 131, 174, 191, 197, 216, 240
Motivation 1, 62, 117, 126, 144, 223, 242
Motive 1, 4
Mountain 20, 101, 232, 246
Mourning 145, 206, 241
Mouth 19, 85, 101
Movement 26, 45, 47, 65, 85, 89, 90, 95, 108, 109, 133, 134, 139, 140, 169, 170, 178, 192, 211, 223, 247, 267
Mud 108, 109, 190, 191, 209, 210
Mundane 8, 9, 51, 58, 112, 219, 235
Murky 106, 120
Music 24, 154
Mysterious 2, 15, 58, 71, 73, 178

Name 11, 19, 70, 72–74, 106, 107, 123, 130, 147, 148, 174, 197, 264
Nameless 70, 131, 172, 174
Nature 11, 71, 161, 189, 257
Natural 12, 59, 68, 130, 186, 227, 229, 230, 255
Near 67, 208, 228
Nebulous 58, 106, 107, 123
Necessary 6, 102
Negative 92
Neighbor 108, 109, 259, 270, 271
Neo-Confucian 124
Neo-Taoist 95, 191, 243
Net 254, 255, 257
New 125
Night 173
Nihilism 2, 9, 13, 92
Nine Li 237
Nine Regions 44, 261, 268
Noble 93, 94, 167, 221
Non-contention 2, 7, 26, 33, 34, 36, 46, 47, 49, 50–52, 54, 61, 90–92, 125, 126, 194, 225, 226, 234, 235, 241, 242, 255, 257, 272–274
Non-being 18, 32, 33, 70, 71, 73, 74, 86, 98, 99, 107, 123, 170, 171
Nondesire 159
None 249
Non-existence 123, 178, 179
Nose 97
Notes 18, 19, 74, 101, 172, 174, 212

Nothing 64, 67, 158, 188, 189
Numinous 58, 70, 167, 168, 176, 218
Nurture 4, 55–57, 74, 96, 97, 111, 120–122, 148, 153, 154, 168, 176, 191, 192–196, 220, 222, 238, 239, 259

Obfuscation 110, 264
Objects 106, 107
Obscurity 73, 110, 175, 222
Obsession 190, 191
Obstinate 120
Ocean 148, 149, 235
Odes, Book of 28, 141, 212
Officers 15, 64, 71, 75, 108, 110, 117, 131, 138, 172, 173, 183, 199, 238–240, 252
Officials 10, 23, 26, 78, 91, 136, 186, 217, 245
Old 42, 43, 141, 142, 144, 204, 205, 270, 271
One 11, 30, 46, 106, 107, 123, 125, 131, 167–169, 175, 177, 227, 254, 263
Open 134, 192, 197
Orders 10, 78, 79, 93, 117, 243, 268
Organization 90
Orifice 192, 197, 207
Origin 70, 235
Origination 11, 81, 110, 111, 159
Orphan 176
Oppressive 260
Orthodox 3, 211, 212
Other 19, 74, 249
Overthrow 139, 168

Pacifism 2, 92
Pai Ch'i 28, 42, 141, 142
Pain 15, 36, 181
Palace 63, 101, 217, 237
Pao Hsi 4
Parents 191, 238, 239
Path 199, 240
Pattern 12, 13 (ck), 40, 54, 58, 59, 70, 72, 84, 109, 111, 153, 159, 177, 187, 240, 252, 255, 264, 269
Peace 2, 58, 72, 88, 100, 117, 121
Penetration 4, 15, 58, 97, 108, 110, 170, 179
Penultimate 14, 113
People 5, 6, 14–20, 22–24, 31, 33, 38, 39, 43, 45, 52, 53, 55, 57, 61, 62, 68, 72, 76, 78, 80, 96–98, 100, 106,

112–114, 120, 134, 137, 140, 143, 146, 150, 152, 156, 157, 173, 176, 178, 182, 183, 187, 189, 194, 196, 198, 199, 209, 210, 211, 213, 215, 217, 218, 220, 222, 223, 225, 227, 229, 231, 232, 234, 238, 239, 241, 245, 251–253, 256–258, 263, 264, 269
common 17, 30, 32, 34, 75, 90, 117, 165, 232, 233, 247, 252, 259
Perception 155, 186, 197, 198
Perish 42, 141, 204
Permanent 171
Persistence 125, 129
Perturbation 25, 78, 79, 122, 155, 160, 181, 191, 198
avoiding 23
Pervasive 223
Perverse 26, 46, 91, 204, 213, 214, 223, 256–258, 268
Pestilence 28
Phenomena 72
Pinnacle 11, 39, 110, 131, 133, 136, 137, 139, 165, 204, 215, 216, 241–243
Placid 42, 47, 120, 132, 154, 241
Plan 65, 76, 109, 210, 224, 227, 228, 232, 235, 262
Plants 5
Pleasure 17, 36, 122, 133, 149, 157, 181, 217, 233–235, 252, 270
Pliant 7, 9, 32, 43, 44, 51–53, 77, 93, 96, 117, 125, 126, 144, 151, 156, 157, 170, 171, 174, 175, 178, 179, 197, 198, 203, 204, 206, 212, 234, 235, 260–262, 265–267, 270
Poison 204
Position 37, 246, 266
Possess(ions) 28, 56, 57, 74, 96, 97, 153, 171, 195
Power 2, 3, 8–10, 38, 40, 43, 51, 54, 55, 72, 77, 86, 92–94, 127, 133, 137, 142, 150, 152, 158, 165, 183, 185, 195, 202-204, 209, 212, 218, 220, 221, 235, 238, 242, 243, 246, 255, 261, 266, 267
Powerful, the 30, 176, 177
Poverty 24, 185, 260
Praise 14, 113, 168

Precaution 137, 214, 215, 225, 226
Precede 234, 236, 237
Preparation 32, 33, 49, 99, 117, 137, 173, 245, 270
Present 172
Preservation 39, 50, 93, 124, 125, 168, 169, 197, 222, 243, 245, 249, 254, 261
Principles 5, 13, 23, 40, 46, 105, 111, 116, 124, 179, 187, 222, 225, 263, 273
Proactive 47
Production 74
Profile 215
Profits 21, 22, 25, 83, 118, 143, 182, 196, 199, 200, 207, 210, 229, 242, 268
Progenitor 41, 159, 216, 249, 265, 269
Profound 15, 25, 73, 89, 90, 108, 231, 232
Prohibitions 24, 25, 209, 210
Promise 224
Provisions 32, 200, 247
Punishment 15, 38, 63, 64, 75, 83, 113–115, 158, 166, 182, 185, 191, 217, 222–224, 237, 243, 252–258, 268
Purification 96
Purity 21, 85, 86, 123, 137, 173, 178, 201, 213, 214, 232

Quantity 266, 267
Quickness 228
Quiescent 16, 121, 137, 159, 178, 213, 214, 223, 269
Quietism 3, 247
Questions and Replies 206, 246

Radiant 207, 213, 214
Rain 101, 127, 128, 148, 218, 225
Raise 262
Rancor 20, 51, 61, 77, 90, 127, 202, 208, 224, 225, 232, 253, 267, 268
Rarities 24, 25, 209, 210, 249
Rash 182–184
Ravine 9, 10, 136
Reactive 47
Real 179, 236
Realist 3
Realization 11, 58, 263, 264
Realm 170, 184, 189, 201, 209, 214, 268
Rear 18, 74, 106, 107
Reason 254
Rebellion 3,4, 29, 189, 220
Reborn 212

Rebound 10, 140
Recede 190
Receptive 10, 136
Recluse 9, 86, 95
Recognition 108
Rectification 183
Reduction 33, 53, 156, 171, 179, 262, 263
Regiment 58, 71, 101
Regulation 240, 253, 257
Regiment 58, 71, 101
Rejection 162, 222, 252
Relatives 29
Reliance 57, 74, 96, 97, 195, 213, 214, 263, 270
Relationship 116
Repression 16, 159, 160, 252, 262
Rescue 236, 238
Resolute 26
Resolution 4, 207, 274
Resources 25, 134, 211
Respect 109, 222, 253
Responsibility 255, 257
Responsive 49, 244, 248, 254, 255
Rest 191
Restraint 91, 104
Results 140
Retire 93
Retreat 95
Retribution 255
Return 11, 56, 71, 111, 120, 170, 183, 235
Revenge 6, 31
Reverent 23
Reversion 9–11, 41, 53, 72, 82, 95, 106, 107, 111, 118, 119, 125, 129–131, 136, 137, 140, 158, 159, 169, 170, 177, 197, 198, 213, 214, 223, 227, 231, 266, 270
Revolution 15, 16, 27, 72, 226
Revolve 178
Rewards 64, 75, 117, 158, 243
Rhinoceros 192, 193
Rich 57, 63, 93, 94, 149, 150, 209, 210, 237
Right 5, 20, 34, 35, 55, 74, 144, 145, 152, 153, 232
Rigidity 42, 144
Righteousness 6, 13, 15, 21, 22, 25, 39, 47, 60, 94 ,100, 113, 115, 116, 118, 119, 126, 148, 149, 164, 165, 216, 235, 242, 245, 248, 263, 264, 272
Rites (*Li*) 6, 15, 26, 34, 40, 49, 60, 87–89, 92, 114, 115, 117, 133, 145–147, 164, 165,

188, 219, 241, 246, 268, 272
Rivers 20, 67, 86, 93, 108, 109,
 148, 149, 221, 228, 230,
 232, 234, 267
Road 71, 143,
 228
Robe 186
Robbers 17, 18, 22, 24, 25, 78,
 79, 94, 95, 118, 199, 200,
 209, 210
Room 32, 33, 99
Rooster 130
Root 5, 18, 39, 57, 111, 159,
 170, 210, 216, 249
Rope 45, 134, 270
Rulers 6,7, 9, 10,13–17, 20, 23,
 27, 28, 31, 35, 38, 40, 41,
 44–46, 49–51, 54, 57–59,
 61, 62, 68, 72, 76–78, 82,
 84, 87, 90, 94–96, 100, 102,
 104, 113, 114, 117, 119, 121,
 126, 132, 133, 136, 137,
 140–142, 146–148, 154,
 167–169, 173–175, 178,
 181, 185–187, 189, 196,
 198, 204, 205, 210, 211,
 216, 222, 226, 229,
 231–238, 240, 241, 245,
 246, 249, 254, 256, 257,
 259- 261, 265, 268, 270,
 271, 273

Sacrifice 201, 202
Sage 7, 9, 15, 19, 22, 23, 26,
 30, 31, 33, 35, 37, 40, 42,
 45, 48, 49, 51, 54, 56–61,
 64, 66–68, 70–72, 74, 75,
 77, 78, 80, 83, 84, 87, 88,
 91, 92, 95, 97, 98, 103, 104,
 108, 109, 111, 114, 119, 121,
 122, 125, 126, 132, 134,
 136–139, 142, 146, 153,
 154, 159, 166, 170, 171,
 173, 174, 179, 180, 183,
 186–190, 193, 205, 208,
 209, 213, 214, 218, 219,
 222, 223, 226–230, 233,
 234, 237, 239, 240, 242,
 244, 248–252, 254, 256,
 263–269, 272–274
Sagacity 22, 118
Salary 37
Sapling 67, 227, 228, 230
Satisfaction 175
Saving 37
Scattered 227, 228
Scintillating 213, 214
Seas 120, 221, 234, 265, 266
Seasons 55, 59, 71, 81, 98,
 159, 212, 241

Secrecy 208
Security 23, 67, 128, 197, 228
Seeds 10
Seize 14, 28, 29, 31, 37, 52,
 138, 141, 157, 164, 180,
 189, 202, 206, 209, 210,
 220, 239, 252
Selectivity 101, 102
Self 19, 74
Self-conquest 152
Self-control 79, 97, 119, 149
Self-correction 177, 183
Self-cultivation 7, 8, 40, 58,
 97, 98, 126, 201, 245
Self-discipline 152
Self-preservation 46, 75, 94,
 95, 149
Self-realization 46
Self-transformation
 223
Selfish 2, 40, 76
Selfless 87, 274
Sensation 101, 102, 122, 190,
 191, 198
Senses 19, 36, 188, 194
Shadow 250, 254, 255
Shallow 33
Shame 13, 88, 115, 157, 223,
 256, 257
Shang Dynasty 7, 44, 63, 150,
 165, 202, 237, 261
Shang, Lord 223
Shape 45, 47, 106, 107, 123,
 134, 154, 172, 196, 254
Shapeless 107, 131,
 155
Sharp 81, 82, 93, 94, 199, 207
Shield 15, 19, 29, 40, 48, 74,
 88, 112, 113, 139, 148, 189,
 191, 202, 222, 245
Short 18, 74
Shu 63, 237
Shun, Emperor 23, 79, 80,
 269
Sight 97, 105, 244,
 245
Sign 67, 227, 228
Silence 4, 10, 11, 121, 130, 137
Silk 199
Simple 75, 213
Simplicity 5, 16, 21, 24, 57,
 64, 102, 107–109, 118, 119,
 136, 137, 147, 148, 152,
 159–161, 174, 181, 183, 232
Simplification 22, 24, 80, 118,
 119, 181, 209, 210, 233, 271
Sincerity 5, 7, 15, 23, 25, 79,
 89, 108–110, 113, 114, 123,
 128, 148, 164, 165, 204,
 213, 218

Six Secret Teachings 13, 98,
 217, 229, 243
Skill 21, 24, 25, 118, 209, 210,
 242, 272
Slow 247
Small 46, 56, 66, 67, 110, 147,
 148, 151, 153, 175, 220,
 224, 225, 228, 245, 266,
 269–271
Sneaky 172
Snort 139
Society 2, 8, 26, 38, 189
Soft 147, 203, 262
Soldier 144, 147, 242, 257, 263
Solicitude 62–64, 189,
 236–240, 246
Solid 23, 62, 64, 134, 203, 208,
 216, 236, 238, 240
Solitary 11, 32, 130, 168, 270
Son of Heaven 10, 93, 132
Sons 30, 148, 197, 201
Sophistry 182
Sorrow 9, 34, 35, 145, 146,
 214, 241, 243
Soul 61, 96, 97, 124, 153, 169,
 177, 196
Sound 174, 204, 270
Source 5, 7, 90
South 23, 186
Spears 35
Speech 25, 45, 49, 70, 75, 84,
 133, 150, 198, 207, 234,
 254, 255, 272
Speed 247
Spirit 10, 42, 53, 85, 86, 101,
 126, 136, 144, 146, 156,
 160. 167, 168, 189, 194,
 219, 223, 224, 255, 257,
 262, 268, 271, 274
Spiritual 40, 98, 138, 155, 218,
 219
Spiritual Vessel 28, 138, 139
Split 227
Spoken 238, 250
Spokes 98
Spring 120, 121
Spring and Autumn 94, 135,
 143, 151, 205, 212, 221
Sprouts 67, 103, 181, 198, 228
Spy 152
Square 172, 173, 213, 214, 240
Ssu-ma Fa 5, 100, 147, 205,
 242
Stability 270
Stammering 182, 183
Stand 129
Star 5
State 5, 7, 14, 24, 26, 30, 32,
 34, 35, 39, 46, 49, 51, 52,
 57, 58, 61, 71, 80, 85, 90,

96, 97, 100, 102, 105, 107, 108, 116, 128, 134, 137, 143, 150, 159, 165, 183, 189, 198, 201, 202, 209, 211, 214–218, 220, 221, 225, 226, 228, 231, 232, 239, 245, 258, 259, 268–271, 273
Steppe peoples 3, 100
Stiffness 42, 43, 52, 144, 157, 177, 260
Stillness 11, 130, 189
Sting 203
Stone 168
Stopping 36, 90, 100, 121, 148, 149, 180, 185, 191
Storing 180
Straight 124, 182, 183
Strategy 50, 110, 248, 254
Stream 86, 93, 148, 149, 167, 173, 221, 230, 234, 265, 267
Strength 1, 28, 32, 41–43, 51, 54, 57, 62, 64, 75, 77–79, 140-143, 150, 178, 179, 196–198, 202, 204, 205, 220, 237, 241, 260, 264, 266, 270
Strengthen 53, 156
Stretch 109, 156
Strike 203
Strong, the 5, 26, 28, 30, 42–46, 53, 91, 139, 141, 142, 144, 150, 151, 156, 158, 168, 170, 176, 178, 204, 205, 212, 239, 260, 262, 265–267
Strife 26, 27, 36, 91, 196
Study 29, 187, 188, 202, 227
Struggle 196
Stumble 167, 168
Stupidity 6, 21, 131, 132, 164, 268
Submission 39, 215–217, 239
Substance 16, 109, 117, 119, 148, 173
Substantial 164–166, 169, 172, 183, 213, 219, 272
Subtle 15, 47, 66, 71, 108, 154, 155, 157, 178, 183, 225, 226, 250
Suburb 184
Subversion 213, 214
Success 56, 67, 93–95, 112, 153, 227, 228, 230, 240
Suffering 3, 15, 16, 18, 46, 233, 271
Sufficiency 36–38, 149, 150, 164, 180, 181, 184, 185, 194
Sui Yang-ti 44, 261
Summer 173, 225, 254

Sun 5, 60, 71, 212, 229
Sun Pin 206, 246
Sun-tzu 72, 93, 100, 105, 109, 110, 126, 135, 138, 143, 152, 155, 177, 205, 211, 212, 239, 242, 243, 246, 247, 262
Sung Dynasty 124, 202, 246
Superficial 165, 166
Superior 16, 17, 75, 128, 220, 238, 250, 251, 258
Supplement 188
Survival 12, 43, 233
Sustain 55, 56, 60, 96, 97, 111, 139, 153, 157, 168, 195, 196, 204, 227
Sweet 270
Sword 10, 17, 35, 145, 194, 199
Symbol 194

Tactics 4, 211, 247
T'ai Chi 177
T'ai Kung 4, 215, 217, 229
Talent 10, 136
Tally 45, 134, 135, 267, 268
T'ang 1, 3, 4, 7, 24, 76, 102, 206, 246
T'ang, King 237
Tangled 106, 170
Tao 4–7, 9–15, 18, 20, 21, 26–30, 32, 34, 38, 40–43, 45–7, 49-51, 55, 56, 58–61, 65–67, 70–73, 81–86, 89–95, 106–108, 111-113, 115–117, 119, 121–125, 127–131, 135, 137, 140–142, 144, 146–148, 151–155, 157–160, 164–166, 169–175, 177, 178, 181, 183, 184, 187–190, 193, 195–200, 204, 205, 207–209, 216, 218, 222, 225, 226, 228, 231. 235, 236, 238, 241, 245, 249-251, 254, 255, 257–259, 261, 263, 264, 268, 270, 271
of Earth 106, 111
of Heaven 49, 60, 61, 97, 106, 111, 186, 188, 195, 200, 254, 255, 263, 267, 268,272, 273
of Man 106, 151, 200, 263
Tao Ching 7, 69
Tao Te Ching 1, 2, 4, 7–10, 12–16, 18, 19, 22,–24, 26, 27, 31, 33, 36, 38–41, 46–48, 51, 52, 54–56, 61–66, 70–72, 74, 76, 77,

79, 80, 83, 84, 87, 88, 90. 91, 94, 95, 97, 99, 102, 106–112, 114, 119, 122–124, 128, 131, 133, 137, 138, 140, 142–144, 146, 149, 152–155, 159, 160, 168, 169, 171, 173, 174, 177–178, 181, 183, 185, 188–191, 193, 194, 196, 202, 204, 205, 207, 212, 214–219, 221, 224–226, 229–233, 237, 238, 240–246, 248, 250–252, 257, 260, 261, 264, 265, 268, 271–274
Taoism 2, 3, 19, 114
Taoist 38, 49, 92, 146, 174, 185, 186, 211, 219, 223, 230, 233, 259, 264, 269
Tastes 29, 57, 65, 112, 121, 185, 192, 210, 212, 224, 225
Taxes 17, 18, 25, 29, 64, 75, 114, 148, 189, 200, 216, 217, 237, 258, 259
Te 5–7, 55, 83, 195, 196, 205, 236, 249, 257, 258
Te Ching 7, 83, 92, 163, 216, 221, 223, 232
Teacher 134, 135,
Teachings 7, 84, 176, 250
Teeth 19, 74
Temples 24, 88, 135
Temporary 230
Temptation 22, 82, 95
Ten 269, 270
Tendons 203
Tension 263, 264
Terrain 6, 10, 25, 31, 89, 136, 143, 221, 246, 267
fatal 6, 192–194
Territory 64, 75, 91, 141
Texts 8
Theft 20
Thick 164, 165, 272
Thieves 20, 21, 95, 102, 232
Thin 164, 165, 272
Things 4, 43, 47, 54, 55, 59, 66, 67, 71, 93, 94, 104, 122, 123, 129, 131, 134, 139,157, 181, 198, 204, 205, 227, 252
myriad 5, 33, 34, 44, 55, 56, 58, 59, 61, 68, 70, 73–75, 81, 83, 89, 97, 107, 110, 111, 124, 147, 148, 153, 159, 167-170, 174, 176, 186, 190, 194–196, 222, 223, 227, 229, 230, 235, 254, 255, 260, 264
Thought 19, 119, 188, 232, 240

Threat 3, 194, 257
Three 175, 176
Three Kings 1, 5, 165
Three Strategies 13, 116, 239
Thwart 227, 228, 230
Tiger 192, 193
Timeliness 1, 26, 54, 65, 89,
  90, 171, 229, 230, 270
Tinkle 168
Touch 106
Tower 66, 67, 120, 121, 227,
  228
Towns 24
Traces 45, 47, 70, 120, 133,
  134, 154, 268
Track 45, 133, 134, 223, 267
Training 102
Transcendence 12, 13, 132,
  174, 175, 208, 250
Transformation 4, 57, 59, 71,
  75, 78, 87, 117, 123, 159,
  160, 165, 209, 210, 222,
  257, 264, 268, 270
Tranquil 65, 66, 75, 82, 106,
  110, 145, 167, 178, 183,
  225, 241, 263
Tranquility 10, 20, 32, 37, 50,
  52, 57, 65, 77, 85–88, 90,
  101, 108, 109, 111, 125, 132,
  136, 154, 159, 161, 167,
  168, 170, 181–184, 187,
  189, 192, 198, 209, 210,
  218–220, 227, 257, 270, 271
Transgression 68, 113, 196,
  222, 223, 227, 255, 257,
  259, 268, 265
Travel 11, 131, 132, 186, 187,
  192, 199, 213, 269, 270
Treasure 37, 48, 49, 62, 180,
  188, 189, 222, 236, 238,
  244, 245, 271
Trees 44, 66, 67, 227, 228, 230,
  260, 261
Trigram 177
Troops 1, 5, 6, 30, 31, 44, 64,
  75, 110, 129, 141, 150, 176,
  189, 205, 238, 239, 261
Trust 113, 114, 117, 128, 190,
  213, 271
Truth 12, 131, 167
Ts'ao Ts'ao 63, 237, 238
Tso Chuan 43, 204, 205
Turbid 10, 11, 108, 120, 130,
  152, 191
Turbulence 116
Turmoil 3
Turtle Books 4
Tyrant 100, 104, 143
Tzu Ying 141

Ugliness 18, 73, 76, 116
Ultimate 14, 113
Unadorned 21, 118, 119, 213
Unbounded 10, 11, 131, 136
Unconquered 215–217
Unchanging 11, 130
Unendangered 11
Unexpected 132
Ungood 19, 74, 190, 222
Unimpoverished 154
Unimperiled 130, 180
Unknowing 204
Unknown 251
Unite 109, 194, 207
Unity 61, 96, 97, 169, 177,
  196, 207, 208
Universe 7, 8, 13, 51, 98, 127,
  230
Unlimited 212
Unnamed 106, 107, 147, 159,
  160, 181, 208
Unobtrusive 169
Unorthodox 4, 14, 209, 211,
  212, 247
Unreal 236, 238
Unrest 3
Unrighteous 22
Unseen 155
Unspoken — See Instruc-
  tions, unspoken
Unstable 171
Untroubled 197, 259
Unworthy 75
Upbraid 267, 268
Upper 235
Upright(ness) 14, 57, 64, 65,
  137, 159, 160, 183,
  209–211, 213, 214, 225,
  258, 268
Utility 32, 33, 99

Vacuity 7, 29, 82, 84, 88, 94,
  110, 133, 135
Vacuous 23, 64, 76, 78, 79, 81,
  82, 111, 172, 178, 182, 183,
  208
Vague 124
Valley 10, 85, 86, 108, 109,
  138, 148, 149, 167, 168,
  172, 173, 221, 229, 234,
  239, 267
Valuables 23
Values 18–20, 22, 23, 64, 68,
  79 104, 227, 229, 259
Valuing 68, 78, 79, 102, 103,
  222, 259, 269, 271
Vast 62, 84, 122, 123, 189, 217,
  236, 237
Vessel 28, 29, 32, 33, 98, 99,
  136, 137, 172, 173

Victory 1, 5, 34, 35, 39, 42,
  44–46, 49, 51, 62, 64, 100,
  105, 126, 134, 135, 138,
  142, 143, 145, 146, 151,
  152, 179, 205, 208, 212,
  213, 216, 220, 236,
  238–240, 243–246, 260–262
Village 6, 24, 30, 35, 201, 245,
  259, 270
Violence 20, 21, 51, 129, 204,
  233
Virtue 5, 6, 8–10, 12, 13, 21,
  23, 25, 33, 35, 36, 38–40,
  43, 47, 51, 55, 59–62, 66,
  75, 77, 79, 82–84, 86–88,
  90, 96, 97, 98, 100, 106,
  112–114, 119, 122–124, 127,
  128, 131, 134, 136, 137,
  149, 150, 154, 157, 160,
  164–166, 172–174, 177,
  183, 190, 195, 196,
  201–205, 215, 216, 218,
  220, 225, 231, 232, 235,
  241, 257, 258, 260, 264,
  267–269, 270, 272,273
Visible 72
Vision 39, 47, 216, 238
Void 10, 136

Wagon 32, 269, 271
Walk 129
Wang Chen 1, 3, 4, 9–11, 13,
  14, 17–19, 24, 25, 27, 29,
  31, 32, 34, 36, 38, 40–47,
  50–52, 54–57, 59–62, 64,
  67, 72–74, 76,79, 82, 84, 86,
  89, 92, 95, 99, 102, 105,
  109, 112, 115,119, 122, 125,
  128, 131, 133, 135, 139,
  142, 146, 153, 157, 158,
  160, 166, 169, 171, 174,
  175, 177, 179, 181, 185,
  187, 189, 198, 203, 205,
  206, 208, 210–212, 215,
  216, 221, 223, 229, 233,
  235, 236, 238, 243, 248,
  249, 251, 253, 255, 256,
  258, 260–262, 264, 267,
  268, 271, 274
Wang Mang 44, 261
Wang Pi 12
Wang Yi 141
Warfare 1, 2, 4–6, 19, 26, 27,
  31, 32, 39, 45, 46, 49, 61,
  64, 74, 79–81, 99, 100, 105,
  112, 119, 151, 157, 166, 168,
  180, 185, 205, 211, 216,
  217, 240, 244–246, 248,
  249, 253, 258, 260, 262
casualties 5, 6, 12, 28, 29, 91,

142, 144, 146, 176, 221, 264
causes 7, 19, 76, 118, 252
cessation 5, 12, 13, 37, 40,
  92, 118, 121, 122, 125, 134,
  168, 169, 270–274
enthralled with 5, 30, 49,
  100, 104, 105, 245, 254
forgetting 5, 100, 245
prolonged 105, 205, 206,
  243, 247, 258, 262
sorrows of 1, 4, 5, 6, 9, 13,
  24, 27–29, 105, 117, 142,
  143, 146, 158
Warring States 2, 8, 13, 17,
  23, 26–28, 47, 76, 89, 94,
  142, 151, 211, 216, 221,
  229, 259, 262
Warrior 51, 94, 99, 147, 194,
  241–243
Water 9, 10, 25, 33, 34, 65, 77,
  89, 90, 92, 93, 126, 136,
  138, 149, 158, 212, 265–267
Weak, the 43, 44, 46, 53, 93,
  151, 156–158, 171, 204,
  212, 239, 262, 265–267
Weaken 53, 64, 156
Weakness 7, 9, 32, 52, 54, 77,
  78, 88, 92, 169, 170, 178,
  179, 198, 206, 234, 235,
  260–262, 270
Wealth 17, 29, 37, 63, 95, 143,
  151, 180, 181, 189, 199,
  221, 237, 259, 263, 264, 273
Weapons 5–7, 10, 17, 19,
  22–30, 31–35, 48, 49, 64,

67, 75, 79, 83, 91, 93, 94,
  99, 100, 121, 139–141,
  144–146, 150, 158-160, 165,
  174, 176, 185, 192, 193,
  199, 205, 209, 218, 220,
  228, 240, 243–245, 252,
  259, 270
Weaving 30, 259, 263
Wedding 89
Weeds 17, 199
Weird 213
Welfare, People's 9, 11, 55,
  98, 102, 112, 133, 210, 217,
  226
Wen, Emperor 237,
  ßß 238
Wen, King 202
White 9, 136, 137, 172
Wide 254, 255
Widow 176, 245
Wife 148, 202, 245
Willful 150
Wind 101, 127, 128, 218
Window 32, 99, 186
Winter 108, 109, 225, 254
Wisdom 5, 16, 19–22, 45, 104,
  112, 116, 118, 119, 121, 122,
  128, 134, 150, 151, 174,
  186, 189, 197, 213, 216,
  231, 232, 242, 250
Wise 37, 64, 78, 79, 135, 138,
  149, 176
Withdraw 42, 48, 109, 142,
  172, 173, 244, 247
Withered 44

Without 80
Wood 93
Women 23, 30, 78, 79, 151,
  259
Words 15, 40, 41, 47, 50, 58,
  60, 70, 83, 84, 113, 114, 127,
  128, 154, 178, 222, 248,
  249, 265, 266, 272
World 62, 181
Worry 17, 87, 112, 120, 121,
  183
Worthies 15, 22, 23, 55, 64,
  75, 78–80, 108, 109, 173,
  193, 250, 263, 264, 271
Writing 4, 5, 270
Wrong 19, 20, 74, 232
Wu (state of) 63, 237
Wu, King 63, 150, 237
Wu Ch'i 105

Yang 35, 58–60, 70, 87, 97,
  111, 145, 148, 159, 160, 176,
  177, 218, 264, 272
Yangtze River 212, 235
Yao, Emperor 269
Yellow Emperor 5, 63, 238,
  269
Yellow River 4, 212, 235, 266
Yielding 32, 47, 52, 63, 92,
  121, 126, 247
Yin 35, 58–60, 70, 87, 97, 111,
  145, 148, 159, 160, 176,
  177, 185, 205, 218, 264, 272
Yoga 97, 189, 208
Yu, King 237